P9-DDK-746

PERGAMON INTERNATIONAL LIBRARY
of Science, Technology, Engineering and Social Studies

*The 1000-volume original paperback library in aid of education,
industrial training and the enjoyment of leisure*

Publisher: Robert Maxwell, M.C.

The Psychology of
the Afro-American

(PGPS-103)

Pergamon Titles of Related Interest

Giles/Saint-Jacques LANGUAGE AND ETHNIC RELATIONS
Hall BLACK SEPARATISM AND SOCIAL REALITY
Hall ETHNIC AUTONOMY: Comparative Dynamics
Katz TOWARDS THE ELIMINATION OF RACISM
Ra'anan/Roche ETHNIC RESURGENCE IN MODERN
DEMOCRATIC STATES
Wandersman/Poppen/Ricks HUMANISM AND BEHAVIORISM:
Dialogue and Growth
Wirsing PROTECTION OF ETHNIC MINORITIES:
Comparative Perspectives

Related Journals*

CLINICAL PSYCHOLOGY REVIEW
LANGUAGE & COMMUNICATION
LEARNING AND SOCIETY
PERSONALITY AND INDIVIDUAL DIFFERENCES
SOCIAL SCIENCE & MEDICINE

*Free specimen copies available upon request.

The Psychology of the Afro-American
A Humanistic Approach

Adelbert H. Jenkins
New York University

PERGAMON PRESS
New York   Oxford   Toronto   Sydney   Paris   Frankfurt

155.8496
J415P

Pergamon Press Offices:

U.S.A.   Pergamon Press Inc., Maxwell House, Fairview Park,
                     Elmsford, New York 10523, U.S.A.

U.K.   Pergamon Press Ltd., Headington Hill Hall,
                     Oxford OX3 0BW, England

CANADA   Pergamon Press Canada Ltd., Suite 104, 150 Consumers Road,
                     Willowdale, Ontario M2J 1P9, Canada

AUSTRALIA   Pergamon Press (Aust.) Pty. Ltd., P.O. Box 544,
                     Potts Point, NSW 2011, Australia

FRANCE   Pergamon Press SARL, 24 rue des Ecoles,
                     75240 Paris, Cedex 05, France

**FEDERAL REPUBLIC   Pergamon Press GmbH, Hammerweg 6
OF GERMANY**   6242 Kronberg/Taunus, Federal Republic of Germany

Copyright © 1982 Pergamon Press Inc.

Library of Congress Cataloging in Publication Data

Jenkins, Adelbert H.

    The psychology of the Afro-American.

    (Pergamon general psychology series ; v. 103)
    Bibliography: p.
    Includes index.
    1. Afro-Americans--Psychology. 2. Afro-Americans
--Race identity. I. Title. II. Series.
E185.625.J47   1982   155.8'496073   81-10734
ISBN 0-08-027206-1   AACR2
ISBN 0-08-027205-3 (pbk.)

Printed in the United States of America

Contents

Foreword

It has been a gratifying intellectual experience watching Professor Jenkins develop his theoretical statement concerning the black person in America. He took on a doubly difficult task, for not only is he dealing with an emotion-laden subject in the current scholarly community, but he has selected a style of explanation that has been rejected for several generations by those psychologists who fancy themselves spokespeople for our science. It takes not only ability and integrity but downright courage to analyze a subject matter relating to the repression of a people on the basis of a theory which has itself been repressed. Yet, Professor Jenkins makes the unlikely combination work with telling impact.

It will probably seem inconsistent or surely paradoxical to psychologists who are unfamiliar with teleological explanations to argue, as Professor Jenkins does, that the black person in America has always manifested behaviors reflecting free choice and personal responsibility. There is a general conviction among psychologists, fostered by their empiricistic orientation, that a person is only as free as the shaping circumstances in his or her life make possible. Failing to conceptualize the person as a premising, intentional organism, the psychologist finds freedom to be a "function of" the number of alternatives that have been generated by the environment and input by the person who is programmed to act as a mere conduit or mediator of such unidirectional influences. Professor Jenkins locates the sources of personal freedom in the individual's dialectical capacities to alter, adjust to, or resist (however subtly) these environmental "determinants." Thus, he shows in many ways, drawing on history, literature, and empirical researches, that the black person has manifested these basic human qualities *in the very face of* repressive circumstances.

As Professor Jenkins argues, it is probably more important for the black person than the white person to recognize his/her *true* human nature. Blacks more than whites seem vulnerable to the suggestion that they are incapable of self-direction because of environmental determinants. Psychology has accounted for behavior in terms that are suited to the laboratory context but are of questionable value to the world at large. The person is viewed as a "subject" performing within congeries of situational variables *(sic)* that somehow total to bring about the behavior observed and described in third-person fashion. Psychologists who pretend to be rigorously precise scientists do not make a habit of thinking about behavior from the perspective of their subjects, getting over into the heads of people and viewing things the way they see them. Add the great difficulties encountered when a white psychologist must get into the heads of black subjects and the problem of accurate scientific description becomes acute.

Even so, unless psychologists are willing to look through the life premises of their subjects they run the risk of totally misconstruing that which is observed "taking place" in the laboratory context. Such empirical facts *never* speak for themselves. We need a framing theory within which to put them in proper perspective so that we may understand what we see. Professor Jenkins cuts through the pseudo-scientific pretenses of a mindless empiricism and encourages us to understand things from an altered perspective—combining both a human perspective, first of all, and then a black perspective secondarily. The reader gains a sense of what it means to be a human being in the former, and what it means to be a black human being in the latter. The combined effect is a profoundly insightful experience which can only prove salutary for psychological understanding in the future.

Joseph F. Rychlak
West Lafayette, Indiana

Preface

To view the Afro-American from a psychological perspective requires that one choose some theoretical position from among the various different psychological approaches to the human individual. My background is that of a clinical psychologist trained in a psychodynamic tradition—a tradition stressing the interplay between the conscious and unconscious mind. In recent years I have been influenced by those developments in psychodynamic theory which emphasize the coping aspects of personality rather than primarily the inevitable instinctual dramas that presumably befall personality. Like most other psychologists I am convinced that the coping characteristics are what must be developed if the human race is to survive and fully develop its potential. More specifically, however, the theoretical trends that emphasize coping and mastery seem to me to be sorely needed when choosing a psychological approach to the study of the Afro-American. Giving more prominence to the positive and creative aspects of personality is especially needed because much of the psychological literature (in consonance with American society) paints a view of the black American as being deficient in the mental and emotional qualities that lead to productive and creative living. For many black social scientists, the judgment leveled by the psychiatrists Kardiner and Ovesey (1962) that "the Negro has no possible basis for a healthy self-esteem [p. 297]" does not fit and has never fit the situation of the Afro-American.

There is no question that blacks as a group are still disproportionately numbered among the poor, and suffer and have suffered personally and collectively in the United States. As an old mother says in Langston Hughes' poem:

Well son, I'll tell you:
Life for me ain't been no crystal stair.
It's had tacks in it,
And splinters,
And boards torn up,
And places with no carpet on the floor—
Bare.

[1926, p. 187]

Yet to adopt the typical American view that blacks as a group are unready for equal opportunity does a tragic injustice to the struggles of individual black Americans and their collective efforts. One does not have to turn to a Benjamin Banneker, a W.E.B. DuBois, or a Ralphe Bunche; or to a Jessie Owens or a Kareem Jabbar—names the white community would recognize more readily—to look for competent blacks. The evidence for nobility of the human spirit is seen in the everyday life of common black folk, as with Hughes' old woman:

> But all the time
> I'se been a-climbin' on,
> And reachin' landin's
> and turnin' corners,
> And sometimes goin' in the dark
> Where there ain't been no light.
> So, boy, don't you turn back.
>
> [p. 187]

Black heroes are special cases of the rule, not exceptions to it, notwithstanding the considerable social problems to which blacks have been heir.

Ralph Ellison noted some years ago that he set himself the goal as a writer:

> To commemorate in fiction . . . that which I believe to be enduring and abiding in our situation, especially those human qualities which the American Negro has developed despite and in rejection of the obstacles and meannesses imposed upon us [1964, p 39].

If psychology is to deal accurately with the Afro-American it must have a similar mission. But psychology has not been up to this task for at least two reasons. First, Western psychology has been hampered by racist cultural biases; psychologists as men of their culture have not escaped these preconceptions (Kamin, 1974; Thomas & Sillen, 1972; Willie, Kramer, & Brown, 1973). Secondly, and the point to which our attention will be directed in this book, in the main the reigning model in American psychology has been one proposing that drives and external events are the exclusive shapers of behavior. When this theoretical view is applied to blacks it encourages focusing on the deleterious forces that act on blacks. For when the human individual is not seen as a being who takes an active, coping stance in life, then the tendency not to see active and creative features in the behavior of blacks follows naturally.

Of course, the kind of psychological model one develops to understand black people depends very much on what one considers appropriate for the study of any human being. I maintain that the "commemoration of the human qualities" in Afro-Americans calls for a model that characterizes the human individual as one who can exercise some freedom of choice in life about self-conception even in the face of punishing circumstances. One goal I have here is to make a scholarly statement about the situation of black people in America. Equally important, however, is my objective to encourage Afro-American students to see psychology as a discipline that can go to the heart of issues meaningful to them. The aim, therefore, is to contribute to their understanding of themselves and to their efforts on behalf of Afro-American people.

Acknowledgments

I wish first to acknowledge the financial support for preparation of the book provided by the Ford Foundation, through the particular efforts there of Mr. Thomas Cooney and Dr. Benjamin Payton, and the Office of Sponsored Programs of New York University through Ms. Ann Greenberg. My department chairman, Professor Murray Glanzer, was also supportive of my taking the sabbatical leave that was essential to finishing this book. I spent an earlier leave period at the Center for Advanced Study in the Behavioral Sciences at Stanford, California. The help of the staff there and the Director, Dr. Gardner Lindzey, enabled me to finish an earlier version of this work.

My talks and correspondence with Dr. Joseph Rychlak were of inestimable value and support as I worked on the rather lengthy and fundamental revisions of the manuscript. My colleague and former teacher, Dr. Walter Kass, who has been helpful to me at so many points in my career, and Drs. Kenneth B. Clark and James Moss have been supportive in a number of ways as the work progressed. I am very appreciative, too, of the time that Drs. Ferdinand Jones and Bernard Kalinkowitz took from busy schedules to read portions of the manuscript and offer wise counsel. The ideas of many students have contributed to my thinking, and the help of some of them as assistants in bibliographic review is gratefully acknowledged: Conchita Espino, James Farrar, Michael Hernandez, and Peter C. Zajonc. My thanks, too, to Mary Ann Dishman for her careful typing of the largest part of the manuscript.

Grateful acknowledgment is made for permission to reprint the following materials: from *Selected Poems of Langston Hughes,* by Langston Hughes (copyright 1926 by Alfred A. Knopf, Inc. renewed, 1954, by Langston Hughes, reprinted by permission of Alfred A. Knopf, Inc.); from *Children of Crisis,* by Robert Coles with permission of Little, Brown and Co.; from *Language in the Inner City,* by William Labov with permission of the author and University of Pennsylvania Press; from *Discrimination, Personality and Achievement,* by Robert L. Crain and Carol S. Weisman with permission of the authors and Academic Press; from *The Dynamic Assessment of Retarded Performers,* by Reuven Feuerstein with permission of the author; from *The Psychology of Rigorous Humanism,* by Joseph F. Rychlak, Copyright 1977, John Wiley & Sons, Inc. and from *Black Consciousness, Identity, and Achieve-*

ment, by Patricia Gurin and Edgar Epps, Copyright 1975, John Wiley & Sons, Inc. reprinted by permission of John Wiley & Sons, Inc.

My very special feelings of appreciation—much more than I can say in this brief space—go to Mary Simons Strong for her diligent and sensitive work as my editorial consultant during the revising of the manuscript.

And of course a particularly loving gratitude is reserved for my family, especially my wife, Betty, and my son, Christopher, whose patience and unflagging support in so many tangible and intangible ways went beyond the call of duty.

Introduction

There has been longstanding discontent among black intellectuals with the inadequacy of the concepts used by American behavioral and social scientists in their research on the black experience in the United States. These dissatisfactions gained renewed vigor as a part of the social protests of the 1960s. The concerns and criticisms have centered on two main points. First, the accumulating literature on the individual black person, the family, and the community reflects the common practice of looking within the black community and black people themselves for the sources of social disadvantage affecting their personal and collective destinies. As a result, the victims of individual and institutional racism in the white society are made responsible for their own plight. Where the role of the white society in creating problems for the black minority is analyzed, the onus is eventually placed on blacks for responding inadequately to the situations they face.

The second distortion—one that I am going to make an attempt to correct and refocus in this book—is the tendency to describe the psychological functioning of the black American in negative terms. This stems in part from the almost complete lack of interest in studying the effective and constructive aspects of the psychological functioning of black Americans. The psychological literature has neglected almost totally a serious consideration of the competent and positive aspects of their personalities, almost as if these components of their make-ups did not exist. Instead, the emphasis is almost always on their personal deficiencies—their seemingly endless failings and inabilities to cope with life. Even where the data suggest strengths and capabilities, these traits are often interpreted as defenses to cover up the deficits and insecurities that are "really there underneath." Blacks seem to be in a no-win position. Whatever their behavior, assessments of it in the literature usually turn out to be negative.

It is understandable that at the present time many black scholars want to reject the modern myths about blacks, circulated under the guise of being scientific findings, for their incomplete, false, and dehumanizing characterizations of black people. Indeed, there are now some black psychologists who advocate scrapping the entire body of theory and research on blacks and developing entirely new approaches and new sources of data to replace it.

New approaches to the psychology of the black American have been put forward. It has been suggested, for example, that perspectives derived from African philosophy and culture might prove fruitful. Whether or not this turns out to be a productive route to take, it is my opinion that there are existing viewpoints in contemporary Western psychology that can also be used to make a fuller and fairer assessment of the Afro-American. In other words there are ideas in the social and behavioral sciences that should not be summarily dismissed as promising alternatives to the main theories and body of findings about black Americans. At least I think this is true in the discipline of psychology.

What are these approaches and perspectives in contemporary psychology that might lead to broadening our understanding of the psychological functioning of black Americans? They are the same ones that hold promise for gaining through the research process a fuller grasp of the personalities of all human beings. These more promising approaches look at the human individual from a "humanistic" perspective. They posit a distinctly different image of the human being from that being defined by "mechanistic" conceptions. In the mechanistic image—the reigning one in American psychology—the human individual is portrayed as a passive being whose responses are primarily determined either by environmental factors or by internal physiological and constitutional states. The behaviorist position can be most clearly identified with the mechanistic tradition. In this approach, behavior is seen as a function of innate or learned drives, or as a function of controlling environmental "contingencies." (Contingencies refer to circumstances in the environment that reward or punish an event and thereby determine its likelihood of occurrence.)

Even though psychoanalytic theory is quite different from behaviorist theory in important ways, Freud's voluminous writing shows clear evidence of *both* mechanistic and humanistic trends (Holt, 1972). The mechanistic components reflect Freud's efforts, which were heavily influenced by the natural science of his day, to develop a metapsychology that would describe the basic forces governing human functioning. One aspect of Freud's mechanistic side was the positing of instinctual drives as the primary motivating forces in behavior. He, like many of the behaviorists of today, considered drive reduction a primary aim of behavior. The reduction of such universal and inevitable drives—such as sex and aggression—was in Freudian theory the primary focus of personality function and development. Thus, there are strong pulls in Freudian thought to portray the person in mechanistic ways.

Counterposed against this notion of humankind portrayed in the passive mechanistic voice is a trend of thinking that is articulated, for example, by psychologists who could be called humanists. One such person, Isidore Chein, has described the humanistic view as one portraying the human individual as "an active, responsible agent, not simply a helpless, powerless reagent."

Man in the active image, is a being who actively does something with regard to some of the things that happen to him, a being who, for instance, tries . . . to

generate circumstances that are compatible with the execution of his intentions
. . . a being who seeks to shape his environment rather than passively permit
himself to be shaped by the latter, a being, in short, who insists on injecting himself
into the causal process of the world around him [1972, p. 6].

A number of other psychologists have developed outlooks with similar implications for the human image. Abraham Maslow, for example, took an early
and prominent part in expressing the growing dissatisfaction with the reigning
emphasis of the time on drive-reduction theories of motivation. Maslow (1968,
p. iii) stressed the need for a "third force" in psychology to counter the position
of the other two "forces" that were influential in American psychological
thought, namely, psychoanalysis and behaviorism. He acknowledged that
there were important "basic" physiological and psychological "drives" within
human beings that directed their behavior. However, he felt that when these
drives were satisfied, other sets of motivations emerged, such as strivings for
personal growth and self-realization.

Robert White also leveled a critique at both experimental and psychoanalytic psychologies. He wrote, "Something important is left out when we make
drives the operating forces in animal and human behavior (1959, p. 297)." To
bring back what is "left out," White developed his view that organisms,
particularly the higher mammals, possess the capacity to interact "effectively"
with their environments. This, to White, implied the presence in humans of a
lifelong motivation to strive for "competent" living as a universal characteristic of human development and functioning.

More recently other psychologists have begun articulating views with humanistic implications for the human image. The psychoanalyst Roy Schafer
has in effect countered the mechanistic themes in psychoanalysis by developing
what he calls an "action language" for psychoanalysis (1976). His work
portrays individuals not so much as victims of instinctual forces and neurotic
afflictions but as people who actively, albeit often unconsciously, construct the
meanings, including the pathological ones, by which they interpret the world.
"Action refers to all behavior performed in a personally meaningful, purposive or goal-directed fashion and includes all the forms of thinking and . . .
feeling as well (1977, p. 61)." Schafer's emphasis on the human being as actor is
basic to the humanistic conception of the individual.

Another psychologist, Joseph Rychlak (1977), reminds us that the opposing
views, which undergird the mechanistic and humanistic images of the human
being, predate by far the twentieth century in the history of philosophy.
Rychlak argues, much as does Chein, that it is time to be explicit about the
implications of including a humanistic perspective into accounts of human
behavior. "The tie binding all humanists," he notes, "is [the] assumption that
the individual 'makes a difference' or contributes to the flow of events (1976, p.
128)."

Chapter 1 of this volume is devoted to laying out the theoretical stance and concepts used in the following chapters to evaluate critically the literature on the psychology of black Americans. In my earlier thinking about psychological concepts as they related to black Americans, Robert White's concept of competence seemed to me to be a good one in which to ground a more positive approach to the psychology of the Afro-American. White's concept of competence implies that there is a lifelong process of self-development, one which he describes in rather straightforward psychological terms. While embodying criticisms of psychology, White's approach attempts at the same time to extend but not necessarily overturn all previous psychological work. In Joseph Rychlak's thinking I found a perspective that provided a framework for viewing most of the major personality theorists (see, for example, Rychlak, 1973) and that seemed also to subsume White's scheme. Rychlak's point of view seems to get directly to the heart of the question I wanted to address, namely, how can psychology make a contribution to a changed conception of the Afro-American? Since space allows only a brief orientation to his thoughts it is hoped that the reader will pursue his works more thoroughly. At several points I will illustrate how his humanistic approach can help orient our thinking about blacks.

In Chapter 1, I introduce the key ideas of the humanistic psychological approach that I have used to examine the Afro-American situation. In the chapters that follow I use the humanistic perspective to review some of the psychological literature on Afro-Americans. I have selected studies from five areas of psychology and organized them around the topics that are indicated in the following chapter titles: Chapter 2, "Afro-American Self-Concept: Sustaining Self-Esteem"; Chapter 3, "The Active Intellect: Developing Competence"; Chapter 4, "The Black Speaker: Cherishing Pluralism"; Chapter 5, "The Assertive Self: Emerging of a New Identity"; Chapter 6, "The Wayward Self: Distortion and Repair." Although the findings examined in these chapters are not exhaustive of the pertinent areas of psychology, they are important ones to address in relation to the psychological functioning of black Americans. The extensive notes to the text at the end of each chapter amplify issues raised in the text and provide further references and ideas that the reader can pursue.

Two final notes before beginning. First, even though my attention is directed at what I affirm as universal principles in human psychology, I do not maintain that there are no differences in the psychological makeup of Afro-Americans and whites in the United States. For example, some of the difference in cognitive performance between Afro-Americans and Euro-Americans may reflect different psychological styles of approaching intellectual problems. These differences in turn may stem from the fact that different cultural heritages place different emphasis during development on one or another aspect of cognitive functioning. I will discuss this issue briefly in the chapter entitled "The Active Intellect: Developing Competence."

Second, it is necessary to distinguish the term "humanistic" from the term "humanitarian." The latter term refers to an attitude of benevolence toward humankind in general and a wish to see the best possible social condition and the highest level of personal development for all human beings. The term humanism as used here refers to a philosophical position that puts human individuals and their choices as central determining factors in their fate. Such factors determine the human being's freedom and his/her responsibility (Rychlak, 1979). Individual humanists *may or may not* be concerned with the broad welfare of humankind; in fact some could be more concerned with their *own* welfare. By the same token some mechanists who see the human being only as shaped by external forces might not take a back seat to anyone in their concern for bettering the human condition. Mechanists can be and often are humanitarian in outlook. My values are humanitarian (similar to most psychologists) *and* humanistic. It is my belief, however, that the humanistic position articulates the potential for human development more effectively.

Chapter 1
Afro-Americans: Shaping Their Destinies

The focus of this book is on Afro-Americans as actors or agents who share with all of humankind the capacity to play a part in shaping the contours of their lives. Characterizing individual blacks in America from such an "activist" approach — as people who "make a difference" in the flow of events in their lives—involves raising questions about the usual portrayal of blacks in the social and behavioral science literature. Blacks are commonly described as "reactors" rather than "pro-actors" to the circumstances they face. They are often said to respond either as victims who accommodate passively to discrimination and economic marginality or as aggressors who deal with their individual and group subordination by striking back violently. The options that blacks choose are described as submissive or defensive—as reflecting powerlessness on the one hand or unthinking rage on the other. Such a picture is one of human beings who only react to their environments rather than take charge of their destinies.

In explaining this situation it is typical to point out the debilitating psychological effects that centuries of American racism have had on blacks. An example of this kind of analysis is offered by Roderick Pugh, one of the black psychologists who have written about the psychological impacts of the black experience on Afro-Americans. Pugh (1972) tends to emphasize the negative aspects of the prerevolutionary psychology of blacks, describing the attitudes before the struggle of the 1960s as reflecting "adaptive inferiority." According to him these attitudes derived from the anxiety that had been brought about by negative events associated with black skin color. In other words, the Afro-American's dark skin was the occasion for painful abuse and limited social opportunity inflicted by the majority white population. The anxiety aroused by such abuse became a drive or tension whose reduction was dependent on the learning of inferior modes of social response. Anxiety was also engendered by society's brutal response (and the threat of such response) to any aggressive display by blacks. Blacks learned to avoid the tension of such anxiety by assuming a stance of "adaptive inferiority," that is, inhibiting aggressiveness and presenting a humble demeanor. As black adults instilled this stance in their

1

children, presumably for their own protection, many blacks began to believe themselves to be inferior—the mask began to "stick to the face," as the proverb puts it.

Pugh notes other concomitants of such an adaptive strategy. With white behavior as a standard, emulating a white person in speech, dress, and manners was held up as a goal. In this sense blacks were identifying with their oppressors. Also, much self-rejection by blacks was apparent. In looking at the mannerisms and the eruptions of impulsive behavior by their frustrated brothers and sisters, some blacks were prone to comment on the unreadiness of blacks as a group for social equality with whites. Pugh acknowledged that Afro-Americans may have experienced a sense of worth in some roles, such as teacher, cook, athlete, musician, parent, for example—but not as a black person. However, with the social upheavals of the sixties in the United States, Pugh feels that blacks reclaimed a proud sense of self as persons (individual self-esteem) who are *black* (pride in group identity).

There can be no doubt that the experiences blacks have lived through have taken a heavy toll of their psychological adjustment, and Pugh does make a contribution to the consideration of the psychology of the black experience. However, in discussing the psychology of the black experience prior to 1963, Pugh draws heavily upon time-honored traditions of psychological explanation; traditions which, it seems to me, are heavily laden with the more mechanistic trends in psychology. In his emphasis on how blacks responded to social oppression by assuming an inferior stance he excludes other aspects of black psychological adjustment. (Pugh does use humanistic terms to characterize the post-1963 psychology of blacks, but I believe even his pre-1963 depiction of Afro-Americans needs to be supplemented with more explicit humanistic considerations.)

The traditional drive-reduction theme in psychology may be a good one for understanding such notions as adaptive inferiority. Such concepts, however, only present a part of the picture of Afro-American psychological adjustment, even the adjustment prior to the recent "revolution." Something is missing when one relies solely on drive-construct notions of behavior. I recognize that Pugh was less concerned with the underlying issues of theory construction and philosophy than he was with making a direct statement about the Afro-American situation. But, in fact, points of view about behavior do stem from (often unwitting) philosophical assumptions. I think attention to the kind of assumptions we are using to discuss such issues will pay dividends in our understanding of the black experience.

Now the task is to determine how the humanistic trend in psychology can be turned to advantage in examining the situation of Afro-Americans. This will be done, first, by looking at some ways in which the humanistic and mechanistic perspectives differ on fundamental assumptions about behavior. Doing so will allow the humanistic position to be presented more clearly. For this task, we will use the thinking of Joseph Rychlak because he has probed these differences in a way that can be illuminating as we proceed. Next, we will consider the ideas of the humanistic psychologist, Robert White, mentioned earlier.

AN APPROACH TO HUMANISTIC PSYCHOLOGY

It is Rychlak's claim that any theory of human behavior must of necessity address itself to several key issues on which humanistic and mechanistic psychologists have basic disagreements. Put in the form of questions, these issues are:

What are our assumptions about the causes of behavior?

What are our definitions of meaning?

What is our model for how the human mind and human behavior work?

Assumptions about the Causes of Behavior

The question of what causes a particular behavior or event seems to be pretty straightforward at first glance. What people usually look for when confronted with a question of causation is what the forces or actions were that brought a particular event into being. It may not be easy to find the particular forces that would provide a satisfactory answer to what caused something to happen, but it doesn't occur to most people that the notion of cause itself has more than one meaning. Actually, what antecedent forces bring a thing into being is only one of the meanings of the word cause. There are at least three others. When trying to get a complete understanding of the nature of an event, one can not only look at it from the point of view of the antecedent forces but can also consider, for example, the things it is made up of and even *why* it was made to happen or come into being. All of these contribute to what "caused" a thing to be the way it is. The reason for introducing such philosophical complications is that the adoption of some particular set of assumptions about the cause of an event such as a human behavior makes a great difference in how we understand that behavior.

In trying to get a handle on such issues Rychlak suggests that the four perspectives that can do this descriptive job for us are those developed by Aristotle many centuries ago in his theory of knowledge. It is worth our going into these points in some detail not only because it will clarify the philosophical underpinning of our approach to the Afro-American but also because humanists differ quite sharply from nonhumanists on the relative importance of these four issues in scientific accounts of human behavior. Specifically, humanists are inclined to use all four of the causal principles to account for the investigation of human behavior; mechanists are inclined to use only two. The four causal principles that were codified by Aristotle are those of "material," "efficient," "formal," and "final" cause. Mechanists emphasize the first two—the material and efficient cause, sometimes they employ formal-cause constructs (see Rychlak, 1977); they never wittingly employ the final cause mode of explanation. It will be useful to take the time to illustrate these four principles of causation with some examples from everyday life so that we can see their relevance to the Afro-American.

Substance as a Determinant. As one example let's look at the pencil I am using to write these paragraphs. From the perspective of the first causal principle (material cause) I can see that it is a slender tube made from a hard plastic with some graphite material inside of it. What I can do with it and what I understand about it depends partly on what it is made of. To describe the pencil in this way is to use a material-cause explanation. Now, Rychlak, in trying to capture the fact that Aristotelian causal principles get at the basic meaning that a thing has for us as we encounter it, introduced another set of terms to parallel those of Aristotle. A synonym for the material of which a thing is made is its substance; hence for Rychlak a material-cause principle can be described as a "substance-construct." (In the 1981 revision of his text, *Introduction to personality and psychotherapy* [1973], Rychlak has dropped these additional "Basic Meaning Constructs." I will continue to use them here because they are useful in clarifying the discussion of these issues.) In applying a substance-construct explanation to the realm of human behavior we can note that people's limits and potentials are determined (that is, caused) partly by their material composition, that is, their bodies. What their bodies consist of partly explains what they can and cannot do. Since humans do not have the wings of birds, they cannot fly. However, starting with his feet on the ground, a person can become, for example, a good dancer if, from a substance-construct point of view, he has sturdy limbs and is free of inner ear problems that would disturb his sense of balance. But of course such a perspective, while necessary in understanding what determines a person's choice of behaviors, is far from sufficient to fully account for behavior. Just having legs doesn't mean he will be a dancer.

Impetus as a Determinant. In turning to another use of the term causation, we come to the idea of efficient cause. I can further characterize my pencil by noting that a certain force was applied to the materials that make it up in order to bring the pencil into being. In other words, it is a manufactured item. Aristotle's efficient-cause idea is translated as an "impetus construct" by Rychlak. The efficient-cause or impetus-construct notion is the more familiar use of the term cause. An impetus construct expresses the "push, thrust, flow, bringing-about-in-motion aspect of experience [Rychlak, 1977, p. 5]." Again, by way of elaboration, an individual exercises his muscles over time to become a dancer, and of course he has to get himself to his dance classes regularly by using specific physical means (walking, driving, taking the bus). So we recognize that applying force to material form, as in manufacturing or moving the body in a disciplined way, is one of the causes of things. Note again psychologists who are mechanists emphasize these two causal principles—the material and efficient, especially the latter—when trying to understand and control behavior.

Form and Pattern as Determinants. In looking at the third sense of the causation term we can note that objects and events have a recognizable shape, form, or organization that makes them suitable to certain contexts or uses and that differentiates them from other objects. This is Aristotle's formal-cause principle which is expressed in Rychlak's notion of a "pattern construct." The term "pattern" captures the idea that constituent pieces of a thing or event fit into an organizational whole that has a distinct character. It is possible, for example, to take the same ten matchsticks and arrange them into the simple form of a house or alternately to arrange them into the form of a chair. We say that this is a house or alternately a chair not because the design is made of hard, solid objects (material cause); not because I exerted effort through time to move them from a random pile into a specific arrangement (efficient cause). We call the design a chair or a house because it has the shape or form of one or another of those things. Similarly, the shape of my pencil is quite distinguishable from that of my bicycle and the form of the pencil is such that suits it to certain uses and not to others. Coming back to the dancer, when we watch his professional performances we know he is a dancer. The patterning of his individual movements distinguishes him quite clearly from, for example, the quarterback on a football field, although the activities of both these athletes depend on a high degree of muscular skill. To zero in on the dance further: his practice sessions may be geared to learning the steps of a particular classical ballet. This number will fit together as a pattern that is clearly distinguishable from another classic dance number and will be even more distinguishable from a modern dance performance.

Ends as Causes. The fourth principle, Aristotle's final cause, takes note of the fact that the dancer's practice sessions are geared *toward* something. Implied here is the notion that some events, particularly those having to do with people, can only be adequately accounted for by delineating the reason or purpose "for the sake of which" a substance was formed into a recognizable shape, or "for the sake of which" something was made to happen. Rychlak describes this causal principle as an "intention construct." We can readily see the idea of an intention as being synonymous with a purpose or imagined goal. Looking at my pencil from the perspective of an intention construct we could say that my pencil was fashioned for the manufacturer's purpose of serving the writing needs of a potential user. (It was, of course, also fashioned for the purpose of turning a profit for the manufacturer.) Returning to the dancer: he goes to class with the intention of perfecting his skill and perhaps with the further conscious intention of becoming the best dancer in the country. A Freudian therapist might have occasion to point to the dancer's unconscious intention of winning his mother's not easily gained favor by the dazzling exhibitions he performs for her (and secondarily, in his mind, for the rest of the audience). This last construct, which emphasizes goals or intentions as causal factors in events, has been identified as a "telic" or teleological description.

Teleological concepts have earned a bad name in the history of philosophy and science because a circularity seems involved. Rychlak notes that it is a major misconception of teleology in psychology to assert that telic descriptions must deal with goals that actually exist or that eventually come to pass. It is, therefore, as if an event came about because it exerted a "pull" on the events that preceded it. In fact it is the *positing* of intentions (goals, reasons) in the present "for the sake of which" behavior ensues that is the crucial issue in final-cause considerations. The *accuracy* of these intentions or a goal's literal exist-ence is not the most important thing in a teleological conception. Intentions are not seen to reside in objects or events (thereby exerting a force on the present in a kind of reversed efficient-cause manner). Intentions are actions of human beings. People make premises in the present which then govern the behavior that follows. For example, the goal or intention in the mind of a black youth to become a physician has powerful consequences *now* in determining her ensu-ing behavior. Whether or not she *does* become a doctor is a function of a variety of ensuing factors (some of which may be beyond her control), but this does not negate the fact that she is an active, intending being at this point with respect to this goal.

Another criticism of telic accounts flows from the fact that they involve an "introspective" perspective, that is, they involve a first-person accounting for events because of the emphasis on intentions and reasons. Criticism is perhaps rightly leveled at this tendency when telic descriptions are used to attribute purpose and intention to nature and inanimate objects leading to anthropo-morphism of such phenomena. But humanistic theorists (see Chein, 1972, p. 229; Rychlak, 1977, p. 488) are quite content to anthropomorphize human beings by describing them as intending, purposive creatures, thus bringing final-cause motivations into legitimate consideration in human behavior.

Now, one of the major implications of these considerations for human behavior generally is this: in its historical development science came to rule out final-cause principles as legitimate ways of explaining human behavior (see Chap. 2 in Rychlak, 1979). But personality theorists and psychotherapists often find the need (sometimes unwittingly) to introduce "pattern" and "inten-tion" constructs in accounting for human behavior. In subsuming Robert White's perspective under this humanistic position, I am suggesting that, when he asserts that "something is left out" when drive constructs are made the sole explanatory principles of behavior, he in effect takes issue with the position that substance and impetus constructs (material and efficient causes) are the only appropriate explanatory terms for understanding human behavior. Instead he finds that in order to be more faithful to the complexity of human behavior it is necessary to use what amounts to a formal-final cause construct. Thus, as we shall see when we go into Robert White's material in more detail, there are specific qualities of behavior from very early in life that seem to serve the organism's intention to relate ever more effectively to the environment in the course of one's life. Similarly when Roy Schafer defines "action" in terms of "purposive or goal-directed" behaviors, he too is using a final-cause or intention construct.

I maintain that such a broadening of explanatory mechanisms can be useful in considering Afro-Americans. A mechanistic persuasion would attempt to account for the behavior of blacks primarily in what amounts to efficient-cause terms. A recent essay by Hayes (1980) provides a good example. He uses a "radical behaviorist" psychological position to portray the forces acting on blacks. He argues that such forces (or contingencies) have been brought to bear by whites' efforts to exert "behavioral control" over blacks. "Behavioral control refers to the systematic manipulation of certain environmental events in such a way that the observed effect occurs in a predictable manner [p. 46]." Thus, he points out that:

> During slavery, whites maintained virtually complete control over the behavior of blacks through the use of aversive control [i.e., punishment]. . . . With the abolition of slavery . . . mechanisms of economic control were instituted [in addition] [p. 45].

These mechanisms served to maintain this control. Such a position sees the environmental forces constructed by whites as sufficient, essentially, to account for the behavior of blacks.

A humanist in psychology, however, would see the value of introducing intentions (final-cause principles) to understand the experience as well as the observable behavior of blacks. For example, Powdermaker (1943) notes that, although blacks showed humble and meek behavior in interracial situations historically, the intent of such behavior was often quite at variance with such a demeanor. Thus, at times blacks intended to mock whites by overobsequiousness; in other instances in their meekness they intended to act out of a conception of personal (Christian) dignity ("turn the other cheek") and/or moral superiority.

As an example from a different source, consider a selection from the opening passages of Ellison's *Invisible Man* (1952) in which an old black man on his deathbed says to his son, " 'I want you to overcome 'em with yeses, undermine 'em with grins, agree 'em to death and destruction.' " The writer continues, "They thought the old man had gone out of his mind. *He had been the meekest of men* [pp. 19-20]" [emphasis added]. The humanistic psychological position recognizes that one cannot understand the behavior without understanding the *intent* that contributes to the behavior. To recognize the intentional, purposive quality in behavior is to recognize the *active* role of mind we have been stressing here. Note, it is not that the effect of environmental events on blacks is unimportant, it is rather that such effects are *not sufficient* to understand psychological experience in the humanistic view.

Conceptions of Meaning

A second point that differentiates the humanistic and mechanistic approaches has to do with conceptions of meaning. The dictionary definition of the word "meaning" refers to that which one intends to convey, purport, or signify. In signifying something, meanings point to or reach for "something else"—which can be called a "polar" reference. Two kinds of meaning, demonstrative and dialectical, can be identified for our purposes here. Specific, deductively iron-clad meanings are called demonstrative or "unipolar" meanings. When we say unipolar we mean that a particular meaning "points" in just one direction, so to speak. Let's take a specific item such as a tree to illustrate this issue. From a unipolar point of view the aim is to describe the characteristics that pertain to the word "tree" so as to link it in a one-to-one fashion with a clear item in the real world and keep it from being confused with other items. Being specific and unipolar in our meaning aids in communicating about and controlling things in reality. Unipolar or demonstrative definitions are designed to increase the specificity of knowledge granted a basic set of assumptions. The syllogism, with which we are familiar from elementary logic, is another example of demonstrative reasoning: granted that "all cats are animals"; given a cat, it *necessarily* follows that it is an animal. If one accepts the (ultimately arbitrary) basic assumption then certain things necessarily follow. The form of this argument truly points in just one direction.

The mechanistically inclined theorist is oriented toward identifying the factors, almost always the material- and efficient-cause ones, which will help us be certain about what a thing is. The aim is to show that, with the conditions of observation carefully controlled, the object standing before us is indeed a tree, for example, and not anything else. This mode of thinking has been particulary important in the development of Western science and technology and has given us considerable control of the material environment. This mode of thinking is important for black people, too, as they assess their social situation. While I disagreed earlier with what I saw as the narrowness of Hayes (1980) conception, I nevertheless do agree with him that there are and have historically been formidable environmental forces of a very specific nature acting on Afro-American people which need to be identified in their struggle to develop.

However, as with our discussion above of causal forces, an additional way of addressing the issue of meaning is also necessary for a full appreciation of the human situation in general and the Afro-American situation in particular. I am referring here to the idea of dialectical or "bipolar" meaning.

Rychlak uses the term dialectical (which has been used in a number of ways in the history of Western and Eastern philosophical thought: see, for example, Rychlak, 1979) to refer to that quality in which every specific meaning is seen to suggest either its opposite, or any number of other alternatives. From a dialectical view, meaning is often framed by bipolar referents, that is, a term is defined in terms of opposing possibilities. This is particularly true of those concepts that, although fundamental to human concern, are less tangible or empirically demonstrable, such as those ancient philosophical classics, truth, beauty, and justice. Thus, for example, one cannot have a concept of "justice" without some concomitant idea of "injustice." In a more mundane dimension, the term "up" for the dialectician necessarily implies a concept of "down"; these oppositional poles are indissolubly linked in our definition of a thing's position. Even as specific a material item as a tree in the real world can be considered from a dialectical or bipolar view: assuming the existence of the tree implies other possibilities—for example, "nontree" or "no tree." Thus, one could say, "Is that really a tree out there or is it a figment of my imagination?"

This tendency of human thought to consider alternative possibilities, even in a clear stimulus situation, is a defining characteristic of this use of the term dialectical. It is also basic to human symbolizing capabilities (see Edelson, 1971, Chap. 1) and is central to a humanistic view of the person. (Note that dialectical thinking does not guarantee more *accurate* thinking. Considering alternative possibilities about the existence of the tree does not make them more correct objectively. It does allow for creativity, and keeps an individual from being *only* stimulus-bound.) For our purposes I think it captures particularly well one aspect of human potential that blacks have drawn on to survive. The mechanistic theorist is impressed by the unipolar characteristics of situations that push or pull behavior in this direction or that. A humanistic perspective supplements with a view that notes that even in the presence of unpleasant givens blacks have been able (dialectically) to conceptualize alternative views of themselves and other possibilities open to them. In many instances they have struggled to actualize these alternatives and they have had varying degrees of success historically.

For example, one can understand the ceaseless though often subtle efforts at resistance to slavery partly by recognizing the alternative (dialectical) conception of self that blacks had. Julius Lester (1968) describes this trend towards resistance anecdotally:

Ol' Aunt Jemima was always spitting in massa's soup, while ol' John out in the field couldn't pick up a hoe without it just seeming to break in his hands. And, Lord have mercy, somebody was always running away [p. 36].

Thus, we see that physical combat is only one way to resist.

> In the context of America, it is an act of resistance for a poor black man to buy a Cadillac. To resist is to do whatever is necessary to maintain self-dignity [p. 36].

In this last passage in particular Lester points to the dialectical mode that must be taken into account in viewing blacks' behavior. That is to say, a particular black man's spending his meagre funds on a luxury is not necessarily just an arbitrary and irrational mimicking of (overidealized) wealthy people. It may also represent an act that helps this man define and express a sense of dignity which is different from the external conditions forced on him. In the terms we have been using such an act can at times stem from the bipolar recognition of what *is* (poverty) and what *could be* (material comfort), were his opportunities not unfairly blocked and manipulated by the system. Of course, a major goal of social change would be to enable the poor to gain sufficient resources so as not to have to strain so much in order to sustain a sense of dignity. However, we should recognize the continuing striving to "make a difference" that blacks have brought to their world.

(I recall a white working-class Michigan high school youth some years ago asking me, after I had delivered a lecture to his class on race relations, why poor Negroes spend money on fancy cars and T.V. sets when they don't have money for the necessities of life. From his perspective this was irrational behavior. His point of view was, of course, external to black people and hence an "extraspective" one. The humanist would advocate taking the black person's introspective view. Such a view will indeed be necessary on the part of whites if they are to overcome racist attitudes.)

The dialectical mode is not seen as supplanting the demonstrative one. Many scholars sympathetic to the former mode of thought recognize that an empirical science is necessary for the advancement of knowledge and it has to be based to an important degree on demonstrative and impetus-type meaning constructs. A potential for dialectical thought in the human being, however, was seen to develop along with the demonstrative style. The importance of the dialectical mode is reflected in the fact that it allows and predisposes a person to consider the alternative possibilities. As one contemplates an actual bird "up" in a tree, for instance, one can conjure up many other images in the so-called reality being perceived. In fact, there is a good deal of arbitrariness in what appears to be "true" or "possible" because all ideas have implicit opposites to which they point. (Presumably the greater the salience of certain aspects of a given stimulus event, the greater the possibility for a unipolar and demonstrative definition of a situation. But, while granting this, the dialectician also insists that it is the individual who *affirms* this meaning by conforming to these probabilities derived from his or her assessment of the situation. We shall have more to say about "affirmation" later.) The capacity to contemplate polar referents is fundamental to the creative and symbolizing activities of humankind. It is interesting to note that this attitude of "but—what if . . . ?" which is so common to children and sometimes exasperating to parents, is an important aspect of hypothesis generation in scientific activity. It is the dialectical capacity to take the opposite position about a given circumstance. Such hypotheses when framed clearly can be tested demonstratively in experimental manipulations.

Models of the Human Mind

Now let us turn to the task of distinguishing between two ways of explaining mind and behavior. These can be seen in the philosophical positions of John Locke and Immanuel Kant on this subject. Locke stresses the notion of mind as a blank slate, the familiar *tabula rasa*. In Locke's view, mind begins to emerge by the awakening touch, as it were, of sense impressions from the environment. The development of mind and complex abilities is held to be solely a function of the association and combination of simpler elements "put" there by experience. This is clearly consistent with a passive conception of the development and functioning of mind.

In the Kantian view, on the other hand, the infant is not simply waiting for the kiss of experience. The human individual brings certain "categories of understanding" to life situations from the moment of birth. These categories give form to (i.e., determine in a formal-cause sense) what can be known. This means, for example, that a child is innately able to make distinctions in his or her experience between the notions of "unity" and "plurality." These are not learned as separate concepts and then later associated in experience, although, of course, the words for these concepts are learned only when language develops. The child is born bringing such rudimentary (and dialectical) "meaning-framing premises" to experience. These operate like a pair of spectacles to give form to experience. As the individual matures and interacts with the world, such premises, of course, become more sophisticated.

Thus, mental activity or "mind" involves the *a priori* ability to organize or pattern experience in some meaningful way from birth. (This presentation of Kant's point of view is not concerned with the details of his theory of knowledge, but rather with his broad approach to the nature of mind.) This mental activity involves the ability to "conceptualize." "To *conceptualize* is to put a frame (order, organization, etc.) onto experience, and as such, the frame *fixes* that which can be known [Rychlak, 1977, p. 294]." To the newborn, in William James' words, the world is a "blooming, buzzing confusion." In other words the world does not come in neat sensory packages waiting to be discovered in the form that we come to recognize. We must organize it. What the developing child comes to "know" reflects what arises from both the child's ways of categorizing and the qualities inherent in reality.

It is the child's innate capacity to order things into "one" versus "many," to return to our example, that leads to an understanding that there is a difference between "one ball" and "three balls." This contrasts with the notion that a child learns concepts only by separate experiences, that is, by seeing one ball, one truck, one horse, and then learning *separately* the concept of several balls, trucks, horses. In the latter (Lockean) view concepts are formed additively and the person's experience with groupings of items finally leads to understanding the unity-plurality dimension. The Kantian notion is that the only reason that the child can "make sense" of an arrangement of balls is because of an innate tendency to organize along several dimensions such as unity-plurality, shape, color, for which the child at first, of course, has no words. Indeed, the child's culture will come along to show which dimensions are more important than others, and cultures will vary in their hierarchies of what is important. "What is held to be innate is the capacity to recognize or create patterns (meanings), and when in due time the conceptualizations . . . achieve a certain organization, we can speak of them as ideas [Rychlak, 1977, p. 294]."

As part of their consideration of American psychology some black writers have been particularly critical of what we are calling the Lockean emphasis in American psychology (see, for example, C. Clark, 1972; Boykin, 1977). (Locke of course was only one of a number of philosophers—Hume and Hobbes were others—who adhered to a point of view identified as the British Empiricist School of Philosophy.) This critique can be made clearer by noting the distinctions between Lockean and Kantian positions on the observer's role in acquiring knowledge.

The Lockean perspective can be associated with a thoroughgoing "realist" position in philosophy. It assumes that there is a specific order to be known in physical reality and that it is the task of human beings to discover this reality through careful scientific observation. In this view our senses in principle transmit the real impression of the world; the observer registers things as they "really" are. Kant by contrast thought of himself as a "critical realist" because he, too, firmly believed that a reality is "out there." But more important for him was his insistence that what *we* know as reality is what we have organized through our sensory and especially our conceptual apparatus. (This latter position associates him with philosophical "idealism" in the minds of some critics.)

The conceptual "spectacles," to use Rychlak's term, that we bring from birth necessarily provide the order that characterizes our knowledge. We are always on "this side" of the spectacles as we observe nature; reality is always on the "other side" of the spectacles. In this view reality doesn't come packaged in neat units of time and space, for example; these are ideas that we impose on it. What we know is subject to the initial conceptual biases we use to frame it. While two people looking into a small furnished room may be able to communicate about the room, they see and come to know (and thus remember, incidentally) the room differently because they bring slightly (or greatly) different perspectives to it as they observe it. And who is to say which of them sees it as it *really* is—particularly if one includes aesthetic features of the room as aspects of what the room is like?

With this in mind let us turn to some of the particular objections that black psychologists have raised. The argument against the Lockean perspective is that it leads observers to believe that they are standing outside of nature, as it were, registering it dispassionately, presumably free of their own biasing value systems. In assuming that scientific observation involves observation of things as they *are,* the Lockean runs the danger of forgetting that things are as they have been observed, *given certain basic assumptions;* these assumptions are in the minds of the observers. (It is not being maintained here that either blacks or psychologists were the first to recognize that science is not free of cultural values. But the implications for Afro-Americans are important enough—and it is often enough forgotten—that it is worth raising again.) Too often, the critics argue, Western psychology can be shown to have forgotten some of its limiting assumptions. It has fallen into the general Western pattern of assuming its own cultural and behavioral framework as the standard, defining all patterns that are different from Western cultural norms as being somehow deficient.

The Lockean position epitomizes for some of the critics the "European" ethnocentric bias which has tended to be pejorative in its judgment of the behavior of people of African heritage. Thus there is the call for discarding European philosophical perspectives in describing the Afro-American. In fact, it is not *necessary* for a Lockean to be culturally biased. Such observers could recognize the limits of their measurements and assume that they had simply not observed enough to know what the real situation is in other cultures. Because the Kantian philosophical perspective recognizes *in principle* the degree to which people bring their conceptual biases (their values) even to scientific observations, it should be better prepared to meet other cultures on their own terms. This is one advantage of the Kantian perspective in viewing the Afro-American (Boykin, 1977). Thus, as I suggested earlier in this chapter, one does not have to throw out all of psychology's Western heritage in order to retain a useful framework for viewing the Afro-American. The Kantian view is European also.[1]

It is an interesting development that even the so-called "hard sciences" have modified their stance on what scientific observation entails. "Modern science has become more open to Kantian-like terminology because of its recognition that what one observes in the 'hard reality' is due at least in part to what one presumes from the outset. This is clearly a recognition of the telic factors in the work of science or the scientist-human who does the work [Rychlak, 1977, p. 193]."

The implication for the Afro-American of the Kantian perspective is that blacks, like all human beings, come to the world with mental equipment oriented toward conceptually organizing experience, not just accepting what is given. While behavior is partly shaped by environmental and constitutional factors (sometimes to a great degree), people also bring a readiness to impose their own point of view on a given situation as well. A continuation and development of this readiness through the elaboration of the intentional and dialectical potentials of the human mind throughout life is what has helped blacks to survive in America.

To sum up the discussion so far, I have been saying that a full understanding of the history—and the potential—of Afro-Americans calls for supplementing the modes of explanation that are typical in American psychology. Humanistic psychological approaches that have been developing can be useful in providing the needed corrective. Thus the humanist posits that behavior is at least partly governed by subjectively derived intentions, factors that can be just as impelling as "instinctual" drives and environmental contingencies. A person's intention to reach an imagined goal can determine behavior "come hell or high water," as the saying goes. Furthermore, the human individual brings an actively structuring mind to the world, one capable of seeing alternative meanings in any given object or event. This enables the individual in principle to rise above the environment and to create or at least imagine something new and different. Since any one event can be interpreted in different ways one must know how the individual conceives that event. Looked at this way the survival of black Americans can be understood as depending to a significant degree on their capacities to imagine a dignified sense of their humanity in spite of external circumstances.[2]

COMPETENCE AS A HUMANISTIC THEME

We will now turn to a consideration of Robert White's concept of competence as a further way of viewing the psychological literature on black Americans in a humanistic light. His development of the competence concept amounts to a humanistic critique of extant psychological theory. In his examination of conceptions derived from both laboratory experimentation and clinical psychoanalysis White found that there was a failure to account for important aspects of behavior. White developed a perspective to supplement the themes emphasized by these two most popular traditions in American psychology. It seems to me that his perspective has clear humanistic implications. This is the concept of competence. In choosing the term "competence" to embody this orientation to behavior White was referring to its familiar connotation of skilled performance of a task. However, he used the concept to talk about broad aspects of behavior and development.

White does not assume that the baby springs fully competent from the mother's womb. Rather he argues that the basis for competence is present in some of the human infant's modes of interacting with the environment from the beginning of its life. Traditionally, comments about the waking behavior of the young infant concentrated on the activity that occurs as a function of (usually irritating) internal drive states which prompt responses from the caretaking environment—some adult, usually a mother, checks on the infant when it cries. In this way the child comes to learn which of its responses are associated with reduction in drive tensions. While the learning that occurs through drive reduction is an important part of the scenario of early development, White calls our attention to other ways the child learns—and here we can see the relevance of competence strivings. The very young child gradually spends more and more of its time awake and in a state in which its drive tensions are met. White argues that such states are also conducive to important learning. He notes that it is particularly in such states, when the child is comfortable in its crib with its biological needs taken care of, that it is amenable to turning its attention to the dangling objects left there for amusement.

If, on the other hand, the child were very hungry it might indeed grab its rattle and try to suck it, but finding the rattle unsuitable for gratifying hunger the child would be likely to discard it quickly and move on to see what else could be sucked and swallowed. In so doing, that is, in interpreting reality objects only in terms of pressing drive tensions, the infant would be very unlikely to learn the many interesting and important non-drive-related aspects of reality that there are. However, in a mood free of basic drive tensions the child is able to evaluate these objects in their own right. Within certain limits of stimulation those objects that it can *do* the most with (in terms of movement, sound, and visual change) are those it gives the most attention.

The more the baby's interactions have pleasing *effects* the more it is likely to repeat and expand its activities. As the child does so it becomes more skilled in achieving such effects: that is, it becomes effective with its interactions with the environment. White calls this kind of activity "effectance" behavior; the emotion that accompanies the opportunities for effectance behavior is a "feeling of efficacy."

> Effectance thus refers to the active tendency to put forth effort to influence the environment, while feeling of efficacy refers to the satisfaction that comes with producing effects [1963, p. 185].

An important consequence of this behavior is that it leads to the formation of psychological structures, so to speak; "it leads to an accumulating knowledge of what can and cannot be done with the environment [p. 186]."[3] The "meaning" (the infant's understanding) of this interaction is not waiting there to be discovered by the infant but arises from the action sequences (effectance interactions) that he or she imposes on it. "The child has a kind of beginning capacity to organize experience, to contribute something to it *from birth,* and then he builds on this organizational capacity to bring more and more knowledge to bear in an ever-expanding intellectually active sense [Rychlak, 1977, p. 92]." Obviously the child's activity does not create the rattle, but its "capacity to organize experience" does determine what the meaning of its interaction with the rattle will be.

The neonate is confronted with a myriad of possibilities and uncertainties ("a blooming, buzzing confusion") and has to develop gradually the categories for stabilizing its experience. As Rychlak notes, "This quality of open alternatives in experience demands that the human being *affirm* [emphasis added] some·. . . meaning at the outset for the sake of which behavior might then take place [1977, p. 295]."

The connotations of an act of affirmation are important for both Rychlak and White. Affirmation can be used to describe a person's choosing, presuming, or deciding that a thing is so or that it has a certain character (among the possibilities conceivable in the given situation). Affirmation is "one of those *active* [emphasis added] roles assigned to mind by humanists, because which pole of a bipolarity is affirmed or which item of unipolar experience is singled out for identification is up to the individual and *not* to the environment [Rychlak, 1977, p. 295]." It is in this sense that affimations are arbitrary.

In introducing the concept of effectance behavior White describes one of the processes by which the infant actively comes to terms with its environment. Effectance motivation is a way of describing one kind of premise that the newborn child brings to its experience, and in White's view it is a premise that the human individual continues to bring to his or her experience throughout life. When the baby reaches out to make contact with its rattle—an (unconscious) act of "affirmation"—the contact is accompanied by an implicit "affective assessment" of the situation as being pleasing, that is as one it "likes."[4]

With repeated experience the child gradually becomes more effective in achieving this experience as it evolves towards competence. Effectance motivation has clear final-cause or intention-construct implications in that behavior is pursued for the sake of the feeling of efficacy. Eventually, as the mature person develops a sense of "self," he or she begins to order life in terms of enhancement of effectance and competence.

Through repeated and expanded contacts with the world the child develops wider ranges of effectiveness appropriate to its emerging developmental stages. In other words, the child acquires an actual competence and a "sense of competence" about his or her dealings with the environment. A person's competence represents the existing ability to interact effectively with the environment.

Competence is the cumulative result of the history of interactions with the environment. *Sense of competence* is suggested as a suitable term for the subjective side of this, signifying one's consciously or unconsciously felt competence—one's confidence—in dealing with the various aspects of the environment [White, 1963, p. 186].

We can reserve the term *feeling of efficacy* for what is experienced in each individual transaction, using *sense of competence* for the accumulated and organized consequences in later stages of ego development [1963, p. 39].

Striving to enhance competence in one's dealings with the physical and social world is ideally a lifelong process and is characteristic of human functioning in all cultural contexts.

Because the crux of the effectance concept is action on the environment, White's developing human being is, as Chein [1972] would put it, no "passive reagent" but clearly one who, even from the crib, seeks to "generate circumstances" and inject him- or herself "into the causal process of the world around him [or her][p. 6]." While White seems particularly concerned with motor behavior, it should be emphasized that, in the humanistic sense being developed here, action refers to intellectual activity as well. It may or may not involve action in the sense of bodily movement but it does involve the individual as premising "causal agent." In fact, for Roy Schafer (1976), "mind" refers to all the things that a person does in the way of purposive and directed efforts to come to terms with the world. "Mind" represents one's continuing efforts to structure situations conceptually and affectively in the process of living. Schafer [personal communication, March 1, 1980] has suggested that White's emphasis on motor transactions with the environment is too limited to do justice to other kinds of changes in human behavior such as shifts in understanding, i.e., the active restructuring of the way in which one looks at the world. This is the sort of thing that presumably happens in psychodynamic psychotherapy. While White's perspective may be limited in this sense, the scope of his concerns does seem to fit into the framework we are considering here.

The fact that behaviorally induced effects and their consequences are important in White's framework could be seen as making this position close to a (mechanistic) Skinnerian model with its emphasis on how the environment "shapes" emitted behavior.[5] However, the difference is that for White considerable weight is placed on the evaluating, experiencing individuals purposefully orienting themselves toward certain features of the environment and gradually developing a "self-conscious" sense of what kinds of activities do and do not enhance a (subjective) sense of efficacy and sense of competence. The introspective and "telic" terms are important to Robert White also, as they are to humanists generally.

CONCLUSIONS

Thus the humanistic theory we have been describing is a "psycho-logical" theory. That is to say, it is a theory that proposes mind (psyche) as an entity imposing an order, a logic (logos), on events (thus a formal-cause determinative principle). This patterning or conceptualization gives events their meaning and is "that for the sake of which" behavior and further understanding follow. Thus human individuals create the "reality" to which they respond (Edelson, 1971). A student may approach college with the intention of becoming a doctor. This intention, spelled out in a set of steps held in mind—a plan of action—existing now in the present, becomes "that" which makes an essential and determining contribution to ("for the sake of which") the behavior carried out. Such behavior would involve choice of courses, choice of study habits, perhaps choice of summer jobs. Such an intention is not sufficient, of course. Native ability (a substance construct) and sufficient finances are necessary. Also the person must have freedom from competing contradictory plans. For example, becoming extremely active in sports while leading an unusually vigorous social life might very well not be in keeping with the intention to negotiate a pre-med sequence with academic honors.

I have suggested that one of the universal patterns that emerges in child development is the effectance-competence striving. I have argued here that seeing blacks as imposing an order of their own making on events, one that has premises of competence striving in it, helps to make clearer their psychological survival through history. Furthermore, I would propose that one of the major contributions that a stable African background gave to the slaves and their descendants was a basis for a sense of competence as human beings. This is what stable cultural forms give to persons by the very nature of their stability and structuredness. In other words, all people look to a norm to provide the grounds ("that") which can be the initial premise for which later behavior follows. Specific cultural contents with their associated ideological components (such as specific religious and political practices, family organization patterns) which vary from culture to culture may also be supportive.

Thus, specific beliefs that all persons are equal in the sight of Allah or social practices that distribute tribal authority among women as well as men (Carey, 1979) can be supportive to individual tribal members. Kunta Kinte, as described by Haley (1976), maintained a consistent sense of self not just because he was raised an African but because his stable African background gave him the grounds for premising himself as a competent person worth more than the treatment he was getting in the United States.

What I have been trying to demonstrate is that a humanistic focus can contribute a great deal to our understanding of the Afro-American. The humanist in contemporary psychology emphasizes the active role of the individual coming to terms with the environment. According to this view the individual makes choices in situations that are seen as presenting more than one possibility for understanding an action. In making choices individuals are not simply responding to environmentally determined factors but are attempting to carry out intentions and purposes of their own. As we look at the history of blacks, we find that they have responded to the situations they confronted with underlying premises of self-worth and competence even though external circumstances did not seem to warrant positive self-appraisals. When Pugh (1972) states of blacks in history that "the form of resistance—when present—was largely passive," he seems to dismiss such forms of black resistance. But even passive resistance is an *act,* an act borne of a conception of self that was different from that which whites had of blacks. Blacks took the kind of action they were able to take under the circumstances.

Again, the focus on a drive-reduction or environmental-contingency psychology tends to see Afro-Americans only as passive victims. It is very true that blacks have been and continue to be victimized by this society. The more mechanistic psychological views may be able to speak to this fact rather well. However, this focus overlooks other important aspects of human psychology and, therefore, other psychological explanations necessary to understanding blacks' survival. Humankind's tendency not to simply react to stimuli—its tendency to be an "active agent," stems from almost irrepressible urges to create an effective relationship with the environment. From birth on, people take actions that eventually grow into actual competences to deal with the world. Such a conception does not preclude recognizing the individual's relationship to the environment based on drives and their primary satisfaction— including anxiety and its reduction. Rather the humanistic theme that places emphasis on the independent striving to affirm and to make contact with the world is a necessary supplement. A psychological conception of *all* human individuals as potentially active shapers of their worlds makes it easier to understand how blacks survive. It is this that is missing from much of the theorizing about the psychology of the black experience.

Whether in the form of violent revolt or passive resistance; whether engaged in the effort to make themselves competent artisans, farmers, or professionals; throughout history blacks have struggled to realize a sense of themselves that was meaningful to them. A conceptualization of the person that can encompass the fact of survival of Afro-Americans must include this quality of striving or "motivation." Chein (1972) asserts:

> The essential psychological human quality is . . . one of commitment to a developing and continuing set of unending, interacting, interdependent, and mutually modifying long-range enterprises [p. 289].

Slavery, poverty, and racism have been and are dehumanizing to the extent that they lead one to give in to being continually preoccupied with the miseries of the present. Such conditions are dehumanizing to the extent that they lead "to the abandonment of one's claims on, and one's program with regard to the relatively distant future [Chein, 1972, pp. 289-290]." At times this has happened to some black people under the bombardment of the efforts of American society to achieve just this. But many Afro-Americans have managed to use their creative human capacities in modest or striking and socially contributive ways to resist being dehumanized.

NOTES

1. There is some indication in literature on African culture that the Kantian perspective is compatible with the African view of a human being's relationship with nature. In the African world view there is much more recognition of the harmony between humankind and nature. People are not seen as being able to step outside of the natural world (Mbiti, 1970). This sounds much like the idea that we are identifying with Kant here, that knowledge is partly a function of what the observer brings to the observing situation.

2. Some would argue that such intentions have been sustained by blacks having maintained African cultural traditions in as many spheres of life in America as possible. To what degree distinctive African cultural features are a part of Afro-American life is for research and scholarship to determine. The Afro-American's capacity to imagine the opposite of what is presented to them makes it quite possible in principle for blacks to have sustained African cultural perspectives of themselves in spite of the "obstacles and meannesses" imposed on them. Such a dialectical situation is partly implied in DuBois' famous statement that the Afro-American "ever feels his two-ness—an American, a Negro [1961, p. 17]."

However, from another dialectical perspective the Afro-American can be seen to be a *new* cultural being, a blend of the African and the European in which elements of the African influence are quite recognizable but melded into something different from either simply African or European forms. A unique cultural product of the blending of these heritages is the development of jazz, a music form that has African roots yet has evolved beyond those origins in the American setting. Ellison has argued in various places (e.g., Ellison & McPherson, 1970) that blacks have made so many contributions to American popular culture that in many ways it is not possible to call this culture ethnically "white." Similarly, second-generation American citizens of other ethnic extractions are not simply transplanted Italians, Japanese, Swedes, and so forth, either. They are different culturally—and perhaps in some ways psychologically—from the persons of the "Old Country," though they are culturally distinct as groups to some degree among themselves here in this country.

3. Put another way, important consequences of effectance behavior are the building of the child's conceptions of reality and the steady exercise and development of what the psychoanalysts would call the "reality testing" function of the "ego" system. This function has to do with the ability to perceive and make judgments about the world accurately, distinguish between what is a part of oneself and what is not, and use thought and action with repeated reliability in dealing with the world.

4. Affective assessment is an important concept in Rychlak's learning theory and is an example of dialectical functioning in human activity. As we shall see in Chapter 3, a considerable amount of research has been done using this theoretical notion. Affective assessments are judgments with a distinct feeling (hence, "affective") tone that human beings are able to make from birth. Such judgments give one's affirmations about experience a positive or negative affective meaning value. There may be differences in degree of positive or negative assessment (i.e., "very positive" or "rather positive"), there may be mixed feelings (ambivalence), but the dialectical view holds that

there is no indifference point on the dimension of affective assessment. Rychlak maintains that any time an individual conceptualizes a situation, that is, organizes it meaningfully (s)he concomitantly applies an affective assessment or affection to the situation. An affective assessment is a part of every conceptualization. Thus, a person's commitment to a belief always involves affective as well as intellectual components.

In this theory "affections" are different from "emotions." The latter have more of a physiological, and therefore material-cause, quality. Affections, as judgments about experience, "are purely mental phenomena, ultimately *arbitrary* and up to the person who levels such idiographic judgments from his or her (introspective) perspectives on life [Rychlak, 1977, p. 317]." Rychlak derives this notion from the Kantian idea of "transcendence" which refers to the capacity of the mind to "double back on itself," as it were, and evaluate its own evaluations. We experience emotions (e.g., anger, sadness, elation) as a function of the physiological responses that are tied to certain events in our world. Affective assessment or affection, on the other hand, refers to our capacity to reflect on our emotions in a meaningful way. The bashful, lovesick teenager gazing raptly at a picture of the high school Homecoming Queen feels crushed ("blue") that she hardly notices him, much less returns his affection. Yet for a complex of reasons he feels good (he has a positive assessment) about being in such a bad way over someone like her. He assesses his doleful *emotional* state as largely positive and proceeds with the activities that allow it to continue (keeping her picture pinned up in his locker, following her home from a safe distance, etc.) until he develops a different conception of what is important in his life. To return to the neonatal situation, the baby in the crib experiences not only the tactile, visual, and auditory sensations that are the direct occasion for pleasure but brings the at first rudimentary/capacity to evaluate this joyful situation as something to be repeated. White's "feeling of efficacy," the pleasure at recognizing that one is effective (and that for the sake of which behavior continues), is an affective assessment.

5. In the Skinnerian framework when an organism makes a random response an experimenter can increase the probability that that response will be repeated by rewarding the response. By selectively rewarding what were at first random ("emitted") responses (or, at least, responses that didn't fit the experimenter's design) the experimenter can elicit a set of responses that fit the pattern of the experimenter's intentions. This is called "operant conditioning" because it is learning that occurs by affecting the organism's operations on the environment.

For Skinner the meaning of an act is determined by the consequences—the externally observable result—it produces, after the fact. Thus a pigeon's peck of the red not the blue dot is "food-worthy" in meaning only in connection with the reward that follows. But to the humanist things are more complicated for people. A person can anticipate the consequences of an action in advance and choose to proceed or not. Thus a person might say, "Of my two favorite foods I expect the taste of pizza rather than Chinese food will satisfy me most tonight." Previous experience is necessary for the decision but not sufficient to explain this night's choice. For a more extensive critique of Skinner from his humanistic perspective, see Rychlak, 1977, pp. 255-270; 1979, pp. 85-98.

Chapter 2
Afro-American Self Concept: Sustaining Self-Esteem

When I draw a white girl, I know she'll be okay, but with the colored it's not so okay. So I try to give the colored as even a chance as I can, even if that's not the way it will end up being [Coles, 1967, p. 50].

This was the way Ruby explained to the psychiatrist Robert Coles why she rarely used the black and brown crayons when drawing herself and other black people. Ruby was a 6-year-old black girl—the eldest of six children of lower-class parents—and one of the first children to desegregate a New Orleans school in the late 1950s. Coles was in New Orleans attempting to evaluate the impact of school desegregation on black and white southerners who were participants in the profound institutional change of desegregation. In gathering his data he used some of the clinical methods familiar to him as a psychiatrist—primarily one-to-one interviews with people, conducted over a period of time in informal settings where rapport could be developed. With young children his interviews were put into the context of play and included asking the children to draw pictures of the life situations they were in or whatever else they chose to draw. Drawings are a natural mode of expression for children. In the case of their pictures of people it is assumed that the kinds of figures they draw represent aspects of their self-perceptions. For example, the drawing of relatively larger figures with intact bodies is thought to indicate that a person has a relatively secure sense of self—presumably a positive self-image. As to what Ruby's crayon drawings looked like when she and the researcher first started their regular meetings, Coles wrote:

She drew white people larger and more lifelike. Negroes were smaller, their bodies less intact. A white girl we both knew to be her own size appeared several times taller. While Ruby's own face . . . lacked an eye in one drawing, an ear in another, the white girl never lacked any features (p. 47).

Ruby was the center of great controversy when she entered 1st grade in her New Orleans school. Almost all of the white parents chose to withdraw their children from the few desegregated schools that first year. Some joined the crowds of shrieking adults who picketed school property and lined the walk to the front door of Ruby's and other schools. Consequently, Ruby's first few years of school, which should have been joyous ones, were instead full of traumatic experiences affecting both Ruby and her family.

Ruby undoubtedly realized that she was the focus of so much attention because she was black. The desegregation drama had brought her face to face with racial slurs and violent threats expressed openly and unequivocally. One might easily have attributed her diminished representation of black figures and her cautious use of certain colors to the disturbing effects of being the target of racial hatred during the school desegregation crisis. That would have been too facile an explanation, because other evidence showed up in some earlier drawings made by Ruby when she attended her all-black Sunday school class. When Coles examined some of these earlier pictures, which had been made before he or the desegregation conflict had come into her life, he found that she had been drawing black people in a similarly incomplete way and had been careful about using the dark-colored crayons when she was a preschooler. It could only be concluded that these characteristics of her drawings reflected something relatively longstanding in her feelings about race that were not simply referrable to the immediate crisis.

Ruby's preschool desegregation drawings placed the onset of her lowered self-image at a time previous to the time she entered first grade when she was 6 years old. Racial group membership, Coles concluded after his extended observations of Ruby and other children, had a distinct and deleterious impact on these black children's conceptions of themselves from early preschool years. But other things were going on in their lives. In Ruby's case, she was of course frightened and saddened by the events surrounding her, but she maintained an amazing degree of poise during those trying times, much more than could have been expected of a 6-year-old child under so much pressure. In fact, her sleep, school work, and play with her friends were not disturbed. (We shall talk later of a psychiatric symptom that did develop for a time.) Like any other child she was going through the various stages of social-emotional and intellectual growth in a particular family, making good progress in many areas, and hitting some snags in others.

The example of Ruby illustrates rather well one of the dilemmas posed by the seemingly contradictory findings in the literature on the self-concept of Afro-Americans. For, on the one hand, Ruby's self-esteem connected with racial membership appeared to be quite shaky from her drawings, while at the same time she seemed to be getting along well and doing a good job at growing up. By the same token, a good deal of the research literature has reported that the self-concept of blacks has been heavily damaged by racism, while at the same time other findings have indicated that black self-esteem has been relatively high. These contradictions in the research literature have been frequently noted and have become more and more the focus of inquiry of black behavioral and social scientists. The direction that the reconsideration of the data has taken has stemmed from conceptual and methodological critiques. In this chapter an attempt has been made to apply a humanistic perspective in psychology as a way of supplementing and clarifying some of the current reappraisal of the data on black self-concept.

RESEARCH: LOW SELF-ESTEEM IN BLACK CHILDREN

Many observers have concluded that there is a considerable amount of "self-hatred" in the black community, even among black children. This rather widely held assumption about the low self-esteem of Afro-Americans is based partly on research done from the late thirties through the mid-sixties. According to these studies evidence of negative self-esteem can be elicited from black children of nursery school age. Of the various methods that have been used to measure racial awareness and self-evaluation of black youngsters (Brand et al., 1974), one of the most frequently employed has been the doll-preference technique used by Kenneth and Mamie Clark in their famous series of studies. The method consisted of presenting a pair of dolls, one brown and one white, to black children, age 3 to 7 years, while asking them questions about the dolls to get at their knowledge of racial terms, their understanding of what racial group they belong to and other aspects of their attitudes toward the dolls (Clark & Clark, 1952). Assuming that the answers to these questions would have implications for the children's racial feelings, the Clarks found that preschool black children had considerable knowledge of racial labels ("colored," "Negro," "white"), and preferred the white doll as the "pretty" doll and the more desirable object of play. In general the Clarks concluded that there was evidence here of a negative attitude toward racial identity on the part of a large number of these children.

Several decades of research using variations of the doll study design produced evidence that seemed to corroborate the Clark findings about the poor self-image of black children. In recent years, however, there has been a good deal of criticism both of the methodology used in making the doll studies and the rather bleak conclusions drawn from them about the negative self-concept of black Americans. Although this criticism was well justified when applied to some of the studies, it was not so appropriately aimed at the work of other investigators who had already recognized the methodological deficiencies of the first wave of doll studies. What had emerged from the newly designed research, however, were findings about black self-esteem that were quite similar to conclusions of the earlier studies, although the interpretation of the findings was more cautious and qualified.

For example, Judith Porter (1971) had already taken into account the methodological weaknesses of the Clark design in her study of a large sample of northern urban black and white nursery school children in the late sixties. To make the play situation more natural she had a small manipulable doll scene built and engaged the children in making up a "story for TV" (this was adapted from the "Movie Story Game" of Evans, Chein, and Hogrefe [Evans & Chein, 1948], developed to measure racial attitudes in elementary school children). In the course of this "game" in which the children could use a set of dolls for their TV dramas—there were grown-up dolls and child dolls, both brown and white skinned—the children were asked questions meant to reveal racial attitudes. Employing more sophisticated statistical analyses than most of the previous research, Porter also introduced controls for social class and amount of interracial contact in the classroom. In addition she controlled for other potentially extraneous variables about the dolls such as their sex, hair color, and color of their clothes. This enabled her to say with some degree of confidence that preferential doll choice had racial implications, particularly for the black children she studied.

From among her several sets of findings, of particular interest to us here was that black children showed a preference for the white doll. It was not clear, however, whether preference for a white doll always meant *rejection* of the brown doll. In a situation where the children *had* to make preferential choices between brown and white figures, white choice, Porter hypothesized, might have reflected neutral or even moderately favorable attitudes toward both dolls with a somewhat greater preference for the white one. But there was no doubt that rejection of the brown dolls was involved for some children since it could be heard in their spontaneous comments while at play.[1]

On the matter of social class influence on doll preference Porter reported the interesting finding that attitudes toward the dolls varied by social class. Working-class black children showed greater preference for the brown dolls than did the middle-class black children. Porter interpreted this as reflecting the fact that working-class black families living in predominantly black environments were themselves stable and had access to the supportive features of stable institutions in the black community. In contrast, middle-class black families were more likely to have more contact with middle-class white families than the working-class group. In comparing themselves with such families middle-class blacks would be under the strong pressure of American racial mores to see themselves as being of a lower status than whites even though both black and white families were middle class.

In a series of studies using a different kind of methodology Williams and Morland (1976) also found that young children—both black and white—in various regions of the country expressed a preference for light-colored objects, animals, and people over dark ones. Using pictures of black and white animals rather than human figures in one research design, they asked the children to give semantic evaluations of a pair of different-colored animals after listening to a story fragment about each pair (The Color Meaning Test). (Semantic evaluations here refer to asking subjects to rate a given stimulus item using different evaluative adjectives such as good, clean, and nice versus bad, dirty, and naughty.) Children of both races expressed a white-preference, black-avoidance tendency. A similar white-color preference was indicated by older children. Black children at the 6th-grade levels rated white more positively when they were given other tests of semantic evaluation. White-color preference has been found generally to be less strong in blacks than in whites in these studies.

Further studies related semantic evaluations to photographs of persons with white European ("Euro") and Afro-American ("Afro") characteristics using the Preschool Racial Attitude Measure (PRAM). Williams and his colleagues found that black and white nursery and early elementary school children expressed a more positive attitude toward "Euro" characters, although again the Euro-American children clearly showed more "Euro" bias than did the Afro-American children. More black children had scores in the "no-bias" range. (Porter had also noted that, on the whole, preference for the white doll was not as strong among the black as among the white subjects in her study.)

Using a variety of measures in her study of self-concept and racial attitude in Afro-American children, McAdoo (1977) also found a moderate white preference among various groups of children. Her samples consisted of 4- to 6-year-old groups of children from an all-black, rural Mississippi town; a residentially segregated suburb outside of Detroit; and children from the Washington, D.C., area. Her study was an extensive one which included retest data on her sample. We will have more to say about her research later.

Overall, carefully designed studies have consistently indicated some out-group orientation in the attitudes of young Afro-American children. In other words, when children were required to express a preference for dolls or pictures of lighter as opposed to darker people or animals, they tended to choose the lighter ones. As was indicated, what seemed to be preference for the lighter did not necessarily mean a broad rejection of themselves by these children. However, since some of the preference questions had to do with physical attractiveness and preference as play objects or play partners, the data have been taken as reflecting some ambivalence about the self. (Banks and his colleagues [1979] still feel that there are unanswered questions about the validity of the "white preference" phenomenon notwithstanding Williams and Morland's rejoinder [1979] to Bank's previous critique [1976] of research in the area of racial attitudes in children.)

RESEARCH: HIGH SELF-ESTEEM IN BLACK CHILDREN

Meanwhile other kinds of evidence had been accumulating which indicated that black children felt neither ambivalence about nor rejection of their own group and that their self-esteem was in fact high. Hraba and Grant (1970) and Ward and Braun (1972) found that northern black children tended over-whelmingly to prefer the dolls of their own race when they were presented with the Clark paradigm. Fish and Larr (1972) and McAdoo (1977) also discovered that the figure drawings done in the 1970s by black children showed an increase in indicators that would identify the figures as being black. All of these researchers interpreted their data as evidence of the positive effects of the Black Revolution on children's self-image. What seemed to show up was a new pride in themselves and their racial identity. Thus it appeared that their self-esteem was changing for the better. (Banks [1976] has raised the question of whether greater own-race doll preference represents greater [and healthier] racial pride or greater [and not necessarily healthier] ethnocentrism.)

In addition, a number of reports (Bachman, 1970; Baughman, 1971; Po-well, 1973; Taylor, 1976) indicated that, in large-scale studies, self-esteem was at least as high among black children of varying social backgrounds as it was among white children. In one of the better known of these studies, Rosenberg and Simmons (1971) administered a six-item Gutman-type self-esteem scale to a large urban sample of 3rd- to 12th-grade black and white school children in Baltimore and related the results to other social and personal characteristics gleaned in the course of extensive interviews, including questions eliciting direct statements of feelings about themselves. Not only was the self-esteem of black children high, but more black children reported feelings of high self-esteem than did white children of the same age.

Contrary to the studies reviewed in the previous section this recent research indicated that a sense of competence as reflected in high self-esteem was characteristic of black children. These findings appeared to be in clear contra-diction to those studies that had shown that some black children expressed either negative feelings or at least a degree of ambivalence about some aspects of themselves. While only a sample of the more often cited or the better designed studies have been presented here, they are sufficient to illustrate the conflicting trends in the literature on self-concept and self-esteem in Afro-American children. (For a more exhaustive review of most of the studies done on self-concept and self-esteem among Afro-Americans, see Gordon, 1977).

SELF-CONCEPT: A MANY-FACETED ENTITY

Let us turn our attention to a reconciliation of what seem to be contradictions in the findings about self-esteem in Afro-American children. To some extent, trying to compare studies has been difficult because they have used different methodologies for examining self-concept (Gordon, 1977; Wylie, 1974). But equally important to how we understand the results of these studies is our understanding of what the terms self and self-concept refer to—that is, we have to clarify some underlying conceptual issues about the self before we look at the research.

In our rush to have something definitive and useful to say about self-concept and self-esteem we often forget that people are complex. The concepts we use to account for behavior sometimes oversimplify, rather than take account of the complexity needed to do justice to the human person. It is one of the tenets of this book, for example, that trying to conceive of the human being as *only* an object that can be manipulated like a machine—even a complicated one—is an oversimplification and has disadvantages for the way we think about black people. While we cannot devote a lengthy discussion to this topic of the self, we can set out some basic ideas here that will help us reorient our conception of the self in Afro-Americans.

Traditionally, the term self refers to those aspects of experience which the individual considers to be "I" and "me." Gradually, through experience with the world, what is self comes to be distinguished by the person from everything that is experienced as "not me." Now, there is a kind of (dialectic) paradox in the idea of self. On one hand self implies that in every person there is the feeling of being a functioning unit organized to achieve certain goals in life (White & Watt, 1981, pp. 148–149). On the other hand this organization or patterning is made up of a variety of different personal tendencies and characteristics. Self and self-concept, while standing for the cohesiveness of the individual, are also multifaceted. Thus, a person's self-concept is an interconnected collection of the various ideas, images, and feelings that (s)he holds about the self.[2] This collection is organized; that is, the different parts are meaningfully interrelated as far as the person is concerned—they are not just present in a haphazard fashion. (What is illustrated here is the "one-in-many" quality of events that dialectic focuses on. This particular unity-in-plurality notion dates back at least to the ancient Greek philosophers. The idea is that there is a oneness [identity] in the manifoldness of events. Self is a unity but patterned of many personal tendencies. See Rychlak for further discussion of this one-in-many aspect of dialectics [e.g., 1977].)

One very important aspect of the self-concept is self-esteem. Self-esteem refers to self-evaluations; that is, it refers to judgments that we make about our worth. Self-esteem consists of affective assessments about the self. These assessments are judgments that give our conceptions a positive or negative feeling tone or valence. So the affirmations about oneself that are a part of self-concept, for example, "I am a girl," "I am a six-year-old," "I am a black child," get important meaning from the positive or negative valence (or the ambivalence) attached to them. Just as people have feelings about all the aspects of their lives that are meaningful to them, so they have feelings about all aspects of their self-conceptualization. Some aspects of self-concept are not conscious and so some aspects of self-esteem are not conscious either. As a result people may hold different feelings about themselves at different levels of consciousness. People strive to keep self-esteem at a positive level generally in order to support their daily encounters with the world (Epps, 1975; Epstein, 1973). We do this partly by trying to be effective in the world through activities and social relationships that we can find rewarding. One's sense of competence is another way of talking about self-esteem. (People whose personal development and social circumstances are or have been difficult may attempt to maintain self-esteem through various types of psychological distortions of their experience called "defenses." All of us use such maneuvers to some extent.)

Granted that maintenance of positive self-evaluation is a basic striving, there are different things that people can do to sustain this feeling:

> The individual may choose from among a number of characteristics in his efforts to maintain self-esteem. . . . One's self-esteem may be based upon such varied characteristics as athletic prowess, dress and physical appearance, attractiveness to the opposite sex, skill at verbal repartee, and skill at fighting, as well as academic achievement [Epps, 1975, p. 305].

These multiple bases for establishing self-esteem reflect the idea that self is many-sided. People value such components of themselves differently according to their personal history, the opportunity structure (the realistic chances for making use of educational achievement, for example), and ethnic and social class group membership. Black and white persons probably value some components of self-concept differently (Baldwin, 1979).

But, even more important, the individual can develop varied and even conflicting components of self. For one thing this has implications for the measurement of self-esteem. Since self-concept is varied and components are differentially valued, tests of self-concept that measure a person's general level of self-esteem are not necessarily good at describing a more specific aspect of self-esteem. For example, if you use global measures of self-esteem you are less likely to be able to predict academic achievement than if you use specific measures of academic self-esteem (Epps, 1975).

Related to that measurement issue is the fact that self-esteem is affected by the situation a person is responding to (Gordon, 1977). For example, students may justifiably be able to think of themselves as academically competent in one context, say in a small high school in the rural South. But upon entering a different setting, let's say a large prestigious black college, they may find this aspect of self-esteem being challenged considerably by the more rigorous classroom demands and the better student body. This would call for a different conceptualization about themselves. Both the lack of specificity of a test and the situational quality of self-esteem may be reflected in the contradictory literature on self-esteem in black children.

Even when measurement issues are taken into account, the fact that self-esteem is multifaceted and situational does not mean that the self and its attributes are simply a random collection of characteristics. Rather the implication is that people define themselves from a number of different perspectives while still maintaining a sense of continuity as a person. Speaking to this point Cross (1978a) suggests that a "multiple reference point" perspective may account for many of the contradictions in the literature on self-concept in black children. By this he means that black children have available and make use of different reference groups and their associated values in assessing themselves. Based on his review of the literature, he argues that on the one hand much of the research done before the late 1960s reflected black children's *racial* reference group attitudes, that is, their attitudes toward their own group and towards whites. It is primarily from these studies that conclusions about low self-esteem in black children have been drawn. On the other hand studies in which test items tend not to raise issues of racial group membership have consistently yielded positive self-evaluation among black children. These studies tap *personal* self-esteem rather than racial self-concept.

What happens when racial and personal self-esteem measures are included in the same study? The results are mixed, but the larger studies (McAdoo, 1977; Porter, 1971; Rosenberg & Simmons, 1971) tend to indicate that when black children have some degree of low self-esteem about race they do not necessarily have a correspondingly poor concept about other aspects of themselves. In other words, racial and personal self-esteem can be different. Based on such data Cross suggests that, while sense of *personal* self-esteem among Afro-American children is and always has been high—at least as high as among whites—regarding racial self-evaluation prior to the late sixties, many young black children seem to have used whites instead of blacks as the reference point for what was positive. It may be that this racial outgroup orientation among blacks is changing as a result of events of the last decade or so. (It is this aspect of self-esteem that would be consistent with Pugh's analysis [1972]. Such a trend is suggested by the Hraba and Grant [1970] and Ward and Braun [1972] studies. However, the rather blunt presentation of questions used in such Clark doll design studies may be less useful as a technique these days when children are so sensitized to conscious racial pride messages. Porter's method [1971] seems more subtle and more useful in contemporary contexts.)[3]

In sum, what we have been saying so far is that self-concept is a multifaceted sense that one has about what one is. It is a theory about oneself. Self-esteem is a set of affective evalutions about oneself; people try by their actions to keep self-esteem at a relatively positive level. Apart from the problems of measurement of self-esteem in general, and among minority persons in particular, the contradictions in the literature on the self-esteem of black children partly reflect the fact that self-concept is multifaceted. Persons have available to themselves a variety of vantage points (or "anchor points," as Cross says) which they use to conceptualize themselves and their place in the world at any given moment. The data reflect the complexity of self-esteem and the fact that black children have used more than one set of reference points to evaluate themselves depending partly on what they were being asked to do. If the reference point was self-esteem from the vantage point of racial group membership, it might contain some negative feelings, while at the very same moment they might feel quite positive about other parts of themselves.

SELF AS ACTIVE AGENT

The next thing we need to do is see how some of the humanistic concepts that we have developed in Chapter 1 can help us understand the complexity of self-concept and self-esteem still further. What is required here is a clear picture of the *active* quality of the self. The self-concept, the (relatively static) view that we develop of ourselves as we turn our gaze toward ourselves—as an object, so to speak—is not the only sense we have of self (Keen, 1970). We are also aware of ourselves as agents. By agents I mean we recognize ourselves as persons who take action, take initiative, make decisions, and make choices from among possibilities. Thus self is also a way of talking about our capacity to come to a situation that is full of possibilities (as most situations are) and make a choice in that situation. As we do this we shape the course of our lives.

This can be seen even in young children. Let's take as an example of this choosing and affirmation activity a hypothetical 7-year-old boy, physically well coordinated, whose acknowledged enjoyment of vigorous muscular activity and his vivid imagination are fulfilled by his active interest in baseball. He avidly follows the exploits of his local major league team which, let's say, is clearly on its way to the World Series. Every chance he gets he plays baseball, draws pictures of his favorite team, uses his still rudimentary reading skills to follow the scores in the paper and to devour simple books on the game, and he watches (as much as his parents will let him) the televised games of *any* major league team instead of the Tom and Jerry cartoons or *Sesame Street* which he used to enjoy. He plays ball with his friends as much as he can and gets his parents to play catch with him as often as he is able to entice them to do so.

The choices he makes, given various options around him, are determined by ("for the sake of") his intention: "I'm going to be a major league (i.e., competent) baseball player when I grow up." As we look at him we can see a consistent pattern to the choices he makes, in this sense "the self is a kind of 'logical thrust' . . . which organisms under our observation bring to bear as they 'come at' the world [Rychlak, 1977, p. 350]." From our aspiring young ballhawk's point of view—that is, from an introspective point of view—the self represents "that sense of orientation and *identity* in behavior which mechanists are prone to consider illusory experience [p. 351]." He has a clear sense of where he wants to go and of getting there by trying to be like Reggie Jackson or Willie Stargell as the case may be—hence the wearing of baseball wrist bands to bed and to school, and the ever-present baseball cap and the shirt with his hero's number on it. The point here is that the choices he is making—to get the most exposure to baseball-related things that he can—determine his activities and the skills he develops. It determines the kinds of friendships he makes—to the exclusion of other possibilities. He is actively shaping what he is becoming. Although he is conscious of his intentions—intentions that of course may not come to fruition—that is, he may never be a major league class ballplayer, one does not have to assume that he is aware of the process I am describing here as such, that is, of contributing to his self-development. Nonetheless he *is* the product of his choices. As he affirms with pride, "I am a good baseball player," this little boy is developing aspects of his self-concept. This is a rudimentary example of what is even more true of the older adolescent or adult individual, namely, that people are active in their own creation.

In his poem, "The Road Not Taken", Robert Frost (1964) captures the idea that to some degree we are responsible for our lives by how our intentions guide our choices. He describes a traveler (a metaphor for the self as I am viewing it here) who stands at a point where the path diverges in two directions. The traveler decides to take one of the paths—the one that is less worn by travel, and later comes to recognize that this choice "has made all the difference" in his life. In one sense a person's development proceeds through time in the selection of one or another "path" or option for carrying out one's life. My example was of a little boy, since we are talking of children in this chapter, but it certainly applies even more to people as they gain greater intellectual and emotional maturity and become better able to appreciate the environmental options, their own skills, and to anticipate consequences. Self-concept is like the "trail" one can recognize as one turns to reflect on the steps one has taken. That trail is made of the active decisions that have brought one to this point. The trail of choices is part of the answer to the question, "What am I?" The self is the particular "logical thrust" that a person's intentions give to his pattern of choices. To paraphrase the title of Frost's poem, self is "the road *taken*." Thus we are the products of the choices we make—the paths we take. We are self-creating beings to an important degree.

These ideas highlight an important characteristic of human psychology, namely, the creative activity and creative potential in every human being. Now, in what sense do I mean this? As I said earlier, in imposing a conception on events, all human individuals create the "reality" to which they respond (Edelson, 1971, esp. Chap. 1). Self-creation is an important example of this, too, and is a fundamental aspect of the humanistic conception. Interestingly enough such a notion has long been implicit in Judeo-Christian thought, though unrecognized. In the biblical story of Creation, as Chein (1972) calls attention to it, all acts up to the creation of humankind are represented as being commanded simply by God and then as having been completed: "And God said, Let there be light: and there was light." The creation of humankind, however, is heralded by, "We will make Man," a statement that is a literal translation of the Hebrew text. For the first and only time God uses the plural subject and the future tense. There is no statement in the text of the completion of humankind's creation as there was with the creation of other aspects of the world. The "we" form is seen to indicate that God took human beings into partnership, and the future tense indicates that this creation is far from completed. "What more magnificent creation, short of the creation of the universe itself, can be attributed to God than a self-creating being? [Chein, 1972, p. 42]." (While Chein indicates this as an aspect of occidental thinking, such an idea is fully consonant with many other religious and cultural traditions as well.)

In drawing on this illustration I want to highlight the fact that Afro-Americans have been very much engaged in the business of their own creation through the intentional, dialectical activity of mind. Our task in living, then, is no less than for each one of us to reclaim our creative heritage and potential in our daily living. The notion that all human beings create their worlds implies that creativity is not just a special activity reserved only for a few gifted individuals. It is true that the nature of a particular creative product is a function of the degree of self-development or special talent of a particular individual. However, the humanistic psychological tradition underscores the idea that our usual honorific notions of creativity are really a special case of what every human being does or could do to a more limited degree.[4]

It could be argued that a model that puts emphasis on choice and self-creation does not properly describe the young child's situation on two counts. First, it seems to run counter to the conventional wisdom that self is a social product, that is, that the self is the result of the influx of social experience. Second, this model may seem to be particularly inappropriate for the ethnic minority child in a hostile society. Now, it is true that self-development is heavily influenced by the actions and attitudes of important persons toward one. "Important persons" here means family, peers, and other people in society whom one recognizes as having some authority over one. In fact it is hard to think of a sense of self developing outside of a social context. G. H. Mead stressed this particularly in his description of self as "the generalized other," literally a self that is the reflection of the social group (1952).

It is also true that development of sense of self is a difficult task for children. This is all the more so in the early years of life when equipment for understanding the world and one's place in it is not well developed. In the face of uncertainty and openness in experience, all people, and especially children, feel the need to establish as much regularity in their lives as quickly as they can in new situations. This would seem to point to the fact that children are especially vulnerable to the influence of more knowledgeable and powerful adults.

Such notions of social influence *on* self-development and functioning emphasize a more passive and Lockean stance toward the self. A humanistic approach insists in complementary fashion on the importance of the active (choosing, affirming) aspects of self. To say that self-concept could not develop outside of a social milieu simply means that the social context serves as the grounds or the basis for the child's self-conceptualizing. A child is surrounded by a variety of options for self-development. All possible human options, however, are not open, and so the child is, of course, limited by the nature of the culture that is making the options available. Yet within these limits the child develops in ways not fully accounted for by the environment alone. The child also develops by selections made based on the personal constructions (meaning) (s)he places on what is presented by the environment; that is, the social scene serves as grist for the child's mill, so to speak.

Thus in considering the origin and development of self-concept for the purposes of this book I would shift the focus and say that children turn to the world in search of meaningful guidelines for fashioning and patterning their sense of self. It seems likely that this is guided by what seem to the child to be effectance behaviors. While it is true that self-concept is a product of social interaction, the phrase "turn . . . in search of" implies an *active* taking on of values in the service of growth and self-development. Drive and environmental contingencies play an essential part but the individual as affirmer is also necessarily a part of the process—usually more and more so with developing maturity.

What I am suggesting is that formation of sense of self as represented in self-concept draws on the processes of choice that are active in other areas of life. More and more as the child grows, the intentions that govern self-development become increasingly well formed (although still they are often unconscious). These of course are conceptualized within the framework of the language and materials of the child's culture. One cannot fully understand objectifiable aspects of self-concept choice without understanding the (active) intention that governs that choice. For example, it is one thing to choose a self-definition of "little ballerina" in order to fulfill the intention of being "mommy's little girl," and it is quite another to base such a choice on fascination with the visual and rhythmic aspects of the dance itself and the intention of reproducing these by one's own activity. In self-development one tends to make choices that seem to help one to "live and grow" within one's milieu. The Afro-American child, like all children, brings an active orientation to his or her encounter with experience and uses the social environment as grounds—as reference points—for behavioral and conceptual choices that get adopted into the sense of self. Of course where pleasing social interactions are few the child may develop an orientation of avoiding the anxiety of unpleasant interactions with the adults (s)he needs so much by withdrawing or by stunting self-development. Drive reduction as a motive (here, the reduction of interpersonally based anxiety) becomes primary; but even so, as the individual purposefully withdraws (see Arieti's concept of "teleological regression," 1974), (s)he has an active role in "making something" of himself or herself.

Some critics would argue that a child is so constrained by the influence of parents and by its rudimentary equipment for understanding the world (a material-cause notion) that choice cannot be said to be a factor. The behavior "chosen" is the only one possible in the situation "as the child sees it." But the latter is just the point here. The behavior is constrained not only by the realities of the situation but by how the child "sees" (i.e. construes) them. The form of this conception, a pattern construct, governs the behavior in a very rigid way. As soon as one acknowledges that how one behaves is a function of how one sees things, one has to admit of a variety of possible ways of construing a given situation. Thus one cannot rule out the active shaping by the mental process of the very young child which leads to behavior that cannot be accounted for simply by the facts of the external environment. Of course, "how one sees things" is a function of developmental maturity. The older individual will see things in ways that will allow more effective behavior. But this does not rule out the principle that, throughout life, behavior is partly dependent on how one "sees" things, that is, how one conceptualizes them.

SELF-CONCEPT: A PRODUCT OF DIALECTICAL ACTIVITY

Having highlighted the active aspects of the self, let us now examine how the dialectical idea fits in with this notion of activity for a better understanding of the complexity of self-concept and self-esteem. The process of self-creation that we have discussed is guided in individuals of all ages by the striving to harmonize various facets of the self with the purpose of maintaining a sense of consistency and positive self-regard in self-conceptualization. People accomplish this at least partly by drawing on the effectance strivings that develop very early in life. In other words, human beings—children and adults—move toward activities that allow them to exercise effectance behaviors in their interaction with the world. The fact that some of the conceptions black children may adopt reflect some of the negative experiences that the culture exposes them to is a part of the multifaceted nature of self-esteem and does not negate the positive strivings in black children. The positive data that Taylor (1976) and Cross (1978a) point to suggest that in the process of self-creation blacks in America have not simply been at the mercy of a single (unipolar) definition of themselves. Even when white doll choice reflected negative racial connotations this did not constitute the black child's only basis for self-evaluation. While black children showed an outgroup orientation in some contexts they showed considerable genuine skill and self-enjoyment when functioning in other contexts. Children have a variety of aspects of self to draw on as they develop self-esteem. A dialectical view recognizes the basic human capacity to see the alternatives that life poses, thereby making individual decision and affirmation possible. If observers recognized the existence and use of this capacity among blacks in the developing sense of self there would possibly be less surprise and less need to explain away either the positive or the negative side of the data on self-esteem. Thus, a child might in some contexts make a choice reflecting an outgroup preference but that does not mean he devalues his particular friends, his ability to draw or to throw a ball, or his sense of being loved by his family. This capacity to take alternative routes in self-definition is one aspect of dialectical functioning.[5]

There is another aspect of the dialectic perspective that is relevant to this discussion. Although different facets of the person may surface from time to time the individual usually has the experience of continuity or identity in the aspects of self that are manifested. This is partly what we mean by a sense of identity. Although I recognize that I tend to be one way in one situation and another way in a different situation, it is still *I* who am that way. We are aware of a oneness in the many sides of ourselves.

One aspect of the continuity and cohesiveness of self is the striving to grow, to be competent, to be self-enhancing. These terms reflect the person's balancing the positive and negative aspects of experience to try and "come out ahead" in their sense of self as much as possible. The little boy for whom being a baseball player is the most important thing in the world right now still recognizes other aspects of self—that he is a black child, that he is an American, for instance. He also recognizes that he is not so good an arithmetic student or a swimmer as he is in other things. These are all aspects of himself that he recognizes. He may, at his parents' bidding, work to improve some of the things that he doesn't care so much about, but he still maintains his own hierarchy of what he thinks is *really* important. He may get into some difficulties with parents and teachers if they don't like his choices as to what is important and this may lead to psychological conflicts for him as he struggles with the problem of possibly losing his parents' love and support if he pursues what *he* thinks is important in self-development.

Part of the problem of measuring self-concept (leaving aside for the moment inadequate measuring instruments) stems from the fact that from one occasion to the next, when asked, the subject may come to measurement situations from a different perspective about self and abilities. From the humanistic perspective, this shift does not mean that there is no internal consistency to the self.

Much of what is called the unreliability of traits or self-concepts in predicting across different situations . . . stems from the dialectical ability of the individual to press more than simply one premise at the [choice point] in any given circumstance. . . . The extraspective theorist presumes that what must be identical across situations is the observed behavior and not some premising identity guiding even differential behaviors from circumstance to circumstance [Rychlak, 1977, p. 352].

Viewed subjectively, there is a consistent orientation, an "identity" in the "logical thrust" that self brings to events. For black people, then, though they have experienced themselves as having many facets, they have also experienced themselves as having a continuity of identity as individuals. For many this continuity has included the striving—the intention—to sustain a sense of competence in whatever areas of life they could. Sustaining competence involved exercising their sense of agency. Some chose rebellion and were punished; some chose escape and were successful. Others became competent farmers and artisans where they were. Many, whatever other course they took, struggled to establish stable families as havens for themselves and their children. Of course choices were determined by available opportunities. But such opportunities did not force behavior in one direction or another. Opportunities were filtered through personal processes including the particular manifestation of competence strivings in different individuals.

In the course of emphasizing self-activity in the form of competence strivings, it should also be recognized that the contributions of the self to behavior are not always positive. History gives ample testimony to the fact that the choices one makes—self-contributions—in trying to have an effect on the world too frequently take the form of wishes to dominate and destroy others. Self-contributions can be selfish. However, to note that self-contributions *can* go awry from an ethical or social viewpoint, does not mean that they *must* go awry. It is almost impossible to get around the notion that individuals make choices (at conscious and unconscious levels) that govern their behavior (Schafer, 1976). Self-activity exists as a function of being human. Granted this humanistic view of people is not necessarily a more optimistic view. Whether self-activities develop to their fullest and, if so, develop as prosocial competence rather than simply skills at manipulating physical and social reality for personal advantage, depends on a number of factors, not the least of which is how the social environment responds to the individual's effectance efforts.

THE BLACK FAMILY AND SELF-CONCEPT

The black family has always had to deal with the corrosive impact of racism on its members throughout their lives. Rearing children in a hostile environment has confronted parents with the particularly difficult task of giving their children an opportunity to develop positive feelings about themselves, their families, and the black community. Shielding infants and very young children from bigotry and discriminatory acts was a technique adopted by many families. But the development of positive self-images in black children has involved a great deal more than that. From what is known about how the family contributes to personality development—and this is far from complete—it can be said that the children's attitudes towards themselves—their self-concepts—are crucially related to their experiences in the family. More specifically, it has been demonstrated that self-esteem is higher among those children who report better relationships with their parents (Bachman, 1970; Rosenberg & Simmons, 1971). It seems reasonable to expect that families that are more stably structured will provide the supportive relationships necessary to positive self-concept development. By stable structure I mean a household where some adults—one or two parents, a grandmother, or other relative—are consistently available and working to provide for members' basic physical and emotional needs. Of course, a stable family unit is not the only contributor to self-evaluation, nor does such a family guarantee positive self-esteem for a child. But such a setting certainly has a head start on fostering the kinds of parent-child interactions that lead to positive personal self-esteem.

Some writers have chosen to highlight the idea that disproportionately large numbers of black families were disorganized by the ravages of both the slavery and postslavery periods. According to this view the inability to develop the level of stability typical of other (white) ethnic groups in America made it hard and often impossible for black families to provide security for family members and to carry out properly the tasks of socializing Afro-American children (see, for example, Moynihan, 1965). Alongside these findings about the black family are the findings that black children have developed a positive evaluation of many aspects of themselves. The question arises, then, of whether or not in the main the black family is to be discounted when we look for sources of the development of positive self-esteem in black children. The answer, of course, is that we do not have to skirt around the black family in our search for institutions in the black community that contribute positively to the average black child's development.

In fact, there has been considerable rebuttal of the recently resurrected deficit view of the black family (Billingsley, 1968; Hill, 1971). Of particular interest here is the scholarship that indicates that blacks throughout their history in America organized their family and kinship patterns in ways that allowed them to support the development of their children and provide emotional security for family members (Cross, 1978a; Gutman, 1976). These patterns may have been similar to those they were familiar with from their African background. The research suggests that after slavery, from the end of the nineteenth century through the first quarter of the twentieth, the kinds of family organization developed by blacks were as stable and functional as those in families of other ethnic groups. And among the comparatively larger number of female-headed households existing among blacks in recent times there is considerable use of extended kinship networks or of nonkin who are regarded as kinfolk to support and stabilize the functioning of the family unit.

This revised view of the black family states that the black family has long had a structure that would enable it to nurture the personal aspects of self-esteem and self-concept. What black families seem to have done historically is engender a sense of personal worth in their children by separating the personal sense of themselves from the negative perceptions the racist society has attached to racial group membership (Billingsley, 1968; Pettigrew, 1964). This keeping separate of aspects of self-evaluation is consistent with the findings that indicate that self-concept is complex and that people have varying sets of attitudes toward different parts of themselves. In the interest of survival the black family has worked to present the black child with frames of reference that were alternatives to those imposed by white society, thereby allowing these children other ways of evaluating their worth. W.E.B. DuBois, writing in *The Crisis* magazine in 1926, was very clear in his suggestions to black parents about how they should go about setting up such alternate frames of reference:

> At least in your home you have a chance to make your child's surroundings of the best; books and pictures and music; cleanliness, order, sympathy and understanding; information, friendship and love,—there is not much of evil in the world that can stand against such home surroundings [Diggs, 1976, p. 390].

Many black families have made great effort to follow DuBois' admonitions. This has not been limited only to the literate and well-to-do in the black community. An unlettered Mississippi woman was perfectly capable of analyzing a complex social issue when asked by her preschool age children about racial inequities. She reported her explanation as follows:

> I tell the children that it's a confusing world, and they have to get used to it. You have to try to overcome it, but you can't hide it from the kids. When they ask me why colored people aren't as good as whites, I tell them it's not that they're not as good; it's that they're not as rich. Then I tell them that they should separate being poor and being bad, and not get them mixed up. I . . . remind them that the Lord is a mighty big man, and what He thinks is not the same as what white folks do. . . . I tell them, and I hope that makes them feel satisfied, so they don't dislike themselves. That's bad, not liking your own self [Coles, 1967, p. 64].

In this excerpt she separates being poor, which is an aspect of social role status, from the personal sense of being a good or bad person. Presumably she was also explicitly helping her children separate being *black* from being bad too. She thereby implicitly imparted the message that they have some choices in how they conceive of themselves and consequently how they approach the world. That is to say, their feeling good about themselves does not depend solely on the stereotypic evaluations of others, particularly not by others who are outside of the circle of people who love and appreciate them.

In the previous two sections we have said that even though there are pressures toward a negative assessment of self, blacks have pursued avenues of self-definition guided by a competence theme. Consistent positive self-evaluations emerge alongside the negative ones as a result of the capacity to pose mental alternatives to those presented by some aspects of the racist culture. I said next that it is legitimate to view black families as being strong enough historically to have made the kinds of contributions that would strengthen their children's self-concept development. Now the question arises as to *how* the family makes its contributions to the black child's self-concept development.

Concerned parents and educators have always tried to influence the development of children's sense of self by making loving and positive contributions to children's experience. This is part of what is reflected in DuBois' assertion that the quality of the home can be a bulwark against the negative psychological influences of a hostile society. Providing positive models and values that the child can adopt is certainly important. This tends to put an emphasis on the flow of good things from the environment into the child, as it were. The humanistic theorist feels the need to supplement this, however. The old saying, "You can lead a horse to water but you can't make him drink," when applied to behavior and development, recognizes something else: the child must be active (intentional, at some level) in taking on the values that surround her or him.

Here, of course, is where our humanistic perspective comes in. Earlier I made reference to self-concept as a theory that the individual *has constructed* about him- or herself (see note 2). Later, in my discussion of Frost, I emphasized that the individual *chooses* his or her path from among alternatives. Both of these descriptions emphasize that the individual is active in developing himself or herself as "constructor" or chooser. A key aspect of the notion of self for the humanistic theorist is the active (conceptualizing, choosing-among-alternatives) quality of the self. I submit that what families do implicitly, that is, without always being conscious that they are doing it as such, is to stimulate children to become more active in their own development partly by becoming "aware" of their potential for active influence in their lives.

The Black Family and Self-Awareness

Most of us can appreciate the fact that we are actively involved in determining the course of our daily lives. But young children and many adults are usually not "aware" of themselves in this way—that is, while people are *conscious* of what they do they are not necessarily *aware* of themselves in a special sense of that word that we shall use here. Awareness can be defined psychologically as "appreciation of the arbitrariness in experience" or, in other words, "knowing that something else might be taking place in a life circumstance [Rychlak, 1977, p. 354]." Self-awareness would imply the recognition that, although I choose to act or be *this* way in this circumstance, I *could* be or do something else. Many persons experience themselves as only being forced into one or another avenue by physical and social forces around them. However, when they do so they are at some level (often unconsciously) *choosing* to accept environmental factors as given rather than being externally forced to comply with them. Having done so, they find that many aspects of life become easy and automatic and fall into a pattern determined by their initial choices. To some extent such automatic responses are necessary for functioning in everyday life. We do not become aware that our patterns of behavior rest on choices we have made until something happens to challenge the premises that govern our habitual acts. However, this does not negate the fact that such habits are based on initial premises we have, perhaps long since, accepted.

As I have indicated earlier the same is true for a person's development of self-concept. One's view of one's self is made up partly of one's selection from (and acquiescence to) environmental factors, and it is also made up of things one imagines (proposes, intends) one would like to be. (Note that even a person's acquiescence represents *his* or *her* [often unconcious] decision to go along with certain conditions.) The individual plays an essential part in the development of self-concept. When a person realizes that who (s)he is becoming is composed to an important degree of choices that (s)he is making, then one is *aware,* as that term is being used here. (Awareness characterizes action not only regarding self-development, of course, but all aspects of intended behavior.)

> For the person to develop . . . self-awareness, he must see the contributions he *makes to* experience, depending upon what sort of meanings are affirmed [in the given situation]. In this sense the self must be *intended*—that is, the purposive meaning of *self* must be brought to life by the individual, who cultivates it and furthers it *or not* [Rychlak, 1977, p. 355].

While self-awareness concerning all of one's behavior is not always desirable, for most people and for the developing child broadening awareness of the degree to which (s)he is an active contributor to his or her own life is a worthwhile goal. At the same time to be truly aware of the degree to which one's conceptualizations have causal power in one's actions is a heavy burden. It reduces the degree to which one can externalize blame for one's life. It is in this sense that Schafer (1976) notes how most of us shy away from recognizing how much *we* are the gods in our lives—the self-creators in Chein's image.

I submit that the black family has nurtured a sense of personal self-worth in the black child partly by "bringing to life" a sense of self as an agent able to propose and affirm hypotheses about potential which are at variance with those white society offers. The family does this, for example, through exposure to values in the home and community that express alternatives. DuBois suggests that one can control some of the important values children are exposed to, thereby giving them choices. One can also respond to children in ways that give them choices about their affairs, small though these may be. They can in this way get the sense of having an impact on events through their choices. Thus through contact with "the best surroundings"—including cultural information about Afro-Americans and their historical contributions—and the recognition of the possibility for individual and group choice, I suggest that "self-awareness" is enhanced and personal self-esteem is potentially improved. The family has been one institution that nurtures a sense of self-awareness—a sense of self as capable of setting its own intended goals—and the family helps expose the child to the means of carrying these goals out. (That a sense of having an impact on the options affecting one is related to academic achievement is supported by Coleman et al. (1966), who found that a sense of "fate control" was positively related to school achievement in black children.)

Social circumstances have put an extra burden on blacks as they struggle to survive. In the service of their own and their children's self-realization, however, black families *have* expended this energy more than is usually acknowledged. Clearly these efforts of families would be enhanced by changes in social policies and social institutions. For example, increased employment opportunity would enable persons to raise their standard of living, provide security for their families, and make tangible contributions to a sense of self-worth. A more benign social atmosphere allows more room for people's effectance motivations to guide their actions. Notice the phrasing here. There is a particular kind of interaction between social institutions and the psychology of the individual. Social conditions provide a set of environmental options and limitations. An individual with self-awareness can decide to abide by the pressures implied in a given set of circumstances or that person can act out of a different sense of self and fight even strong odds. (For example, the odds against graduating from college if you are a rural black youth has not kept such persons, with the support of their families, from trying—and succeeding in many instances.) The environmental circumstances do not *force* the individual's choice, they do make a particular action less likely—particularly if (s)he is unaware that (s)he can choose. This is *not* to say that blacks are primarily at fault for not having done better against the great social odds confronting them. It is rather to describe from one perspective the individual processes that have enabled them to do as well as they have. It is also to indicate how much more they could do if given a fair chance by society. In fact the system is still very much to blame for the plight of Afro-Americans (and the poor of various racial groups). Enhanced social opportunity would expand the arena in which natural effectance strivings could operate.

OTHER ASPECTS OF RACIAL SELF-CONCEPT DEVELOPMENT

I do not mean to imply that self-concept development in blacks is simply a tug of war between society with its noxious pressures on the one hand and the black family seeking to instill feelings of pride and self-worth in its children on the other. Such a view tends to imply that the family is successful when it can isolate the black child from the larger society, which in turn implies that the black child's problems stem from external influences alone. While it is clear that institutions in American society are structured so as to transmit easily racially prejudiced attitudes, things are not as simple as that. There are other factors in the child's life that both aid and hinder efforts to sustain and develop the sense of competence.

For example, psychoanalytic theory based largely on clinical observation of children and adults stresses bodily impulses and the way they are handled by family members as important to the development of self-concept (Kovel, 1970). During socialization normal preschool children often develop attitudes toward their bodies and skin that intertwine with racial perceptions (Harrison-Ross & Wyden, 1973; McDonald, 1970). From the perspective we have been developing here we could say that children's active efforts to make sense of the world draw on sense impressions and abundantly communicated information around them. We have seen that young children are attentive to such issues in the racial sphere. With their comparatively limited cognitive and social sophistication (which is another way of saying: with their uncertainty over the most probably correct alternative of the many that occur to them about given events), children normally develop ideas about experience that are idiosyncratic. Such notions may appear as distorted notions about themselves and social reality and may lead to personal problems if not corrected.

Ruby: "My skin or me?"

Coles (1967) gives a striking example of just such an interaction between developmental perceptions and racial concerns in the life of Ruby, the little girl with whom we opened this chapter. As I indicated earlier, she had to brave a mob of white protestors who formed a veritable gauntlet in front of her school each morning shouting invectives at her. At one point she developed a severe appetite loss and began to ask repeatedly whether it was "only" her skin that made her the object of such daily persecution. It became clear over the course of time that one of the picketers kept shouting a threat to choke and poison her. Of all the nasty things yelled at her this one seemed to "hit home," probably because it happened to mesh with her normal struggles in her family to control her ordinary naughtiness toward her siblings. Such behavior on her part included verbal (oral) aggression toward them; her parents on occasion punished her by withholding her favorite foods or by offering the stern observation that she might well "choke" on her hostile words. Her question, "Is it only my skin?" indicated that she had become confused for a while as to whether only her skin color was what was "wrong" with her or whether she was the object of abuse for more deepseated faults. The racial trauma had begun to confound her racial and personal identities.

How can children be helped to resolve such difficulties? In the course of children's efforts to achieve a sense of self in the larger world, many confusions and distortions can arise. Parents and educators can help children differentiate between racial perceptions about their acquaintances and themselves on the one hand and their own natural developmental lapses of the moment on the other hand. Adults can do this by dealing forthrightly with situations as they arise. For example, one little Afro-American child was reported to have remarked to his mother that he didn't like the brown rice served to him because it was the "color of 'do-do.' " She answered by acknowledging that the rice was brown and that this is the color of a waste product from our bodies but went on to note matter-of-factly that many things that he likes are brown including the skin color of himself and his loved ones. She reminded him further of one of the books he liked called *Brown is a beautiful color* by Jean Carey Bond (1969). Here the mother dealt straightforwardly with her child's concerns and showed him the range of associations—many of them positive—that accrue to brownness.[6]

As Coles notes, Ruby's symptoms passed with time. Certainly this was partly because her family helped her in important ways. Although her parents were generally firm in their expectation that she be a well-behaved girl during the crisis, they also were supportive and loving. In addition, although she knew that the immediate family was vulnerable (her father was fired from his job because of her attendance at the desegregated school), she was given a feeling for the larger supportive clan they could fall back on. She had been told of her maternal grandfather, a Mississippi Delta farmer, who was described to her as a person who could provide a haven for them: "Momma says . . . her daddy is the strongest man you can find. . . . She says not to worry, we have a hiding place and I should remember it every day [1967, p. 49]." This was reflected in her drawings. In contrast to her drawings of other blacks at that time, she drew her grandfather as a large powerful man. Thus, her family (and possibly other institutions such as the church, for example) provided a needed context in which she could work out the difficulties facing her.

Fortunately, however, there were other things working for her as well. For one thing the city began to quiet down over time as white children began to return to the schools. But in addition she undoubtedly achieved some gains in personal maturity from the exercising and developing of social and cognitive skills in the real world, as difficult as that world was. When Ruby was 10, several years after her eating disturbance, Coles who had visited with her and her family regularly during this time, engaged her in some reflection on the nature of her growth during those years. Specifically he commented on the different and more complete quality of her drawings of black people now that she was older. "Do you think," he asked, "there's any reason for that, apart from the fact that you're now a better artist in every way?" She answered:

Maybe because of all the trouble going to school in the beginning I learned more about my people. Maybe I would have anyway; because when you get older you see yourself and the white kids; and you find out the difference. You try to forget it, and say there is none; and if there is you won't say what it be. Then you say it's my own people, and so I can be proud of them instead of ashamed [1967, p. 51].

Coles goes on to note:

Her language was so clear, so pointed; and she somehow seemed both content with herself as she was and determined to make something of herself in the future [p. 51].

Recent research supports the notion that racial self-concept in black children changes with age. In a retesting five years later of the children used in her Michigan and Mississippi samples, McAdoo (1977) found that the children's previous outgroup orientation had shifted significantly in a pro-"Afro" direction such that the older children, who were now 10-year-olds going on 11, were either neutral or were somewhat positive toward the "Afro" choices. To test the effect of age on racial self-concept Williams and Morland (1976) asked a sample of black children ranging from the 6th to the 12th grades to give semantic evaluations of the term "Black American." They found that among the older age ranges the rating of this term was clearly more positive than among the younger students. The indication is that as Afro-American children grow they are able to apply the feelings of efficacy which they have gained from other areas of living to their sense of racial identity.

What I am suggesting is that as black children get older a more defined sense of self in other aspects of living helps them get a different perspective on racial group membership. A part of this perspective comes from a somewhat greater self-awareness as we have defined that here. This feature may come not only from family interactions but also from children's recognition that as they grow and gain more skills they are actually able to exercise more options and are able to be more independent than they have been before. Also there is growth in the ability to understand the messages coming from their own culture as well as from the dominant society regarding racial issues. Ruby's development was partly a function of her recognition of being older and having the skills appropriate to her age and partly a function of the ability to use some of these skills to understand her social situation better. As one of Ruby's teachers noted at this point (four years after entering school), "Ruby is an exceptionally alert child." In short, Ruby and other black children illustrated in the research are negotiating Erikson's developmental stage of "industry."[7]

The sense of self is made up of various facets, some of which may function somewhat independently in the interests of sustaining healthy adaptation. In that sense the family's role has been seen in this chapter as helping the black child ward off society's negative attributions regarding race by bolstering other aspects of the self. However, I am saying also that there can be an interrelation among aspects of self. One's sense of efficacy in one area of development can spread to other aspects of one's sense of the self. Thus, the efforts of the family and other supportive social contexts that work toward the stabilizing of a sense of competence in various of one's personal attributes may have a positive effect on aspects of self-concept related to racial group membership.

The preceding summary comments suggest that one way of modifying racial attitudes of black children is by providing good experiences for them in other areas of life. Change in attitude then would be an indirect effect—a by-product of the positive experiences in other areas. The question arises of whether or not it is possible to tackle attitude change in black children head-on outside of the family.

Since the late sixties considerable attention in the black community has been devoted to raising the level of black people's self-esteem. Some have claimed that this general emphasis on black pride and in some cases the institution of specific programs have been responsible for attitude changes in Afro-Americans (Hraba & Grant, 1970; Sacks, 1972). However, direct efforts are not new in the black community although they are possibly less dramatic. For years many black families have made a point of introducing their children to juvenile literature about Afro-American heroes—material notably absent from the established texts of American history. Furthermore, it was not an uncommon experience for children raised in the segregated schools of the South in the first six or seven decades of this century to have learned a good deal about black history. These kinds of exposures had as their purpose the effort to fill the vacuum in positive information about blacks and to combat directly the negative information and attitudes that are a part of the warp and woof of American society. The same idea is behind many of the small "freedom schools" that sprang up in black communities in the seventies. There was an added emphasis in these schools on Afro-American and African history and Swahili along with the usual basic educational skills.

Along these lines some researchers have argued that self-esteem may be higher in segregated school situations than it is in desegregated ones (Rosenberg & Simmons, 1971; Taylor, 1976), although others argue that the evidence is equivocal on that point (Epps, 1975). A crucial factor that would make these data hard to interpret is the issue of what the definition of an integrated situation is. For example, Pettigrew (1971) argues that one must distinguish desegregated from "truly integrated" settings. In the latter kinds of situations adults set a tone of encouraging interracial acceptance in which children can learn about and appreciate one another's cultural differences. Pejorative expressions toward one another's differences are firmly, but nonpunitively dealt with—they are not ignored—and thus opportunities to respect one another and themselves is enhanced. A "merely desegregated" situation is one in which children sit in the same classroom but little attention is given to structuring the social situation. In some desegregated schools children go to the same school but may be tracked into different classes which resegregate them anyway. There are probably few truly integrated situations in the United States. It is likely that most of the research about the effects of "integration" on children's self-esteem has been conducted in *desegregated* situations, *not* in truly integrated ones. Thus we do not really know as much as we think we do about the effect of integration on children's self-esteem, and we won't know much until we do more than simply desegregate.

There have been efforts to modify racial preference attitudes in black children experimentally. Among these studies are those using the procedures developed by Williams and Morland (1976) whose theoretical orientation is in the mechanistic tradition using behavior modification techniques. Generally the research involved individually administered procedures in which a child's response was followed by an immediate "reinforcer"—either a reward or a punishment. Two kinds of research designs have been employed. In one type the effort was made to change racial attitude by directly changing the children's "pro-Euro/anti-Afro" bias toward photographs of people. In the other type of design the attempt was to change racial attitude—the attitude toward Euro and Afro figures—by changing the child's preference for the color white. These studies have yielded some success in moderating racial attitudes. Material rewards and punishments (winning and losing pennies) along with verbal reinforcers have been found more effective in changing children's color attitudes than verbal reinforcers alone (Reeves, 1976). There is some evidence that change persisted in follow-up measurements. By contrast, attempts to alter the pro-Euro bias in young children by using special curriculum programs in the classroom have not been as successful.

Although we have a good deal more to learn about effective modes of intervention, there is good reason to believe that racial attitudes in chidren can be modified (Katz, 1976). There are many things that parents and educators can do in their relating to children and in structuring institutions that can enhance the development of black youngsters. The humanistic framework we have been developing would also suggest the specific value of helping a child become more self-aware—as someone who is an active, choosing being. To the extent this attitude is nurtured and developed the accompanying sense of competence will lead toward effective ways of interacting with the world that will enable the child to throw off the negative connotations offered by a racist society.

NOTES

1. The question has been raised as to whether or not these studies actually measure racial feeling in Afro-American children. The data from "racial awareness" questions in some of these studies are useful in clarifying this issue. As one method for getting at racial attitudes, one can ask a child what (s)he knows about racial terms—the words "colored," "white," "Negro," and "black"—as applied to people. Or one can find out whether or not the child will sort differently colored dolls or pictures of persons into correct racially based groupings (a "racial classification" question). Further,

one can find out whether the child knows what racial group he or she belongs to. These tasks would appear to tap the amount of information children have at a "cognitive" or knowledge level. Apart from their feelings about such information the data indicate that children are aware of racial differences as early as age 3; correctness of classification increases, of course, with age and stabilizes at about age 6 or 7. Proportion of correct classifications by age and race is a function of the measure used.

The data from the "racial similarity" questions used in some studies ("Which doll looks like you?") indicate that preschool Afro-American children have tended less often than white children to choose figures of their own race as those that look like them (Porter, 1971; Williams & Morland, 1976). Similarly, preschool "Afro" subjects in some studies chose own-race figures less often as looking like their own parents than did "Euro" children (Williams & Morland, 1976, Chap. 7). This seems not to be simply a function of faulty knowledge because even some black children who used racial categories correctly in classifying themselves tended to label themselves as being similar to the *white* doll. Afro-American children made this particular outgroup selection considerably more often than did the white children.

Racial similarity data combined with Porter's "color salience" measure seem to indicate that racial feeling is involved. Color salience for Porter refers to the degree to which skin color of the dolls was a more salient variable for grouping them than sex of the dolls or the similarity of the color of the clothes they were dressed in. So, for example, in the clothes-skin color control, in the course of play with the dolls a girl was presented with four dolls, two black and two white, but with contrasting clothes (a white and black doll with a red dress and a white and a black doll with a blue dress). For boys similar contrasts were made with boy dolls. The children were then asked, "Which two look most alike?" leaving them with the option of picking the dolls with similar skin color or the dolls who were similarly clothed as being "most alike."

Porter found that skin color of the dolls tended to be more salient for black children than for white children in these comparisons. (The fact that skin color was an important variable for black children—yet they tended to make an outgroup choice in doll preference—indicated to her that at least some black children were making negative or at least ambivalent *affective* assessments.) Furthermore, analyzing her data on a more individual basis she found that black children for whom skin color of dolls was more salient were *more* incorrect in their racial similarity matching of themselves. This indicated for Porter that there was special feeling about race on the part of these black children and that the racial similarity measure seemed to carry an important part of the weight of this feeling. As a corollary to this she found further that children who had favorable attitudes toward the dolls of their own race (high own-race preference) in the story-game procedure were the ones who were highly likely to be correct when asked to choose the doll whose color was like theirs. However, if own-race preference was *low,* correctness of racial similarity choices tended to be *low* even when the children demonstrated that they knew correct racial terminology. This too was more often the case for black children than for white children.

It seems clear that racial awareness involves affective assessments as well as cognitive (knowledge) issues for children. Porter's data led her to conclude that a *specific* affective issue was being tapped by the racial similarity measure. This was that the more frequent incorrect racial similarity choices by black children were an index of some ambivalence or even clear discomfort with their racial group membership for some of these children. Note again that such terms as "ambivalence" and "discomfort" do not mean "self-hatred" as a global construct, but do indicate a mixture of feelings and hence complexity in the self-concept.

2. Epstein suggests that self-concept should be seen as a "self-theory." "It is a theory that the individual has unwittingly constructed about himself as an experiencing, functioning individual, and it is part of a broader theory which he holds with respect to his entire range of significant experience [1973, p. 407]." In the terms introduced in Chapter 1, self-concept is a "conceptualization"; it is one of the most central conceptualizations that an individual develops in life. As noted in Chapter 1, the purpose of a conceptualization is to bring a sense of order and stability to a particular aspect of experience. Thus, one's self-concept is a conceptualization that stabilizes and

organizes the feelings and thoughts that a person holds about his or her existence as a physical and social being. It represents the way a person has mapped out his or her psychological territory, so to speak, and represents the way a person accounts for himself or herself—it is the individual's sense of "what I am" (Keen, 1970). With this kind of map (or frame of reference, or psychological orientation point) the individual is better able to carry out a fundamental characteristic of living which is to grow—to become ever more effective and competent in his or her milieu.

3. This point regarding children's sensitivity to parts of the research design that are peripheral to the researcher's intended thrust raises the question of what Martin Orne has called "demand characteristics" in research (1962). Orne found that his (college age) subjects persevered in the meaningless experimental tasks they were given long after he expected them to. When Orne questioned them later they indicated that they stuck with the tasks because they were concerned about being "good subjects" and making a contribution to science. The typical psychological interpretation of this occurrence is that subtle but inevitable cues in the situation (such as the figure cut by an obviously earnest young student trying to complete her dissertation research, or an impressive looking older person in a white lab coat) *elicit* behavior from the subject in an efficient-cause fashion. An alternate view is that the subjects' persevering behavior was in the service of ("for the sake of") intentions they imposed on the task not simply called out by the explicit manipulations the experimenter placed on them. The experimental situation is a "two-way street." "The subject is virtually always thinking about his role in first-person terms, asking himself questions like: What is he (the experimenter) up to? What's he trying to get me to do? What am I getting into here? What's the worth of all this? What's the trick? [Rychlak, 1977, pp. 322–323]." The teleologist sees the individual as being active in the research situation and acting for the sake of intentions of his own as well as those of the experimenter. Such concerns influence the way the subject responds and must be taken into account in a thorough understanding of the data.

Coming back to the racial preference studies: young children are not as mature in the range of intentions they bring, yet they are active in similar ways. One writer, a child psychiatrist, asks:

> What is a three-year-old child to think is going on when an adult, a comparative stranger who serves no understandable purpose in his life, as parent or teacher, surprises him with a series of strange questions such as: "Which doll do you prefer? The brown one or the white one?" and then takes away the test dolls he has just given him, supposedly to play with? [McDonald, 1970, p. 31].

The child is not simply a passive object being manipulated by the experimenter—no more so than in daily life outside the laboratory. While the researcher's controls do set limits on the options for a subject's behavior, it is quite likely that even a young child is engaging in an active, if relatively unsophisticated, search as to what is going on. This search is governed by and influences his or her conceptualizations about the situation. For example, the wish to please the examiner is a relevant intention in children, particularly in view of the heightened authority relationship between the (adult) experimenter and the (young child) subject. In this regard, with an older sample, Dansby (1980) reports that responses of black college students to a racially oriented questionnaire were more militant when the interviewers wore an Afro. (This doesn't mean that children are always cooperative. The Clarks [1952] report strong emotional reactions and negativism on the part of some children regarding the task presented to them. As we shall see in Chapter 3 Rychlak and his associates [1977] report that a subject's dislike, i.e., negative affective assessment, of an experimental task can reliably affect performance on important aspects of that task.)

One aspect of responding to the examiner is noting his or her race. Researchers working in the area of children's racial attitudes frequently attempt to control this factor, at least partly, by having same-race examiners test the children. Porter used a black examiner in some instances with those subjects who were from predominantly black classrooms. Where a white examiner was used in such settings, she found that black children tended to misidentify the doll more often than they did with an examiner of either race in a desegregated setting. Race of examiner had no effect on results with children in desegregated classrooms. Katz and Zalk (1974), however, using the Clarks' design, found race of examiner influenced doll choices of both black and white children. Williams and Morland report not finding race-of-examiner effects and feel that such effects can be pretty much ignored with young children (1976, pp. 306–307). But I believe that this is a premature conclusion when one looks at the variety of research designs in this area and the potential children have for attending to these and other cues.

The recent emphasis on racial pride in the black community may have highlighted certain issues for young children such that the direct questions in a forced-choice format are more easily met by children's intentions to be positive racially. Porter's technique, on the other hand, which involves a more elaborate, semistructured play situation, may engage a broader range of children's feelings and has the potential for enabling an expression of feeling in greater depth. This is not to say that feelings that are more conscious are less real; rather it is to say that feelings about self are complex, as we are emphasizing in this chapter, and they are held at many levels of awareness. Various ways of getting at them are probably necessary to get a full picture of self-concept.

4. The idea of conceptualization, which is central in the humanistic approach here, can be used to further illustrate this notion of creativity. Conceptualization implies that the human individual responds in reality in terms of his or her symbolically created conception or idea of reality rather than to "real" reality as such. As Edelson notes, "While 'real' external reality may be presumed to exist independently of its apprehension, it cannot be known except symbolically—as part, then, of psychic reality insofar as psychic reality is constituted by symbolic processes. Even the experience of simple sensations involves interpretation in a framework of meaning (1971, p. 27)." Such constructions of reality can be illustrated in as fundamental and seemingly simple a process as how an individual begins the day. For example, when I am awakened in the morning by the alarm clock, I may have the experience of not knowing for a moment where I am. I have to actively organize, that is, conceptualize, the sense impressions around me. Doing so involves making affirmations, that is, taking a stand about my situation. I must search for the perceptual clues that will tell me what's going on. Having done so I have meaningful anchor points ("Oh—I'm at home in bed. It's morning already!") to help determine my next steps. Note, however, it is not finally the external *fact* of morning that determines my next steps; it is my mental *affirmation* of that fact with the associated feelings that determines my next moves. The process of achieving full wakefulness involves some mental *activity* on my part. As we have postulated earlier, to the extent that a situation is conceptualized, that is, organized meaningfully, it is always accompanied by a further kind of subjective judgement—an affective assessment (for example, "Darn it! It's Monday!"). Such assessments can "set the tone" for my day (as in ideas and beliefs about "Blue Monday") and affect how I cope with my day by helping to pattern the way I view events, although it is likely that events will come along that will contribute to a change in my initial outlook during the day. This example can be taken to characterize the many other activities of self, too.

5. The psychodynamic psychologist is aware of another aspect of the multidimensionality of self, too. No one, including adults, has perfect self-esteem. All of us make judgments about ourselves as having aspects that are less desirable than we would like them to be. These negative affective assessments about ourselves represent low self-esteem. (Note that studies indicating similarity in level of self-esteem between blacks and whites do not imply that self-esteem is perfect for either group, though it may be at a "healthy" level.) One way of dealing with those aspects of ourselves that we do not like is to alter awareness of them, that is, withdraw attention from them or eject them from consciousness. The tendency for people to alter and in fact distort awareness of disturbing (anxiety-arousing) aspects of their experience to regain a sense of well-being is partly what psychodynamic personality theorists mean by "defense." To some extent we all must defend against certain (internal) thoughts and feelings or (external) events in order to keep anxiety from paralyzing our adaptive efforts. So we tend to shut out the more unpleasant assessments about ourselves.

The sense of imperfectness and uncertainty about self that all people harbor to some extent should be even more true of children whose sense of self is less stabilized and developed. It should not be surprising that young black children might manifest some effect of the highly charged racial scene in America. Depth interviews and personality assessment techniques have been able to pick up *some* degree of anger and depression regarding racial group membership. Thus, differences in levels of personality function tapped may account for some aspects of conflicting results. Porter's methodology may have tapped broader ranges of children's functioning than some other studies.

6. The psychoanalytic point of view suggests certain inevitable instinctual drive factors which in the course of development may get expressed in racist ways. Williams and Morland (1976) have a different set of speculations about universals within the individual that can set the stage for racial attitudes. They argue that the attitudes toward black and white as colors—distinct from attitudes toward light- and dark-skinned people—are not dependent on social learning. If they were dependent on learning, they point out, then older and brighter children would be expected to show such attitudes with greater strength than duller and younger children. This is what we would expect for a learned behavior. But, according to the Williams and Morland studies, there is no correlation between the measures of color attitudes and either age or IQ. This suggests that the light-preference phenomenon, which shows up cross-culturally, may come from an experience universal for the human species. Specifically, they postulate that the human tendency to associate pleasure and activity with daylight hours and to associate fear and withdrawal with the darkness of night may be a source of the black-white color preferences. Thus, people are primed phylogenetically for contact with American social institutions and racial mores. The feelings about dark and light which come from attitudes toward daylight and its absence get emphasized and placed in a value hierarchy in this multipigmented, status-oriented society. Of course Williams and Morland acknowledge individual differences and the fact that differing individual experience will accent or moderate such potential. For example, a generally more fearful child might be expected to manifest the day-night attitudes more sharply. Also darker-skinned people with positive associations to other dark people (in their families, for instance) might be less prone to transfer such negative attitudes as strongly to colors and relationships with people. This lesser degree of transfer is probably reflected in the lower amount of dark-color avoidance in Afro-Americans reported by, for example, Williams and Morland and by Porter.

7. In Erik Erikson's development scheme (1963) the years spent in elementary school in our culture (what Freud called the "latency" period) are a time when a child is learning a sense of "industry," a necessary feature of development toward maturity. Negotiating this phase of growth involves learning the basic tool skills of the culture and learning a sense of pleasure in work completion, as Erikson puts it, necessary for eventual adaptation as an adult in a given cultural setting. Erikson defines this phase in a way that is similar to White's ideas about competence. The child comes to take a certain amount of pleasure in being effective in the kinds of graded tasks that the society presents. Such tasks are presented in formal schooling in many cultures. Children who do not develop a healthy sense of "industry" are prone to a sense of "inferiority" as the opposite possibility. Of course, as continua, these developmental stages are conceived in terms of *degrees* to which an individual succeeds or fails to negotiate the tasks; this is not an "all or none" conception of attainment. In childhood, especially, successful progression through the stages depends on the social milieu providing the right balance of nurturance, opportunity, and disciplinary structure to enable the child to mature in the ways the culture sees as properly representing achievement. A sense of inadequacy or inferiority can stem from a family life that hasn't prepared a child for school or a school life that does not value what the child has learned to do well. Of course a major social issue today is the concern in minority communities about the failure of schools to be able to enhance the potential that young black children bring for development of a sense of industry.

Chapter 3
The Active Intellect: Developing Competence

The assumption can be made that cultural and economic backgrounds of pupils do not constitute a barrier to the type of learning which can reasonably be expected of normal children in the elementary schools . . . [Clark, 1965, p. 139].

The evidence of the pilot projects in "deprived" schools—odd though it may appear to many—seems to indicate that a child who is expected by the school to learn does so; the child of whom little is expected produces little [p. 132].

The lagging school achievement of Afro-American children from inner-city communities persists as a major educational and social problem in America. Despite the promising educational experiments that Kenneth Clark cited in *Dark Ghetto* more than 15 years ago, the schools have been unsuccessful in keeping the children of the poor from falling further and further behind in the grade levels expected of them for their age. As one black 5th-grader observed in commenting on how little learning was going on in her classroom, "By the time we get to sixth grade, boy, we be dumb [Gouldner, 1978, p. 64]." "Dumb" is a classification now applied to many black children—a larger percentage of them than white children have been labeled as retarded in intellectual functioning. Is this an accurate reading of the intellectual capacity of black children?

Some educational psychologists feel sufficiently satisfied about their grasp of the facts to state that black children are innately limited in their intellectual potential. Jensen (1969) has presented this view in his postulation of a distinction between Level I and Level II types of intellectual ability. Level I abilities presumably consist of associative skills primarily such as are involved in the (potentially quite accurate) mental registration of stimuli and the faithful reproduction of such information. Everyone has and needs such skills. If a man wants to reach someone by telephone he has to be able to remember the seven-digit number the operator gives him. This is rote memory. Level I ability also includes trial-and-error learning which does not necessitate sophisticated problem-solving strategies. Children do not seem to differ consistently by race or socioeconomic class in Level I abilities. If anything, lower-class children sometimes do better when tested for these skills.

Level II abilities involve the more complex capacity to pick out the relationships among stimuli. In a concept-formation test a question might be, "How are a wagon and a bicycle alike?" Another kind of Level II test might offer the possibility of using a set of relationships in order to solve a problem. A favorite example here is to require a child to learn a list of items presented in random order (coat, cat, teepee, dress, bear, igloo) all of which can be grouped into a smaller number of abstract categories. Noting the categories and using them (spontaneously) to group the items helps the subject to memorize them more efficiently. Those who do well on such tasks are seen as having Level II abilities. The average black and lower-class child, in Jensen's judgment, is genetically deficient in Level II abilities—the "average" black and lower-class child, because it is not maintained that all blacks are without high-level intellectual abilities. Rather it is posited that a significantly larger number of black and lower-class persons are without such abilities and are thus limited to a Level I style of approaching intellectual problems. Looked at this way, a person who is both lower class and black is in double jeopardy of being intellectually limited.[1]

From the humanistic perspective there is an interesting implication regarding this supposed deficit in black intellectual capacity. It has to do with the difference between the Lockean and the Kantian conception of mental functioning. The reader will recall that the Lockean view is that mind develops primarily as a result of the flow of stimulation *to* the individual. The person registers it and responds to it. We have pointed out the passivity of the individual in this conception of mind. The Kantian view emphasizes that from the beginning the infant "comes at" the world with structuring activity which interacts with the reality it confronts, and so the child contributes to what it "knows."

The view that Afro-Americans are limited to Level I, or primarily associative abilities, implies that their intellectual functioning is adequately described in a rather simplified version of the Lockean model. In other words, it implies that Afro-Americans only function effectively in the mode of rote reproduction of what is fed into their mental systems. The concept of learning by association, with its emphasis on how recently and how frequently a particular stimulus occurs along with another, has been important for traditional psychology. In this regard Rychlak notes, "This mechanical—often purely accidental—bonding of one item to another is what humanists consider to be a passive characterization of mental associations [1977, p. 333]." To conceive of blacks' intellectual capacities as being primarily associative is to consign them to a model that emphasizes passivity of intellect. On the other hand the implication would be that middle-class white persons are properly described in the Kantian model which posits the capacity to actively unearth and apply the dialectical options available in a given intellectual situation. (For some mechanists more sophisticated Lockean models might be in order. See the references associated with note 5.)

Of course this book argues quite a different view—namely, that people of all races and social classes are best described by including Kantian terms. More specifically, the view is that blacks bring into the world the kind of actively conceptualizing mental equipment that gives them the capacity to achieve intellectual competence. It is true that the performance of lower- and working-class black children is frequently lower than that of white and middle-class children in standard testing and teaching situations. But a considerable number of researchers feel that this is not a true estimate of the basic capacity of black children.

There is evidence to indicate that, rather than being genetically determined in the main, such disparities stem from different learning experiences that these children have had. This throws doubt on the validity of putting people irrevocably into these Level I and Level II categories. This is a basic point in Feuerstein's intriguing book (1979) on the "dynamic" assessment of children whose intellectual functioning is below par. He argues that such children *learn* to restrict themselves to Level I functioning, or at least they do not learn other ways of responding. Speaking of these children, he notes,

[The child's] limitation to a reproductive modality of interaction with stimuli results directly from his perception of himself as a passive recipient of information rather than as an active generator of new information and ideas by inferential and constructive mental acts.

[Such a child] often considers appropriate reproduction a virtue, and whatever deviation is produced by his creativity he considers inadequate. This basic attitude is reflected in a state of passivity vis-a-vis the world and the incoming stimuli. . . . He does not attempt to produce the relationships that would organize the stimuli into meaningful categories [p. 81].

The variety of things that can contribute to what amounts to a *style* of Level I functioning will be the subject of a large part of this chapter and a portion of the next.

One of our tasks in this chapter, then, will be to review a selected sample of the evidence that indicates that black and other minority children can think and learn in abstract as well as rote fashion. In short we shall argue that they are potentially active in their approach to intellectual situations just as they are in their definition of self. (I acknowledge that the humanistic perspective being used to discuss the intellectual functioning of Afro-Americans here is only one way of trying to organize this material. Many psychologists prefer not to be explicit about theoretical biases in this area. My use of this theoretical approach is an expression of my belief that the humanistic approach with its emphasis on active, coping features of human behavior provides a point of view that is quite compatible with the tenor of a certain portion of the research on intelligence in blacks. That is the portion that stresses the equal overall intellectual capacities of Afro-American children with other children.)

Traditionally in psychology the term *conceptualizing* is used to refer only to the abstract, problem-solving thinking abilities, those seen as higher level skills, associated with Level II capacities. The humanistic position, however, uses the term somewhat differently. From the beginning for all children the interaction with the world not only involves passively registering what is "there" in reality, but also involves actively meeting experience "at the level of sensation (input) with a creative capacity to *order* it via patterns that constitute meaning and meaningfulness [Rychlak, 1977, p. 326]." This is the particular way in which we have defined the term *conceptualizing*. As we are using it here it is a term that can be employed to subsume the various components of thinking activity, or, as thinking is often called in psychology, "cognitive" activity (see the definition of cognition below, under "Cognitive Components of Intelligence"). So, for example, reasoning and memory are two quite distinguishable cognitive activities but overall they can be seen as cognitive tools by which a person structures the world. In other words, eventually the child comes to be able to mentally organize events in front of him/her into relationships and causal sequences (reasoning) and comes to reapply his or her earlier organization of a situation to a past event (memory). Psychologists have spent considerable time delineating other specific ways that conceptualizing goes on (see Rychlak [1977, Chap. 8] for a discussion of memory and classical learning principles interpreted from within his framework). But the main point here is that *some* rudimentary form of organizing *activity* begins at birth. We know things because of the (prior) conceptual activities, the spectacles so to speak, that we bring to an experience. A person is active in coming to know about the world.

In the humanistic theory adopted here, learning (which is an important aspect of intelligence) does not simply result from something falling into our mental storage bin, as it were. It involves actively extending the meaning framework that we have developed to new situations in order to make sense of them. When we have made sense of them, that is, imposed an order on them, we have learned something. What we have learned may not be correct according to some external criterion, but it does represent a mental reshaping of the situation. Of course we are required eventually to bring our learning into line with social and physical reality if we are to be effective in the world. But in principle the humanistic view is that a definition of learning needs to include what the subject understands and intends, not only what an observer sees from an extraspective point of view as behavior. So, for example, a toddler seeing a four-legged creature standing before her meowing may call it a "doggie" which is her name for the general concept of all four-legged creatures with tails. With loving interventions from parents and others the child eventually comes to make the correct distinction between dogs and cats, "Yes, good girl, that's a kitty!" In such a parent-child context positive affective assessments can get associated both with the act of learning and specifically with the idea of approaching domesticated four-footed animals.

Throughout life, learning proceeds by extending forward the meanings of previously established conceptualizations of a situation along with some feelings about them, positive or negative. If a football enthusiast decides he wants to learn more about the rules of rugby, he probably does so in terms of his knowledge of football, which rugby resembles. He probably extends his knowledge of rugby from the similarities and differences in American football. And he develops, let's say, an appreciation (a positive affective assessment) for the game. (He would have to bring forward some other orienting conceptualization if he knew nothing about football.) Someone else attending their first game may also learn things about rugby based on their knowledge of American football. This person might learn—that is, extend the understanding—that rugby is just as "brutal" as football and the action of a bunch of men running up and down a field and suddenly falling on one another is just as "senseless." Here a negative affective assessment is being extended from one situation to the next. This person is learning, too. A firm set of understandings is being extended and influences ways of looking at particular sports activities.

Learning, then, involves actively "bringing forward" previous conceptualizations and personal intentions in a new situation. (Although Rychlak does not say so, it seems to me that these ideas about the role of conceptualization are very much akin to Piaget's concept of "schemata" and related to principles he has advanced regarding "accommodation" and "assimilation." See, for example, Flavell's text on Piaget [1963] and also Kagan [1976].) Rychlak calls this approach to learning "logical learning theory." This name emphasizes the view that a conceptual pattern or order (a *logos*) provides the framework that guides behavior. We understand a situation, and perhaps act in it, primarily in terms of our conception of it, not just because of its "real" characteristics.

One of the important aspects of this view of learning is that learning does not occur simply because a child happens to be standing there when an event—let's say, the passing of a fire truck—occurs. Learning is not simply a process of automatic (passive) "bonding" of events that are accidentally present. The child doesn't learn that that thing rushing by is a fire truck, even if her mother says so, unless she is *actively* involved and intentional in extending forward the pattern she has developed to this noisy, bright, fast moving object that she sees ("What's that, Mommy?"). Further, her learning in this situation involves extending the conceptualization about trucks and cars, not the ones about trees and flowers that she has developed. If she has no conceptualizations for trucks and cars she is probably not going to learn much about the fire engine. Learning involves proceeding from where we are and extending what we have already organized to the new and (not too) unfamiliar. Included in the learning about fire trucks may be a happy excitement about the noise and flashiness (a positive affective assessment) or an aversion (a negative affective assessment) to such commotion. Meaningfulness in any humanistic theory, not just Rychlak's, is a very important term. It signifies that the individual decides, often subconsciously, what is important in a situation, according to his or her intentions and learns along lines that (s)he has already developed and is pursuing. This of course is how we described the development of the self in Chapter 2.

This model of learning and intellectual functioning postulates that all groups of human beings bring active conceptualizing processes to experience.[2] When it is defined this way intelligence is not a special capacity that only some privileged groups of children have, although indeed people may vary in the efficiency with which they use this capacity. This kind of conceptualizing is a part of everyone's mental activity. As we shall see later, Feuerstein has found that by using such a conception of intelligence he has been able to help many children develop intellectually who were abandoned as being unable to learn—that is, abandoned as unable to bring forward previous experience to new situations— children labeled as hopelessly retarded.[3]

In summary, then, it can be said that black and poor children as a group bring active conceptualizing capacities to intellectual situations. Children learn best when they can see the meaningful connection between the conceptualizations they hold and the situation they are being asked to learn. If the learning situation is framed in unfamiliar ways or if the situation is associated with negative affective assessments and seems strange and forbidding, then learning and intellectual performance are likely to be hampered. On the other hand, it is known that other settings and approaches can have dramatic effects in helping children realize their intellectual potential.

TESTS AS SAMPLES OF BEHAVIOR

Judgments about intellectual potential are usually made on the basis of how a person does on tests of "intelligence." A test is a sample of behavior. In order to be efficient a test cannot ask all the possible questions about a given content area to see how much a person has learned; or it cannot pose too long a list of problems to test a person's skill, let us say in spatial relations. So it has to select a limited number of items that presumably represent the wider domain of knowledge that is under investigation. Now, this issue, which is fundamental to all psychometric testing, is particularly important to the testing of minorities. The accuracy of the test (its "reliability" and "validity" in psychometric terms, see Anastasi [1976]) depends on knowing what the domain being sampled actually encompasses. For example, what do we *really* mean by the term intelligence? What does intelligent behavior really encompass? (We will not get into a lengthy discussion of the problem of defining intelligence in this chapter. Useful discussion of this topic can be found in Feuerstein (1979); Loehlin et al. (1975); and Samuda (1975).) The accuracy of test items that are selected to measure a particular ability depends on having a good idea of what that ability involves. Further, even if one has a good idea of what is involved in a particular domain the limited sample of questions used have to be justifiable as a representative selection of that larger domain or universe. Critics note that standard intelligence tests tend to fall down on both of these counts, especially when it comes to testing minority and poor children. We try to measure with certainty something we don't clearly understand—intelligence—and the test items we use on standard tests are not necessarily representative of "intelligence" across human groups.

The most widely used of these tests yield a score, a standardized numerical weighting, called an "intelligence quotient" or IQ. Briefly, an IQ score is determined by comparing how a child does on the test items with the performance of a group of children who were used to provide the "norm" or the standard for the test. The test items pose differing levels of difficulty for children at a given age. This is an empirical approach to intelligence in that it lets the data from the testing of a large body of "representative" children determine what the criterion is for being more or less smart.[4] The average IQ is set at 100. If one were to give such a test to a random sample of children, the individual scores would range considerably from high to low. In this range we would find that blacks and lower socioeconomic persons tend to score lower than white and middle-class persons on the average.

What do such results mean? There are different parts in the answer to that question. Some educational psychologists put particular stress on the fact that IQ scores are good indicators of potential for profiting from schooling, particularly at advanced levels. The high scorers are seen as good risks in school and the low scorers are seen as poor risks. Now, there is relatively little argument over this contention when the discussion is confined to the issue of the immediate readiness of a child to profit from the standard classroom situation typical of American schools. Such tests predict academic performance in the classroom quite well. There is less argument over this point because today's test score makes a (more or less) accurate statement about what a child is ready to do in school *today*. When a score is looked at this way the possibility still exists that providing remedial help or changing the classroom setting will trigger the learning potential of the low test scorer to improve *tomorrow*.

The real controversy begins with the insistence by some psychologists that the differences in IQ scores represent relatively immutable and fixed intellectual potential. The conclusion from such a premise is that there is little we can do to help today's low scorers become ready for higher levels of education tomorrow (Jensen, 1969). Such a perspective has a long history in our society

(Guthrie, 1976; Kamin, 1974) and has been fostered by decades of a numerical measurement, or "psychometric," approach to intellectual ability testing. It has led to a way of thinking about intellectual ability as if it were a kind of quantity. Unfortunately professionals and laymen alike have adopted these ideas. The IQ test score, then, is almost literally seen as an indicator of how many units of that finite substance called "intelligence" the individual has. Such a perspective seems to assert that intelligence is adequately defined and measured by IQ tests.

It is clear that such a definition has had elitist consequences and its exclusive use has led to testing procedures that have failed to take account of the potential of black children. A more useful view of intelligence is that it is a concept, a hypothetical term, used to account broadly for what we observe about a person's potential for solving problems in life situations. The important thing here regarding measurement is that this potential may or may not be reflected on an IQ test. Whether or not it is depends on a variety of factors. In a multicultural society such as ours, however, differences in cultural background can influence the way intellectual potential is manifested. Thus, in contrast to the view that IQ test performance is the best measure of the potential for intellectual development, it is plausible to interpret test performance as reflecting how an individual *uses* his or her intellectual or thinking capacity in a given situation. Whether or not an individual has more thinking or problem-solving capacity than is used at any one moment is something that these tests, in and of themselves, are not very good at telling about for lower-class minority children. To get a clear perspective on the intellectual functioning of black children one has to recognize that children can have more intellectual competence than they apply to a given situation. Many things determine whether they do in fact make the application of their capacity to the intellectual problem they are presented with.

THE ANATOMY OF INTELLECTUAL PERFORMANCE

For some people IQ test performance is the accepted standard of intellectual ability. Many others do not think it is a straightforward measure of thinking ability. Instead they view the standard intelligence test as a "polyglot sample of behavior that is influenced by three empirically related but conceptually distinct collections of variables [Zigler & Trickett, 1978, p. 792]," namely, (1) those that are so-called purely formal cognitive ones, (2) those that demonstrate what knowledge or information the person has been exposed to and learned—what can be called factors of achievement, and (3) a diversified cluster of motivational and affective variables influencing how a person acquires and/or expresses what (s)he knows in a given situation. Looked at this way the standard intelligence test is far from a straightforward measure of thinking ability.

In the next sections of this chapter I will be concerned with a selection of studies pertaining to these three sets of variables. Our focus will be on lower- and working-class black children for the most part. My aim is to select studies that will allow us to further our humanistic theoretical perspective, and show the capacity for active intellectuality in black children. My purpose here is not to confine the discussion about intellectual ability to the arena of tests, but rather to find a way of grouping the studies about the intellectual ability of black children that will be consistent with the humanistic perspective. Specifically the sections deal with "cognitive components of intelligence," "learning and achivement in intellectual performance," and "the impact of affective and motivational factors on intellectual performance."

Cognitive Components of Intelligence

Cognition is an important term in psychology. The developmental psychologist Jerome Kagan suggests that cognition

> refers to the processes involved in the extraction of information from both the outside world and the internal environment, the application of existing knowledge to the construction of initial representations, the storage and retrieval of that information, the integration of new with old structures, the application of structures to deal with problems, and, most important, the creation of new knowledge [1976, p.1].

The processes of formal cognition can also be described in such terms as reasoning, memory, abstracting ability, speed of visual information processing, and others that psychologists have identified.[5] For many people these components are what overall intellectual ability is really about. Such factors are often thought of as being the true representation of native ability. Even though people may be willing to acknowledge that other aspects of functioning contribute to intellectual performance, the cognitive abilities are seen as the bottom line, as it were, of an individual's intellectual capacity. Even though the role that such factors play must be put into context, as we shall see, there is no doubt that formal thinking abilities are fundamental to intellectual performance.

Jerome Kagan notes (1976) as a principle underlying the development of cognitive or thinking abilities the idea that "the major cognitive processes . . . mature in a regular way in *any* natural environment [p. 2, emphasis added]." A "natural environment" for Kagan is one that contains people and objects— "even if the people know little of what a child requires and no object is manufactured [p. 2]." What this means is that different cultural and social class settings are not necessarily deficient in the different ways that they structure the world for their offspring. At any given point in time children from various backgrounds have arrived at different stages of cognitive development. They may also differ in what kinds of cues it takes to show that they have arrived at a certain stage of development of a particular cognitive process. But the potential for developing the process is there; that is—and this is a fundamental assumption—the basic cognitive processes are distributed broadly throughout the human family. Or, as sociologist Jane Mercer puts it, "All ethnic groups have equal potential for acquiring any human culture [1979, p. 53]." Cognitive processes are not limited to persons of a particular race or class, although differences in background seem to affect how and when these cognitive processes are manifested.

Most people would agree that *some* degree of active intellectual potential is present in all human groups. There is disagreement as to whether all groups can achieve the highest levels of intellectual ability of which human beings are capable. Of course to label blacks and other social groups as deficient in cognitive ability is to characterize them as being inferior. It justifies a kind of racist solicitousness towards blacks of not encouraging them to "frustrate" themselves by pursuing intellectual development that is "beyond" their abilities. It justifies tracking them into quick exits from schooling and lower level, dead-end occupations.

Now, it is true that if one leaves the intellectual performance situation pretty much in its standard form, one can find ample evidence that will support the inferior functioning of minority children. What I shall maintain here is that when one alters the form of the performance situation in specific ways, without altering the basic difficulty level of the problem, one can uncover intellectual potential in black children that is missed by standard situations. The studies in this section will be chosen to describe what some of the variables are that influence intellectual performance and how the performance of black and poor children is enhanced when these factors are taken into account. Whether or not a child performs up to capacity depends on whether or not (s)he recognizes the usefulness in a given situation of applying skills that (s)he has but doesn't often *use*. We shall see that differences in background heavily influence such use, and we shall also see that such background factors can be manipulated or compensated for with some patient intervention techniques, perseverance, and, as Kenneth Clark says, a firm belief that these children can learn as well as any.

At this point in our level of understanding in the field there will probably continue to be disagreements about these issues. However, this research does make plausible and quite tenable the idea that basic cognitive capacities are broadly distributed across ethnic groups. It justifies helping blacks and the poor strive for the highest levels of intellectual development rather than using their class or racial status as a sign of uneducability.

Let's turn first to an experimental test of the hypothesis put forward by Jensen that lower-class and black children lack Level II thinking ability. A research team headed by Scrofani (1973) proposed an alternative hypothesis as a way of accounting for the low scores of these children on tests of abstract cognitive skills.

An alternative explanation, according to Scrofani et al., is that black and lower-class children actually possess such high-level intellectual abilities but simply fail to use them in testing situations. If these abilities are lying dormant, they might be activated by some practice or training in how to employ them on test questions.

The design of the Scrofani study was rather complicated, involving a series of steps. A short account of it follows. In the first phase, they administered tests of Level I (rote) and Level II (abstract) abilities to a group of middle- and lower-class, black and white, 4th graders in Prince Georges County, Maryland. The children did not differ in Level I abilities and, according to expectations, the middle-class children scored much higher on the test of Level II abilities which was an IQ test. In the second phase of the study the children were given a different kind of test—a Piagetian test of cognitive development, and on the basis of the results of this test, the children were divided into three groups called categories A, B, and C.

Category A children were middle class, almost all of whom had made perfect or near-perfect scores on the Piagetian test.

Category B children were the 48 percent of the lower-class children who had also made perfect or near-perfect scores on the Piagetian test.

Category C children were the remaining lower-class children who did not complete the developmental test correctly.

Category A (middle-class) children were similar to category B lower-class children in maturity of cognitive development according to the Piagetian test. The lower class B and C children were similar in IQ scores.

In each of these three groups half of the children were given two 30-minute training sessions on the use of concept formation strategies. The training sessions consisted of a number of brief sorting and display exercises. In the former activity children were given the task of sorting a group of pictures into piles corresponding to the conceptual groups they represented (e.g., food, tools, toys, and utensils). In the display exercises the examiner showed the group one or more pictures and children took turns indicating a conceptual category the picture(s) might belong to. The untrained group of children were given exercises that did not involve concept training.

Later they were tested with the kinds of free recall tasks used in Jensen's laboratory to sample Level I and Level II skills. This involved remembering as many of the items shown to them as they could in each of several trials. The items were shown in random order but the items in the Level II task could be clustered by the subject into categories. Two of the categories were those used in the training session but none of the pictures shown were used in training. The trained category B children showed that they had profited from the training. They performed as well as the trained middle-class children on the Level II task and better than untrained Category B children. The trained category C children did not improve very much. When socioeconomic status was controlled there were no differences in performance by race.

What the study seemed to demonstrate was that a sizable number of lower-class children—almost half of them—actually possessed cognitive skills of a higher order but had not made use of them in the IQ test. The results of the developmental cognitive test turned out to be a better predictor of their potential functioning, for after only two half-hours of practice in forming concept categories they were able to perform as well on Level II tasks as middle-class children who had received the same training.

From the humanistic perspective we can describe the middle-class children as being able to extend forward a pattern of dealing with the environment that had been developed in previous encounters with the world. The lower-class children who scored well on the Piagetian tests did not immediately bring forward skills that they had in order to structure the Level II recall situations abstractly. They needed a couple of training sessions to help make the skills more salient. It is as if the practice sessions opened a cupboard door on skills these children had acquired but had shelved, so to speak, as not quite knowing what to do with. How they performed in the IQ test situation was not a good indicator of their potential. Such results certainly ought to make us cautious about the conclusions we draw about lower- and working-class minority children from single intellectual tests.

Questions arise, however, about those category C children who went through the same training procedure as did some of the category A and B children. Category C youngsters were those whose cognitive development on the Piagetian tests was not on a par with the other children in the sample. Their performance even after training suggested that they did not have the cognitive skills that were available to category A and B children. This could be because they had limited genetic endowment. However, we shall look at other possibilities about these performance deficits in the course of our review of some of the research in this area.

Before we take up the category C children, let us turn to the question of why it might be that some children come to intellectual performance situations with cognitive skills they are not able to use efficiently. This, of course, was the situation with the category B children in the Scrofani et al. study. I will spend the next sections discussing research that describes issues influencing the readiness of children to perform cognitively at more advanced levels.

Environmental Background and Intellectual Ability. Although basic intellectual skills are distributed widely throughout the human family, the maturation of specific intellectual abilities may occur at different rates. Apparently some cultural settings provide environments that hasten the rates of development. Whether by the fast road or the slow road, the children eventually reach the same destination. When urban American middle-class children were compared with various groups of rural Guatemalan children, for instance, it turned out that the American children matured in certain skills earlier than the Guatemalan children. Urban Guatemalan middle-class children were also more advanced in some skills than the rural children. But by the time they were 11 years old all the children were at approximately the same level on the skills in question. If predictions of intellectual potential had been based on their scores when they were 5 and 6 years old, the rural Guatemalan children would have been incorrectly called retarded. Kagan and Klein make this interpretation, "These data have implications for America's educational problems. . . . The Guatemalan data, together with those of [studies on urban Western children], suggest that children differ in the age at which basic cognitive competences emerge and that experiential factors influence the time of emergence [1973, p. 958]."

It seems reasonable to assume that for lower-class Afro-American children differences in cultural experience significantly affect their readiness to do well in intellectual performance situations. Sandra Scarr has attempted to assess the relative contributions that environmental as opposed to genetic variables make to the intellectual performance of black children. Based on a study of both black and white twins in the Philadelphia school population, she asserts that genetic factors have less of an impact on cognitive test performance for black children than for white; environmental factors are more influential for black children. Many black children "are being reared in circumstances that give them only marginal acquaintance with the skills and the knowledge being sampled by the tests we administered [1977, p. 31]." This differential access to such skills and knowledge "explains the lower performance of black children as a group [p. 31]." As she put it in an earlier version of this work, "The black child learns a different, not a deficient, set of language rules, and he may learn a different style of thought. The transfer of training from home to school performance is probably less direct for black children than for white children [Scarr-Salapatek, 1971, p. 1294]."

Scarr and Weinberg (1976) made a more direct test of the possibility of influencing the environmental contributions to IQ. In order to separate genetic factors from conditions of rearing, they studied a group of 130 black and interracial children adopted by advantaged white families. The adoptees, whose natural parents were of average educational background, scored above the mean for the white school population in IQ and school achievement. "One reason for the substantial increase in test performance of the black and interracial adoptees," it was suggested by the researchers, "is that their rearing environments are culturally relevant to the tests and to the school [p. 737]."[6] Later we shall see how Jane Mercer has used such notions about cultural difference to try and devise what she thinks is a fairer method for assessing intellectual ability.

What is it about the backgrounds of young children that prepares them to do well in school? Is it the "books and pictures and music; [the] cleanliness . . . sympathy and understanding" recommended by W.E.B. DuBois? Cultural enrichment and good family relations undoubtedly play a part, but there are some other important elements in their experience as well. A pivotal issue in the backgrounds of the children who are ready for school seems to be a particular way of using verbal skills. I am not referring here simply to the ability to be talkative, as such. The evidence indicates that, in circumstances where they feel comfortable, lower-class black children are as talkative as any children. The point is that children seem to differ by socioeconomic class at least in the efficiency with which they use language internally to carry on their problem solving.

Scrofani et al. report as a part of the study we reviewed above that following the experiment they asked their subjects to put the pictures used in the Level II recall test into groups of things that go together. The trained subjects regardless of category were able to do this task. Among the untrained subjects all but one of the middle-class subjects (from category A) did so, but less than half of the lower-class subjects (category B or C) could do so correctly. Of those who did, only a few were able to come up with a precise concept or explanation for their groupings. However, most of the category B and C children grouped the pictures and verbalized the concept when prompted. The researchers note, "These observations suggest that the middle-class children may have specific skills (for example, verbal labelling skills) and know-how that the lower-SES children do not have. Perhaps the attainment of this skill was all the B subjects needed in order to actualize their potential [1973, p. 552]." Thus, although most children bring active intellectual abilities to performance situations, the backgrounds of some children teach them skills that help them use these abilities more efficiently.[7]

This observation concerning the way verbal skills are used is supported by other research. One study investigating intellectual performance among black children found that social class differences in performance did not emerge until about 3 years of age (Golden et al., 1971). This was seen as reflecting the fact that between 18 and 36 months language becomes an important way of dealing with the world, and the forms of language development tapped in standard IQ tests reflect the experiences more familiar to middle-class families. In a study of white preschool boys, Golden et al. (1974) found that the middle-class subjects in the group were better than the lower-class boys at using verbal cues to find a hidden reward. The children did equally well when they had to do the task without verbal cues. The researchers concluded that the specific verbal labels— "The cookie is under the lock (or the valve, etc.)" rather than "The cookie is under this thing"—made the difference.

These studies suggest that, in contrast to less educated individuals, highly educated adults tend to use more specific terminology and rely more on language to transmit information and to regulate their children's behavior. Children whose parents are more educated may acquire a greater set to listen when they are spoken to, to use verbal information to acquire knowledge, and to respond to verbal instructions to guide their behavior than do children whose parents are less educated [p. 91].

It is not that lower socioeconomic status children come from "defective" backgrounds or even backgrounds in which there is necessarily less talking. It is rather that they may come from backgrounds where language has been used in a different way than in higher status homes. This difference in style of language use may make higher status children more prepared to respond to the demands of the schoolroom situations.[8]

Intervening to Support Intellectual Activity. Studies such as those just reviewed compare children with existing differences in social class and intellectual performance. Is it possible to intervene in the lives of children and their families to actually influence their intellectual development for the better? Let us turn to two examples of such efforts.

A Brighter Dawn. A frequently cited example of early intervention is the ambitious and almost heroic undertaking of Heber and his colleagues in the Milwaukee Project (Heber, 1978; Heber and Garber, 1975). In a survey of the most impoverished area of Milwaukee they found that mothers with IQs below 80 produced a disproportionately high number of children with IQs below 80— children, furthermore, whose tested intellectual functioning declined with age. A sample of 40 black families was selected from this area which seemed to have so many children who were at high risk for developing intellectually retarded modes of performance. Twenty of the families were placed in the experimental group and twenty in the control group. There were no significant differences at birth in important features of health and physique of the 40 infants involved in the study. Economic status of the families and number of siblings in the household were also similar.

The program for the mothers in the experimental group included instruction in home and child care and occupational and educational training. Starting in the first few months of life, the children in the experimental group were placed in daycare facilities with all-day sessions, five days a week, every month of the year through age 6. The program for the children was intensive, personalized, and focused on perceptual-motor skills, cognitive-language skills and socioemotional development. The experimental group began to show differences at 14 months when their growth norms were four months ahead of the controls. The controls were about at the expected levels at that time. On tests of learning and language development, children in the experimental group were not only doing better than the controls but on some tests were ahead of the test norms for their age. By the time they entered school at age 6 they were clearly ready to learn. They demonstrated the active approach to problem solving needed to do well in school.

There has been considerable cautiousness in how to interpret these results (Loehlin et al., 1975). Page (1975) argued that these children were being trained in IQ test related skills, not necessarily in the kinds of skills that would lead to broad educational growth. However, the children were followed for three years without further intervention and continued to do well. This blunts that particular criticism. Nevertheless Heber noted that for those children living in disrupted family or social environments with intellectually limited parents it is probably necessary to continue special programs for the children. Even though there may be differences of opinion as to just what factors are most involved in changed performance of the children in the experimental group, such a program as Heber's does show the educational modifiability of economically deprived youngsters. Some writers are inclined to feel that it is primarily in the area of affective and motivational factors that intellectual performance can be boosted. However, it does seem likely that cognitive as well as affective factors were enhanced in this program. Heber's research is very much in line with the idea that basic cognitive processes and the capacity for intellectual competence are universally distributed in human beings, and differences in environmental opportunities are critical to determining when and how completely these abilities will become manifest.

Dynamic Assessment of Active Potential. Following a review of work such as Heber's the question arises as to whether one has to intervene in the lives of children as early as the first few months of life in order to prevent the decline in functioning of those children at risk for becoming retarded performers. For example, the children in the Scrofani experiment were 4th-graders. Are the category C children, the lower-class children of less advanced cognitive development, to be considered lost to any significant intellectual improvement because they are "too old" to change? While almost all psychologists would agree that the earlier an intervention is made in the child's development, the easier it is to achieve significant effects, the work of Feuerstein and his colleagues (1979) suggests that children maintain a significant capacity for intellectual modifiability even into adolescence.

Let's introduce Feuerstein's work with one of his case studies:

> When first referred Joel [who had been institutionalized at the age of 8 with a diagnosis of severe mental retardation] . . . was apathetic and torpid, and only interacted with the examiner in a limited manner. [He] was illiterate, had little orientation in time and space, and lacked self-care skills. . . .
>
> Very early in our assessment and work with Joel, [however,] it became clear that he had a substantial potential for modifiability. Unfortunately, in his 8 years of institutionalization this core of potential had never been recognized or assessed.

. . . we continued to work with him for 6 years. At the end of this period Joel was able to learn a vocation. He is a proficient reader and is able to communicate his thoughts and feelings. Most important, Joel is able to function independently as a self-supporting member of society [pp. 23–24].

The above vignette is presented as a representative example of many cases Feuerstein and his colleagues have worked with. It illustrates the dramatic changes they brought about by applying a different conception of intellectual potential to people whose initial test performance was strikingly below par. Feuerstein's work has been done with the many different kinds of immigrants that have poured into Israel in the last 25 years. The issues he raises are pertinent to dealing with the controversies about the intellectual functioning of racial minorities in the United States, too.

Feuerstein's approach is based on the belief that cognitive processes involved in intellectual performance can be modified. Taking something of a "deficit" approach to substandard intellectual functioning, he starts with a belief that in many instances children do not do well intellectually because they have not developed—they lack—certain specific problem-solving skills. However, he does not believe that the deficits that lead to lowered performance stem from genetic lack or some other physiological disturbance. Instead they are the result of reversible disruptions in the learning process. To summarize his extensive analysis briefly, the cognitive processes involved in dealing with intellectual problems can be divided into "input," "elaborational," and "output" phases. Typical impairments to the cognitive processes may occur in each one of the three phases. (Some of the processes he identifies are very similar to Kagan's (1976) "executive processes").

In order to assess exactly which elements of cognitive functioning are impaired, Feuerstein developed a new method of assessment which he calls the Learning Performance Assessment Device (LPAD). This is a procedure that uses developmental kinds of tasks and a greatly modified examiner-examinee relationship to observe the child carefully. Not feeling bound by the aloof and neutral stance taken by the usual psychometrician, when the child begins to have trouble, the examiner using the LPAD intervenes immediately to see whether or not the child can moderate his or her impaired functioning to some degree by accepting the examiner's suggestions to attend more carefully to the test stimulus, pause longer to reflect on different options of proceeding, deliver the answer in more conventional terms, and so on. The assessment emphasis here is not so much on the product—whether or not the answer is wrong—but on the process—how the failure came about for this particular child.

Viewing intelligence . . . as summarily expressed in the capacity for modifiability or learning, implies that assessment procedures used for educational and social intervention should not be primarily concerned with interindividual differences. Rather, they should enable a full, independent study of each particular individual.

If intelligence is a summation of one's learning and learning consists of being modified, then if one sets about to induce some modification, the speed and accuracy with which learning is produced will correctly indicate the intellectual capacities [p. 50].

This is the essence of a clinical approach to learning and behavior. Assuming that the basic potential for developing high-level intellectual abilities is widely distributed in the human family, the assessment process is oriented toward finding out where these abilities have gone awry in the individual case.[9]

How do these cognitive impairments come about in Feuerstein's view? He proposes that they come from a lack of "mediated learning." Although physiologically intact children have the potential for adequate intellectual functioning, this potential must be brought to full flower. Typically this happens as the family goes about the job of transmitting to the child the important aspects of the culture in which it is embedded. As the family does this it teaches the child not only *what* is important to learn about the world but also *how* to learn. To put it in our terms, in focusing the child's attention on one or another pole of the dialectical world—on hunting rather than sewing for a boy child, or on weather conditions for planting rather than animal tracks for an agrarian society—the family helps the child develop modifiability, the ability to learn and use past experience. This comes from the patient, repeated interactions between parent and child. (In the very earliest months and years the parent responsible for this is typically the mother but certainly not exclusively.) The basic features of intelligence emerge from this cultural transmission process in that the child comes to be modified within its cultural setting and develops the ability to apply prior learning to new problems within that setting.

A child for whom these experiences have been comparatively few can be said to be "culturally deprived" in Feuerstein's view. Such a person or group can be said to be "alienated *from its own culture* [p. 39]." This is to be distinguished from a culturally "different" person or group in which the individual has learned the content and skills of his or her own culture which may not be immediately applicable to a new setting. Feuerstein gives an example from his own experience of the "sudden change produced by the 'flying carpet' program that whisked [Yemenite Jews] . . . to Israel." It became clear that these people were not culturally deprived: "these extremely different individuals were equipped with highly developed culturally adaptive capacities—capacities acquired through their exposure to their own and very different culture [pp.38–39]."

In emphasizing learning as basic to intelligence Feuerstein distinguishes between two kinds of learning—direct and mediated—which are involved in the child's active coping with the world. Direct learning results from the child's own immediate contacts with the world. For example, the child swats at the rattle and comes gradually to develop conceptualizations about it. Mediated learning is defined as "the interactional processes between the developing human organism and an experienced, intentioned adult who, by interposing himself between the child and external sources of stimulation, 'mediates' the world to the child by framing, selecting, focusing, and feeding back environmental experiences in such a way as to produce in him appropriate learning sets and habits [p. 71]."

This need not be seen as a Lockean conception of the child's development. The parent not only feeds stimuli to the child, (s)he also guides the child's active conceptualizing efforts so that this activity is focused on what the culture thinks is important. Mediated learning is seen as being more important than direct learning, especially initially, because, while the child does learn from early on by direct contact with the world, its learning is not very efficient as it tries, for example, to grasp, suck, or bite to find the most effective ways of interacting with a new object. Thus, the parent-mediator intervenes and helps the child focus its attention on the shaking of the object if it is a rattle or the grasping and throwing, if it is a ball. The interactions between parent and child, of course, are not limited to visual-motor ones. The whole range of human developmental experiences is involved. Language development, learning about satisfying bodily tensions, and learning about what other people are like, are all examples.

Mediated learning is prerequisite to engaging in effective learning on one's own through direct exposure to the world: "the more an individual has benefited from mediated learning, the greater will his capacity be to become modified through direct exposure learning [Feuerstein, 1979, p. 71]." It is important to note, too, that there is no special language of mediation. It involves the everyday activities and language used, for example, in labeling— "That's your nose," "Yes, that's a kitty"; in comparison—"That one is red, that one is green"; in locating things in space—"Where's teddy? There's the teddy bear!" and of course many other specific acts. It becomes clear that these are daily events engaged in with infants and young children in most households in cultures all over the world. This lends particular meaning to Kagan's assertion noted above that parents do not necessarily have to be sophisticated in their knowledge about child development in order to provide sufficient background for the unfolding of basic cognitive skills. (It puts all the more responsibility on society for enabling people to achieve the basic living standard that will make it easier to do with their children these things that come so naturally.)

Furthermore the important issue is not so much *what* the child learns about himself, his family, and his culture, important as these things are. "Even more important, however, over and above the specific contents the child might obtain by means of mediation is an attitude toward thinking and problem solving that is actively and efficiently involved in organizing the world of stimuli impinging on the individual from both internal and external sources

[Feuerstein, 1979, pp. 71–72]." This notion of a primary task of educating being to nurture and sustain an active attitude toward problem solving, is, of course, very compatible with our humanistic point of view here. In addition, Feuerstein states that the language and content of the activity are not as crucial as "the *intentionality* on the part of the mediator [p. 71]." The mediator has a purpose in mind which gives a special direction to the relationship between parent and child. In one sense, perhaps, the child, in developing its active approaches toward problem solving, takes on the active image of the parent projected to it.[10]

From the perspective of mediated learning, Feuerstein's approach involves presenting brief task situations in the form of test items to assess the individual's ability to profit from learning experiences. The test items are flexible enough so that finding out about specific cognitive skills can be tailored to an individual child's particular style. On the basis of the assessment a training plan is worked out. The examiner and eventually the educator serve as the mediators for learning what the child lacked in his previous educational experience.[11]

Now, Feuerstein's conception is that insufficient exposure to mediated learning during the course of the child's development is responsible for the cognitive deficits that appear on testing. Several things can interfere with mediated learning developmentally. First, a disturbed family interaction may keep family members from attending consistently to the child. Second, the infant or child may be emotionally disturbed or physically ill itself and thus unable to avail itself of the parents' mediation efforts. Thirdly, a child's socioeconomic conditions may narrow the interaction between parent and child to issues that put him or her at a disadvantage later in school. This may be a way of characterizing the situation in neighborhoods of the sort, in all ethnic groups, from which Heber drew his sample. Finally, disrupted sociopolitical circumstances may lead to disruption of the processes of cultural transmission in the family. One can think of many recent examples of this happening to children in various parts of the world—Viet Nam, Cambodia, Palestine, and many parts of Africa. Although children from poverty environments are at higher risk than others for experiencing insufficient mediation, such disruptions in early learning are by no means confined to poverty conditions. Children from materially privileged environments have been a sizable group for whom mediated learning has not been adequate.

By use of the LPAD Feuerstein and his colleagues have been able to assess the difficulties of and offer learning experiences to children that have helped them develop their intellectual capacities in dramatic ways. He has case examples of persons who have become unusually bright and productive adults by any criterion. Probably most of the children he worked with lived more modest lives but capable and contributive ones, considerably beyond the level of retarded functioning predicted for them by standard testing procedures. Feuerstein's successful experiences in awakening the potential of children from varied racial backgrounds and suffering considerable deprivation certainly suggests that the potential of lower-class Afro-American children could be activated in similar ways.

It is important to note that much of Feuerstein's work has been with children whose IQ level is quite low—below 70. Many of the Afro-American children whose intellectual potential is not being realized do not score that low on IQ tests, although they score lower than they could ideally. The category C children in the Scrofani study had an average IQ score of 91.25 as a group at the lower end of the Average IQ range, not at all different from the IQ scores of the category B children (average IQ, 91). The average IQ of the category A children, however, was 118.75, at the upper end of the Bright Normal range. The relevance of the Feuerstein material is the principle that the various cognitive skills involved in intellectual problem solving are not simply carved into the granite of the child's constitution at birth. What a child develops in the way of thinking abilities depends on how his or her structuring activities are met and mediated by the cultural environment. It is likely that one would not need to make such extensive interventions with most lower-class Afro-American children as the Feuerstein group is prepared to make with the more severely impaired children. There are other ways of modifying the test process for the less impaired children which we shall come to presently in this chapter. It is quite feasible that children performing at average levels and above might improve their performance with carefully conducted, individualized sessions, too. The category A children did not improve with training but those were not very intensive training sessions.[12]

If we look at this from the standpoint of logical learning theory, we understand that certain kinds of environments provide children with opportunities for building conceptual skills that mesh with the expectations of educational settings. It is not that the environment determines intellectual development in a mechanical (efficient-cause) way. Social and physical environments do make important material contribution to development. But "enriched" environments do so to an important degree by providing an arena in which effectance activities, dialectic options, and the development of intentions can have a fuller expression. In an interview J. McVicker Hunt similarly notes, "Development doesn't come just from exposure to environment. It comes from the child's attempt to cope with his environment—from his *experiences* in acting on the things and people around him and getting a response from them [Pines, 1979, p. 59]." Furthermore, enrichment does not only come from the material facts of one's environment. Through exposure to books, television (not to mention trips to the "other side of the tracks" for an inner-city youth), and loving mediators (parents and family), one may facilitate a child's imaginative processes such that (dialectic) alternatives and new intentions emerge.

Whether or not such new developments emerge depends on the nature of the organization of the mental patterns. As children develop their conceptualizations (and the actions that these patterns generate) along certain lines, they become more able to form further conceptualizations along those lines, particularly as the accompanying affective assessments about these experiences are positive. Effectance strivings become channeled through such patterns and children become competent in particular areas. Thus, as young children are supported in developing mental patterns that generate an interest in books and reading, in familiarity with a pencil and with writing, with counting their blocks, and with talking about their activities to other children and to patient, attentive adults—to name a few kinds of things—they find themselves readier for classroom activities. In other words, readiness for new experiences is a function of the kinds of mental organizations that have developed heretofore in the individual. Whether or not exposure to new experiences "takes," so to speak, depends on whether or not these experiences do in fact fit in with existing conceptualizations and thus allow a child to change existing conceptualizations "meaningfully." Thus, the form of a child's conceptualizing activity and the way (s)he manifests that activity on behavior samples called tests is influenced by the kind of environmental background in which (s)he has grown up. The fact that a child does not show the expected level of conceptualizing activity in a particular situation does not mean that (s)he does not possess such ability or the potential to develop such ability. It is of interest that Kagan and Klein (1973) interpret their data from the Guatemalan study using a perspective that is explicitly critical of the predominant Lockean influence on Western psychology. Their support is for "the idea that the child carries with him at all times the essential mental competence to understand the new in some terms and to make a personal contribution to each new encounter [p. 960]." This is to be taken to apply to children from *all* cultures.

Cognitive Style and Intellectual Performance. People from different backgrounds develop distinctive approaches to perceiving the world and thinking about problems, approaches that have been called "cognitive styles." For example, a person may be either relatively "convergent" or relatively "divergent" in thinking. In the case of convergent thinkers, they use conventional reasoning processes to arrive at answers and are more likely to do better on tests that involve finding the one correct answer that, for example, is asked for on multiple choice exams. Divergent thinkers, on the other hand, are more original and novel in their thinking and do better on open-ended questions that allow alternative ways of solving a problem.

Rosalie Cohen and her colleagues have investigated the impact of one such cognitive or conceptual-style dimension on the school performance of lower-class, inner-city children. Conceptual styles for Cohen, as for Rychlak, are strategies for selecting and organizing sense data:

> The analytic cognitive style is characterized by a formal or analytic mode of abstracting salient information from a stimulus or situation and by a stimulus-

centered orientation to reality, and it is parts-specific (i.e., parts or attributes of a given stimulus have meaning in themselves). The relational cognitive style, on the other hand, requires a descriptive mode of abstraction and is self-centered in its orientation to reality; only the global characteristics of a stimulus have meaning to its users, and these only in reference to some total context [Cohen, 1969, p. 829–830].[13]

High reliance on one or the other of these cognitive styles is not related to intelligence; both relational and analytic persons can be very intelligent. However, the dilemma is that schools emphasize the analytic approach to cognitive organization, and the ability to use that style well becomes more critical in higher grade levels in school. Thus, pupils with poor development of such skills or who develop an alternate cognitive style could be expected to do poorly in school early in their careers and do even less well, comparatively, as they advance in grade level.[14]

It is not only in relating to the curriculum—the learning of specific content and the development of problem-solving skills—that analytic skills are emphasized. Cohen argues that the overall ideology and learning environment of the school is permeated by social and psychological correlates of the analytic style. This can be seen, for example, in requirements placed on pupils in school to sit and concentrate for increasingly long periods on impersonal learning materials and to observe and value fixed time-allotment schedules.

So discrepant are the analytic and relational frames of reference that a pupil whose preferred mode of cognitive organization is emphatically relational is unlikely to be rewarded in the school setting either socially or by grades, regardless of his native abilities and even if his information repertoire and background of experience are adequate [p. 830].

Relational patterns of responding tend to be considered deviant and/or disruptive in the school setting.[15]

Behavioral Verve. While Cohen seems to see her work as applying to a variety of lower-class groups, others argue that the conceptual style notion is a good way of accounting for some of the learning problems of Afro-American children in particular [Boykin, 1979; Hale, 1977]. Boykin has proposed the concept of "behavioral verve" as a way of characterizing the conceptual style of lower-class Afro-American children. He uses verve to refer to a higher "chronic activation level" and sees it as being manifested as "an increased behavioral vibrancy and an increased psychological affinity for stimulus change [1979, p. 354]." He suggests that it is possible that lower-class black children would learn better if they were taught in circumstances that provided for more stimulating surroundings.

To test this hypothesis, Boykin gave 3rd- and 4th-grade black and white children cognitive tasks to learn under two conditions, one of which was formal and unvaried and the other a varied one.[16] The varied or unvaried formats had no bearing on the performance of the white children (high versus low scholastic achievement was taken account of), but did make a difference for the black children who did significantly better in the varied presentation situations. The varied and lively context appeared to facilitate their learning, a situation that resembled more closely the crowded homes filled with people and activity presumably characteristic of lower socioeconomic persons. Rather than being a source of distraction preventing children from acquiring cognitive skills, perhaps such lively settings have become the customary environment for learning. When these characteristics of their home environments are missing learning may be more difficult. As Boykin put it, "Schools are relatively unstimulating and monotonous places. . . . perhaps Black students are not as successful in school because they are relatively intolerant of monotony [1977, p. 19]."

Boykin has acknowledged that his results have not made clear which of a number of possible explanations for the responses by the children is correct. It may be that black and white children have the same verve-activation levels, but white children have learned to adapt to the formal, rather dull classroom. Or it may be that the customary level of verve of white children is indeed lower than for blacks. More research is clearly needed here.

The emphasis on conceptual-style difference as a source of educational failure is a departure from the notion that the children have cognitive deficits. These children are seen as capable of developing high-level abstracting skills with the potential for leading productive lives as adults in fields calling for creative thinking—perhaps in some cases in the arts and humanities as opposed to some aspects, at least, of the sciences. Cohen suggests the problem of conceptual style is not so much one of cultural deprivation as it is one of "cultural conflict." In this conception when relationally oriented children attempt to deal with analytically oriented schools the child can be considerably hampered in learning. Here the educational problem is not necessarily to focus on the child and teach him or her to be like the school. Many would argue that the emphasis should be on making schools more flexible so that they can help the child function in the mode that is best for him or her while also helping the child to develop analytic skills as needed.

Recognition that there can be different high-level approaches to problem solving in different people argues for a "pluralistic" conception of intellectual ability, that is, that there are multiple equivalent high-level problem-solving styles. Such a conception challenges us to find ways of accurately measuring the talents of people from different cultures. Perhaps one of the reasons our research has not helped us get a hold on equally valid alternative methods of problem solving is that the American (Anglocentric) culture seems to favor the analytic mode. Alternate modes of approach are often associated with other, non-European cultures—by definition not as "good" as the Western one.

It is clear from these studies that low-performing black children cannot be lumped together in a single group. There can be many reasons why minority children do not perform well in standard educational and testing situations. A child's background may not have helped him or her use language to cue him- or herself into employing the thinking strategies that (s)he has already developed. Or the background may not have helped to develop the needed thinking strategies for effective problem solving that (s)he could develop. Or again background may have fostered the development of an approach that is at a conceptually high level but that is not geared to the task demands of the given situation. Broad stereotypes about the uneducability of black children for higher thinking is refuted by the above ideas. One generalization that is supportable is that these children have the capacity for competent self-expression in the intellectual sphere and if we take the time we can help them to fulfill it.

Learning and Achievement in Intellectual Performance

The standard intelligence test tells us something about what the person's thinking abilities are and also what (s)he has learned. It is difficult if not impossible to separate the contribution of cognitive skills per se from achieved knowledge in the final test score. But it is important to appreciate the distinction in principle between process and content in intellectual performance. So, for example, when one reasons (a cognitive process), one does so with certain ideas and information (content). Achieved knowledge is obviously influenced by a child's particular set of experiences. For example, the test question, "How are a bus and a cable car alike?" does not fairly test the reasoning powers of a young child who has never heard of San Francisco's main tourist attraction or seen a picture of a cable car.

This example touches on a particular bone of contention for many critics of the testing of minority groups, namely, the negative effects of the "cultural bias" of tests on minority children. Cultural bias refers to the idea that the poor performance of minority and economically disadvantaged children stems from their unfamiliarity with the content and format of the tests rather than their lack of the thinking processes needed for high-level problem solving (see Feuerstein [1979], Garcia [1972], Loehlin et al. [1975], Samuda [1975], for a further discussion of issues regarding bias in testing). It has typically been thought that tests emphasizing verbal skills are the most biased or unfair to minority children. Many of the efforts to develop "culture-free" or "culture-fair" tests of intellectual ability have attempted to deemphasize verbal factors. However, it is not a matter of verbal factors alone. Halpern (1973), writing of her experience working with southern, rural black children, noted that even nonverbal portions of the widely used Wechsler children's test proved a challenge to her subjects. What is often not recognized is that "subjects who do not have books or magazines in their homes, whose walls are without pictures, often find pictorial representations of common objects a strange experience. In fact, in many instances, they do not recognize what the picture is intended to represent . . . and so the black subject is at a decided disadvantage when compared with most white subjects [p. 93]."

Robert L. Williams has argued in essence that poor performance is a matter of lack of familiarity with the culture which serves as the reference base for most intelligence tests. His Black Intelligence Test of Cultural Homogeneity (BITCH) has 100 verbal items geared to sampling knowledge about black American culture (the Black Intellectual Test of Cultural Homogeneity: Manual of Directions, 1975, is available from R. L. Williams, Williams and Associates, Inc., 6374 Delmar Blvd., St. Louis, Missouri 63130).[17] As expected, blacks do considerably better than whites on this test, and Williams (1975) has argued that a high score by black children may very well indicate learning potential that is not revealed by more conventional tests. Documentation of the usefulness of this particular test awaits further report. Whether or not one must be as culture-specific as Williams in attempting to offset the onesided effects of mainstream culture, the influence of acquired knowledge is clearly an important aspect of intellectual performance.

While Robert Williams' approach to counterbalancing the cultural bias on tests is to meet the problem head-on by changing their content, Jane Mercer takes an alternate route (1973, 1979). Assuming that the test is biased, Mercer would keep the test but find out what differences from the cultural norm in the child's background make that test biased and give those factors a score in a prediction formula by which the child's learning potential is estimated.

Mercer champions the view that all "intelligence" tests are in fact tests of achievement, since intellectual functioning can only develop in a cultural context. Insofar as intelligence tests measure the degree of exposure to the "American" culture, understanding the problems of testing of minority children requires some appreciation of the cultural history of the United States. In this vein, Jane Mercer (1979) makes one of the most searching current critiques of the influence of culture on standard IQ tests.

The molding of this nation culturally has involved inducing or coercing all immigrant groups to shed their particular cultural backgrounds and conform to the dominant "Anglo" cultural model. In its milder forms anglicization has involved insisting that non-Anglo immigrants learn the English language and adopt Anglo ways. "In its more virulent forms, Anglicization rested on a belief in the superiority of the English language and culture and of the 'Nordic' and 'Aryan' races [1979, p. 15]." School systems in America have been entrusted with the task of developing in non-Anglos a set of Anglo values—Protestant religious values, white Anglo-Saxon social values, and Puritan economic values.

The standardized tests used to determine who can profit from schooling have always been culture-specific to the Anglo-American core culture. The tests, Mercer argues, tend to be heavily loaded with questions requiring "progressively more advanced verbal skills in the English language and knowledge of the history, values, customs and institutions of the Anglo core culture [p. 19]." The tests assume that most non-Anglo cultural groups have had the opportunity and the desire to become assimilated and have indeed absorbed the essentials of American (Anglo) culture. Therefore, when non-Anglo children do not perform well on the tests it is assumed that they *cannot* do well—that is, they do not have the ability to do well, even though they have lacked exposure in their daily lives to what they need in order to do well. If, on the other hand, it is admitted that different ethnic groups are being reared with different degrees of exposure to the kinds of materials used in standardized tests, it means that no single set of norms can fairly assess the learning potential (i.e., the intellectual abilities) of the varieties of children from different ethnic and class backgrounds. It means further that children's intellectual performance should be compared with other children who have similar exposure to the experience needed to do well on the test, similar motivation to learn the material in the test, and similar test-taking experience. Hers is clearly a "cultural difference" approach to assessment.

The procedures that Mercer uses to try and do a fairer job of evaluating the ability of lower-class minority children are included into what she calls the System of Multicultural Pluralistic Assessment (SOMPA). It is made up of some previously standardized procedures and some that she has devised based on her research with black, chicano, and white children residing predominantly in California. The SOMPA consists of scales to tap the child's physical health history and sensory-motor intactness, visual and auditory acuity, physical dexterity, ability in simple geometric design copying; a measure of the child's social behavior (the Adaptive Behavior Inventory for Children—ABIC) to provide information on how the child functions at home, in the neighborhood, and in extracurricular aspects of school life; a standard measure of intellectual ability, to assess academic readiness—the recently revised Wechsler Intelligence Scale for Children (WISC-R) which is a widely used individually administered test; and a set of scales to determine the degree to which a child's socioeconomic circumstances approximate the Anglo pattern.

This latter set of scales (called Sociocultural Scales) is particularly important to the pluralistic approach. Such an approach takes the issue of cultural difference quite seriously and tries to build it into the assessment procedure systematically. These Sociocultural Scales assess qualities of family structure, family size, socioeconomic status, and urban acculturation (Mercer, 1979, pp. 35–38). They are used to determine whether to interpret a child's IQ score according to the norms appropriate for children from the standard American cultural background or whether to use another set of norms to determine learning potential. Mercer's research has shown that, provided a child is physically well and shows adaptive behavior appropriate to his age, the less a child's sociocultural background fits the "core culture" (Anglo) profile (core culture children on the average have IQs of 100, of course), the more likely this child belongs to a cultural group whose average performance on the test is less than 100. In other words, a measurable degree of sociocultural difference from the Anglo standard means that children who in fact actually have average intellectual ability score lower on the WISC-R. Mercer advocates using formulas derived from her research to determine what the predicted average score would be for a particular child. For example, consider a girl whose WISC-R score is 90 and whose scores on the Sociocultural Scale indicate that the average IQ for children from such a background is 80. The score she achieved indicates an above average degree of learning potential even though her attained score puts her barely at the lower limit of the average intellectual ability range according to the standard norms for the test. The standard set of norms used with this girl gives an index of her school functioning level (SFL) and it may be a fairly accurate estimate of how well she will do in the standard classroom without some individualized attention. But the measure derived from the use of the sociocultural norms gives an "estimated learning potential" (ELP).

Mercer would describe such a child as a "bicultural" child—one from a background in which there may be familiarity with a standard English but some degree of limited participation in the core culture. There is considerable internal heterogeneity in ethnic groups, and degree of biculturality can range from recent immigrants who barely speak English but wish to acculturate somewhat to those almost completely Anglicized. Mercer's work shows that a bicultural child can be from any ethnic group—Hispanic, black, or white.

On the other hand, some minority children—considerably fewer of course, especially in Mercer's research sample—are raised in social circumstances characteristic of the core culture. For a black child, for example, this might occur in a family where, among other things, the parents were reared outside the South, and had attained at least a high school education; the father provides the income for the wife and two or three children; and the parents speak standard English and participate actively in community affairs. For such a child the standard norms might well be a fair yardstick of learning potential because the background is likely to have exposed the child to the kinds of things on which performance on this test is based.

There is a third group of children for whom the WISC-R is seen to be totally inappropriate. This group, the "monocultural, non-Anglicized" children, are those "being reared completely outside the White core culture, who are not familiar with the English language, know nothing about the values, lifestyle, or culture of modern America [Mercer, 1979, p. 134]." The families of these children may be recent immigrants or they may choose to keep their cultures apart from the core society. Mercer advocates not using the WISC-R with children whose predicted Verbal IQ average is lower than 75—and great caution should be used in the 75-79 IQ range. These undoubtedly would be the kind of children for whom Feuerstein's approach would be particularly apt.

The implication of Mercer's work is that the evaluation of whether or not a lower-class minority child is "slow" intellectually should not be made from a single assessment perspective. Children whose socially adaptive behavior is adequate but whose intellectual performance is low when compared with the core culture standard probably need to be evaluated with a different set of norms. Minority children should not be labeled retarded or subnormal intellectually unless both adaptive behavior and intellectual functioning as compared with culturally similar children are also subnormal.[18]

Affective/Motivational Factors and Intellectual Performance

The third set of factors affecting test performance involves a child's feelings about the test and about being tested, as well as attitudes toward the (possibly white and/or middle-class) examiner. No educational psychologist would disagree that these factors play some part in performance. The question is *how much* of an impact do they have. Arguing that such attitudes have a considerable impact on intellectual performance, Zigler maintains that the minority child's failure to function adequately can often be traced to "a negative self-image, to a 'can't do' philosophy and to a wariness and/or hostility toward others, that in all too many cases has been honestly come by [1974, p. 158]." Children's cognitive abilities can be masked by these negative attitudes. While recognizing the need to establish rapport with the examinee, some psychometrically oriented psychologists tend to overlook the fact that a testing situation can hold a broad set of anxieties for minority children. For example, Zigler describes asking a child the test question, "What is an orange?"

> The child replied that he did not know and then went on to do everything in his power to maximize the social interaction. This was a child residing in an institution, and what was conveyed was that, given the child's need system and motivation, he was much more interested in obtaining a warm human interaction than he was in playing some game of little interest to him concerning oranges. . . .
>
> Why exactly do children insist on engaging in what our value system tells us to be such self-defeating behavior? . . . Our best hunch is that they are fearful of [examiner and testing situation] and therefore behave in an adaptive manner having as its goal the termination of an unpleasant experience [Zigler & Trickett, 1978, p. 793].

This can be compounded if the child is black and the examiner white. Watson (1972) suggests that the test situation can then come to represent to the black child something of the tension-ridden atmosphere of the wider society, lowering the child's expectation of succeeding and hence his or her motivation to perform to his utmost.

Various studies show that when the motivational setting of the test situation is enhanced, intellectual performance is significantly improved (e.g., Bortner and Birch, 1971; Flynn and Anderson, 1976; Terrell et al., 1978; Thomas et al., 1971; Zigler and Butterfield, 1968; Zigler et al., 1974). (The Terrell et al. study [1978] is of particular interest because it reflects the different angle on traditional problems that black psychologists can bring to issues of cultural pluralism. In showing that social reinforcement enhanced performance on the newly revised Wechsler Intelligence Scale for Children [WISC-R] they found that in a sample of 2nd-grade lower-class black children, receiving a "culturally relevant" reinforcer—"good job, blood," "nice job, little brother"—obtained significantly higher IQ scores than two other groups: a control group receiving no reinforcement, and a group receiving the typical kind of verbal reinforcement—"good," "fine".)

These studies tend to use "optimizing" procedures as the way of influencing performance. Optimizing procedures refer to things the examiner does in the individual testing situation to try and elicit the child's best motivation to perform. They consist of altering the item or subtest sequence of a standard test to enhance the child's interest and to try to prevent long sequences of failures, and making a more liberal use of encouragement than is customary in the standard setting. These procedures do not involve a permissive atmosphere that sets few performance standards, however (Vosk, 1966). For example, the tester may refuse to accept a silly answer that a child might give just to finish the testing ordeal quickly. In such a situation the examiner might state the expectation for the child to try again and do better if it were felt that the child could do better. The examiner's encouraging firmness is a way of expressing respect for what the child can become. Some of Feuerstein's procedures clearly fall within this "optimizing" rubric although he uses tests that are more likely to elicit examiner-child interaction and makes these interactions rather than the final score the primary basis of his evaluation. Optimizing procedures are effective with working- and lower-class children but seem to make no difference in the performance of middle-class children.

The effect of motivation and affect on intellectual performance is not confined to the test situation. Rosenthal and Jacobson's investigation of the effect of teacher attitude on pupil achievement in the classroom indicated that when teachers had been given (false) information about differential learning potential of their students, the pupils' achievement at the end of the year matched the information given the teachers (1968). In this so-called "Pygmalion effect," the data seemed to support the hypothesis of teachers treating their students in accordance with their prior expectations of them. The Pygmalion effect involves identifiable components of interpersonal interaction. When people expect their students, clients, or whomever, to do well, they "[1] create a warmer social-emotional mood around their "special" students (*climate*); [2]

give more feedback to these students about their performance (*feedback*); [3] teach more material and more difficult material to their special students (*input*); and [4] give their special students more opportunities to respond and question (*output*)" [Rosenthal, 1973, p. 60.] There is enough evidence about the stressful nature of performance evaluation situations for blacks and the existence of deleterious middle-class attitudes toward the poor to take the Pygmalion effect seriously. Zigler et al. put it this way:

> Once one recognizes that the performance deficit in disadvantaged children, instead of being invariably due to a cognitive deficit, may be due to a variety of motives, attitudes, general approaches to tasks, and even to psychological defenses that tend to be defeating in the school setting but are generally adaptive to the child's life, then one is ready to seriously entertain the proposition that disadvantaged children are brighter than their test scores indicate [1974, p. 213].[19]

Test Format and Motivation. In our discussion of the cultural biasing of tests, we noted that children do not do well with material with which they are not familiar. We can extend these concerns into the section we are considering now to say that children are less motivated to perform well on test content or tasks that they find less interesting to them or less pertinent to them.

Kagan (1976) points out, for example, that in testing memory span, 3-year-olds were able to recall a sequence of only two or three items when these items were numbers to be orally reproduced. But when the task involved reaching to find a toy, the children could recall under which one of four or sometimes five different receptacles an item was placed.

In another study (Franklin & Fulani, 1979) black high school drop-outs demonstrated high-level thinking strategies (clustering) in a free recall task when materials were included that drew on ethnically relevant themes such as types of dancing and different "soul foods" as well as themes familiar to both black and white subjects (called "Universal Themes"). Under these circumstances the black youths showed a considerably greater use of concept formation than did white adolescents. This was contrary to the level of performance usually anticipated for black youngsters. Rather than concluding that the white students were cognitively deficient, the researchers suggested that the white students were stymied by their unfamiliarity with themes relevant to the black culture. "The seemingly miscellaneous nature of many of the Black items for the White students apparently contributed to the overall poor performance in categorized recall [Franklin and Fulani, 1979, p. 237]." The black students used categorizing strategies on both Black and Universal items suggesting that when the task was interesting they applied their abilities across the board to all materials. The unfamiliarity of a significant portion of the content seemed to freeze the capabilities of the white youth.

It is not necessarily just the special familiarity of the item content that is relevant either. In a study of intellectual and personality characteristics of children, Yando et al. (1979) used a variety of behavioral problem-solving tasks selected to minimize the predominance of academic achievement in the outcome. The tasks used were designed to investigate creativity, self-confidence, autonomy, curiosity, frustration threshold and dependency. The sample consisted of black and white 2nd- and 3rd-grade children, half of whom were economically advantaged and half of whom were disadvantaged. They found that the groups performed equally well across the variety of tasks; the group differences that did emerge reflected stylistic rather than capacity differences. They noted also that disadvantaged children were particularly able on tasks requiring creative thinking. They state: "The present results add to the argument that a better understanding of children in our society who are not middle-class white children can be gained only if we attempt to devise measures and define situations that allow their competencies to emerge [1979, p. 107]."[20]

Cole and Bruner concur in these assessments: "When we systematically study the situational determinants of performance, we are led to conclude that cultural differences reside more in differences in the situations to which different cultural groups apply their skills than to differences in the skills possessed by the groups in question [1971, p. 874]." In other words, persons do not manifest cognitive skills in situations that are not meaningful to them, and they differ in the kinds of situations in which they bring forward the conceptual patterns they have developed. In one sense, to anticipate our next discussion, children perform better in situations they like.

Affective Assessment. As the reader will recall, the term "affective" has a special meaning in the humanistic approach being adopted here. It is used in the term "affective assessment" which is an inborn dialectical aspect of mentality. Conceptualizations, meaningful affirmations about the world, are always accompanied by a "like-dislike" judgment, thus lending a clear dispositional tone to their meaning. This meaning is determined by the person's intentions and standards, not by those of the environment (see Chap. 1, note 4). Much of Rychlak's research has been devoted to demonstrating the effect of such assessments on the learning process and to showing that humanistic concepts can be investigated in rigorous ways. It is worth looking at some of this research because the issues that we have been discussing in this section can be perhaps seen as particular instances of the larger affective assessment concept.

Rychlak calls his operational measure of affective assessment "reinforcement value" (RV). It is one kind of "subject variable" that persons bring to every experimental situation (see the discussion of subject variables in Chap. 2, note 3). The RV measure is derived by asking subjects to rate whether or not they like materials that they are going to be asked to learn or deal with in some way in the experimental situation. A rating of "liking" is presumed to reflect a positive affective assessment; negative assessment is reflected in a rating of "disliking."[21]

While the learning of nonsense syllables was the original domain of investigation for testing his humanistically oriented theories, Rychlak and his coworkers have extended their methodology to a number of other areas including studies on the interaction of RV effects with personality factors and some aspects of psychopathology (1977, Chap. 10). Of particular relevance to our discussion here is the research by the group on RV learning styles in minority and lower socioeconomic status (SES) groups.[22] Several studies have established that black subjects (both junior college and junior high school students) were more influenced by RV considerations in their learning of lists of trigrams than were their white counterparts, and lower SES adolescents were more influenced than were their middle-class subjects. However, class differences did not eradicate the influence of an RV-learning style for black subjects. Reliance on an RV style may reflect strong tendencies within the Afro-American culture to emphasize the basic human affective assessment propensities. Rychlak is careful to point out here that he is not suggesting that a genetic (efficient and material cause) factor is involved in these racial differences.

It is also of interest to note here that "clustering" kinds of measures in free recall tasks have been used in some of the RV studies. Rychlak and his colleagues have found that subjects cluster more frequently on liked trigrams than on disliked ones. In other words, people use a more high-level thinking style on the tasks they like. Having established that black subjects learn more easily along RV lines than AV lines, Rychlak hypothesized that blacks would cluster significantly more—that is, show more of the high-level kind of thinking along RV lines than white subjects. A study designed to test this with a college-age sample found this indeed to be so. Although all subjects showed preferences for clustering liked trigrams more than disliked ones, black subjects showed this RV-phenomenon even more than did white subjects. Rychlak's data are supportive of Franklin and Fulani's finding, which we discussed earlier, that blacks tended to make use of a clustering strategy more than white subjects under certain conditions. This suggests again that when opportunities that are meaningful are presented black youngsters can respond in the active conceptual mode. It may be that in the Franklin and Fulani study, and in Boykin's work (1979) as well, there are reinforcement value effects that are accounting for at least some of the findings.

A hypothesis worth investigating here is that it was not only prior associations to the black community that made for ease of clustering in the Franklin and Fulani study. Perhaps in addition to prior familiarity the black subjects' positive affective assessments helped to trigger an active involvement with the word list and thus facilitated extending a sense of meaningfulness into the materials. Prior familiarity would not necessarily mean "liking" the materials.

It is conceivable that black persons striving to escape association with black culture might have assessed the black list negatively, resulting in detrimental effects on learning those words. For the white subjects the sense of "meaninglessness" they experienced with the black cultural list may have been accompanied by at least mildly negative affective assessments which diminished their inclination to learn them. In Boykin's study black children may have assessed varied stimulation formats positively and unvaried stimulation negatively, making for the better performance in the varied situation. Such a hypothesis would make fewer assumptions about the varied format being like the homes of the black children, although the reason for liking that format could be similarity to the home. In any event both studies seem to exemplify the idea that children learn better in situations they like.

In an effort to extend the work on affective assessment to other minority groups, Garza (reported in Rychlak, 1977) reasoned that other non-white cultural groups in America might show a similar RV emphasis. Comparing a group of Mexican-American with a group of Anglo-American college students, Garza found that the performance of both groups was affected by a tendency to learn the RV-positive trigrams more readily. However, the Mexican-American group was significantly more influenced by this factor than the Anglo-American group.

It is not posited that non-white minorities *inculcate* an affective style.

It is almost too easy to think of RV as a sociocultural product, as a kind of manipulation that is related to the cultural milieu and not actually rooted in the individual's conceptual abilities.

Cultures surely influence the *grounds* for affective assessment (influencing what is considered proper, good, beautiful, etc.) but the RV phenomenon *per se* is no more a cultural product than is the individual's ability to recall in memory that which he sets his mind to remembering [Rychlak, 1977, p. 462].

The fact that nonwhite minority groups may retain RV modes of approaching situations as a salient value does not mean that other modes are not available to govern conceptualizing. The Scrofani et al. study suggests that such modes are available to some degree and presumably have been taught in some homes and perhaps absorbed somewhat from the broader mainstream culture. However, it may well be that groups excluded from participation in all aspects of society's educational and occupational structure come to emphasize less the conceptual modes (such as AV style) that would be useful in advancing within that structure.

Rumsey and Rychlak (1978) carried this line of investigation the next logical step. They considered the possibility that the cultural differences in the salience of an RV style may extend to performance on IQ tests. In addition to the above-cited work with minority groups, such an extension also derives from several studies from Rychlak's laboratory which had indicated that a subject's positive (or negative) assessment of a *task* can alter the usual positive-RV effect in that task.[23]

With this background of research, Rumsey and Rychlak predicted that subjects would score higher on intelligence tests reliably prerated as positive in RV than on tasks rated as negative in RV. More specifically, they predicted that the positive-RV effect would be stronger for lower-class than middle-class subjects and stronger for black than white subjects. If the latter points regarding race and class were so, it would suggest that performance of lower SES and black children on IQ tests is a critical function of reinforcement value factors and thus it is not sufficient to attribute group differences primarily to inherent differences in formal cognitive abilities.

With permission of the test publisher, Rumsey designed subtests modeled on those in the Wechsler Intelligence Scale for Children. She made a movie of two female examiners, one white and one black, demonstrating the tests as if preparatory to administering them. The camera remained focused on the body of the "examiners" from a level below the shoulders; the heads of the women were never in view. After the demonstration of each subtest the subjects, who were 7th and 8th grade black and white children from lower- and middle-class backgrounds, were asked to express their liking or disliking for doing a task of the type presented. Here, as in others of these experiments, subjects' RV ratings were taken twice, with 24 hours separating. Only the reliably liked or reliably disliked measures were used. The children were then administered all 12 subtests of the WISC.

Among the results that emerged from the statistical analysis were that the sample as a whole earned higher IQs on their liked as opposed to their disliked subtests. Contrary to predictions, however, blacks did not increase their score significantly more than white subjects, nor did lower-class children more than middle-class children; that is, RV trends were not significantly greater for black and lower-class children than for their counterparts. Nevertheless the substantiation of the notion that a positive affective assessment has a salutory effect on a standard intellectual performance task is valuable. "An implication of this finding might be that education should cultivate positive interest value for academic tasks and learning, as opposed to merely supplying information [Rumsey and Rychlak, 1978, p. 424]."

With respect to the failure to find racial and class effects, it may have been that the *entire* IQ test situation was negatively assessed by black and lower SES subjects, thus overriding the RV effect. Therefore, it is still an open question as to whether or not a more careful design might show the effect predicted by Rychlak. It should be noted that IQ differences on liked and disliked subtests, while statistically significant, amounted to only about five points. The traditionally oriented psychometrician might well dismiss such a small absolute difference as being unimportant. However, the work from Rychlak's laboratory is consistent with Zigler's research in indicating that affective factors reach "into the very core of a child's intellective processes [Rychlak, 1977, p. 464]." Affective assessments in intellectual situations are a part of inevitable processes that operate broadly in human behavior. As such they are not factors to be dismissed or "controlled out" of situations but rather factors to be accounted for in all human behavior.

The point of this lengthy discussion of the RV research is to highlight in some detail another part of the structuring activities that people bring to intellectual situations. Just as learning and formal cognition are hard to separate in practice, Rychlak's research suggests that affective assessments and cognitive factors are also hard to separate. Affective assessments help determine how an individual's conceptualizing activities are brought to bear on a situation. Rychlak's data provide a broader basis in humanistic theory for understanding the susceptibility among lower status minority children to affective issues in intellectual situations. This doesn't mean that more specific manipulations, such as optimizing procedures, do not have an even more specific effect than the RV variable. It would mean, however, that such procedures are a special case of affective assessment activity.

The theme of this chapter has been that intelligence involves the ability to learn how to bring forward patterns (actively) developed in one situation to adapt to new problem situations. This is consistent with a Kantian view of mental functioning and is seen as being distributed throughout the human race. To some extent individual differences in the efficiency and speed with which one learns are probably a function of genetic contributions, but the ability to extend prior patterns into new situations is very critically dependent on the quality of developmental experiences—the opportunity to apply one's abilities actively in a variety of situations and the opportunity to develop verbal mediation skills to help in the problem-solving process. When such developmental experiences have been lacking there is strong evidence that deficient conceptualizing performance can be considerably improved—even in adolescence. For some children, special attention to cognitive functioning is what is necessary to set them on the right track toward intellectual competence. For others, what is of primary importance is giving consideration to the affective and motivational context in which intellectual learning takes place. Often when the child realizes that intellectual problem-solving situations involve interesting and pleasing challenges posed by supportive adults (s)he decides that the academic situation at hand is the kind of situation to engage actively.

What is called for is a recognition on the part of our educational system of the need to adapt to the pluralism of cognitive styles and cultural backgrounds that children bring. We must also recognize the child's readiness to learn *something* when (s)he comes to school. Just because children are not learning what the teacher wants in inner-city classrooms does not mean that the child is not actively conceptualizing the situation. Learning is going on. "Since the advent of behaviorism learning has been conceptualized as occurring only when there is an alteration of overt performance, which means that some experimentally preconceived criterion of performance has been attained by an animal or human being [Rychlak, 1977, p. 325]." It is the meaningful ordering of the situation (conceptualization) with or without some expected external performance that constitutes the learning. The child may well be learning *not* to learn what the teacher presents. Many minority children come to learn that in the average school situation it is hard to develop feelings of efficacy and fulfill the general effectance strivings that they bring. Negative assessments color the learning situation and get extended to more and more aspects of the school setting. The child begins to learn to express competence strivings in nonacademic situations or in street-game pursuits. It is little wonder that minority youth show intelligence in the extra-classroom pursuits. They are using the same active (native) conceptualization processes that have been thwarted in the classroom! The burden is on society then—not on the children—to make the changes in techniques and attitudes that will help all children to make competent and socially contributive use of the considerable skills that they already possess.

NOTES

1. Jensen's 1969 paper brought to a full boil the long-simmering controversy concerning the intellectual level of black and lower-class children. Jensen stated that low IQ children are genetically as well as environmentally handicapped and that genetic factors account for differences between ethnic and socioeconomic groups as well as within such groups. Jensen concludes that low IQ children *can* be taught if one deemphasizes learning through the use of abstract (Level II) abilities and instead emphasizes learning by rote methods. The idea of genetic inferiority of blacks was not new with Jensen. However, there has been much debate centering specifically around this article, because it is one of the most sophisticated presentations of the argument of racial inferiority to date. From the perspective of self-realization the implication for blacks of genetic limitations on the nature and flexibility of problem-solving capacities is that blacks as a group have limitations on the direction and capacity of their self-development. I will not dwell on the Jensen article and its critique in this chapter. Farber (1981), Feuerstein (1979), Gordon & Green (1974), Lawler (1978), Loehlin et al. (1975) and Montagu (1975), among many others, have provided a range of recent commentary. For this writer, in addition to the weakness of the strong nativist point of view, the particular tragedy of the way this issue has been raised is that it deflects attention away from the many things that *can* be done to enhance the intellectual development of Afro-Americans.

2. Feuerstein's definition of intelligence centers on learning: "We define intelligence as the capacity of an individual to use *previously acquired experiences* to adjust to new situations. The two factors stressed in this definition are the capacity of the individual to be modified by learning and the ability of the individual to use whatever modification has occurred for future adjustments [1979, p. 76]."

3. This is not to deny that some children are indeed retarded, that is, actually limited in their intellectual ability. However, we shall maintain here that the proportion of children who are really hopelessly retarded is small and far smaller than the numbers of minority children now being labeled as retarded.

The term retardation has generally been applied to persons who score below the IQ range of 70–75. It is more appropriate to use the term "mental subnormality" for the broad group of persons falling into that range and then to distinguish between two kinds of mental subnormality (see the excellent articles on this topic by Sarason, 1966, and Zigler, 1968). One kind of subnormality involves a group of persons who on the average have mental scores that are extremely low—on the average about 35 (Zigler, 1968, p. 284–285). This group comprises persons with known physiological defects, such as Down's Syndrome, congenital rubella, phenylketonuria (PKU), to name but a few. This group of persons, which is often identified as the "mentally defective," is a small percentage of the subnormal.

The far larger proportion of the subnormal is a group labeled the "sociocultural retarded." By and large they fall within the 50–70 IQ range and have no identifiable physiological basis for their retarded performance. It seems reasonable to assume that social environmental factors (poverty, lack of access to educational opportunity, etc.) make an important contribution to their subnormal performance. On the other hand, some see limited genetic endowment as making an important contribution to their subnormality. Even with such an assumption, education for some degree of usefulness in society would not be ruled out for these people. What is sometimes forgotten is that people can achieve scores in the retarded range for different reasons. The retarded are a quite heterogeneous group. Some may have limited genetic endowment, but a great many others score low for reasons of environmental history during their development.

4. Other psychologists disagree quite strongly with the IQ approach and argue that the developmental approach to intelligence is the better one. Such an approach is based on *a priori* or theoretical notions about the invariant developmental stages in which cognitive abilities emerge. Jean Piaget's theory of the development of children's thinking is clearly the most influential and comprehensive one in modern psychology. Piagetian theory was derived by careful, intensive observation of the ways that children of differing ages go about solving intellectual problems posed to them. Rather than trying to derive a measure of intelligence level from how many right or wrong answers to specific standardized questions a child gets, the score on a developmental test represents the degree to which a child shows that (s)he has in his or her own way achieved mastery of a particular cognitive task.

One of the more familiar tasks is the mastering of "conservation," an aspect of that cognitive level achieved in middle childhood called "concrete operations." Conservation is the ability to recognize that a given quantity of a substance, let's say a liquid, remains the same even when transferred to a different shaped container. Thus, two pints of water looks like more to the 5-year-old when it is in a tall slender beaker than when it is in a short wide beaker. The younger child does not conserve the quantity even when it is shifted from one container to the other right in front of him or her. Many of the original Piagetian tasks were designed to be presented in an individualized, clinical style allowing for different ways of getting to the answer.

5. Rychlak feels that the term cognition has been too much associated in psychology with a passive characterization of thought processes. Such connotations can be seen in the term "mediation" which is now popular with social learning theorists and cognitive behaviorists, researchers who while having rejected a strict environmental contingency approach still are basically mechanistic in persuasion. From their view individualized cognitive or thinking processes are seen to mediate or filter an incoming stimulus so that a response to that stimulus may be relatively unique and perhaps unexpected. Thus they agree that the response cannot always be accounted for by the present stimulus. But Rychlak argues that cognitive theorists describe mediation in a way that makes it clear that mediation occurs because psychological structures have been developed in the individual through his or her exposure to *previous* stimuli. Mediation, then, is only the process of applying previous input to the present situation. The person never in principle brings a unique response to the situation *de novo* as a truly dialectic option would propose (see Chap. 1 of this volume). The humanistic approach allows in principle for previous stimulation as well as the truly original response—what Rychak calls a "telosponse [1979, p. 140]"—to influence behavior. Thus, modern cognitive approaches are still mechanistic in that they try and account for a person's

behavior on *this* day in terms of yesterday's (efficient-cause) stimulation (see Rychlak, 1977, especially pp. 154 and 217–218, for further discussion of this idea). Granted that the terms must be used carefully, I will use the terms cognition and mediation from time to time here but fully within the humanistic spirit being developed.

6. Of course such a study raises social and political questions. Scarr and Weinberg (1978) note that they are not advocating the adoption of black children by white families. They took the opportunity available to investigate the effects of a different environment on a sample of children. In so doing they demonstrated rather dramatically the broad potential for competent intellectual development that black children share with all human beings. Their assumption probably involved the desirability of trying to see what could enhance IQ and possibly thereby school performance in black children. Their study does not argue against changing the system so that black families can help their own children. In fact it suggests that allowing black families the opportunities to help their children will do some good; these children are able to profit from changed environments. The Scarr and Weinberg study does not rule out approaching intelligence from other perspectives than IQ testing either.

7. No one, including highly educated adults, uses abstract modes of thought all the time. In fact abstract thought probably makes up a relatively small percentage of waking thought. Some writers even question whether abstract thought is always the best way of thinking (Rohwer, 1980). It is *different* from more concrete modes but given a particular social circumstance the concrete mode may be more adaptive. The trick is knowing when it is appropriate to institute an abstract mode. Kagan argues that this kind of sophistication is governed by the presence of "executive processes" in our cognitive arsenal. Executive processes are superordinate cognitive processes that appear later in a child's development and that control the use of the more discrete cognitive functions such as memory, perception, generation of hypotheses, and the like. He lists a number of such executive processes (1976, pp. 20–24). Among these are appreciating the level of complexity of a problem and adjusting one's effort accordingly; flexibility of approach—the ability to shift from ineffective solution hypotheses and search for better ones; and searching for ways of organizing a problem situation so as to deal with it better. In some cases, the strategies that an older child will use are ones that younger children already know but do not use. The younger child's "deficit" is in the *activation* of or *use* of the knowledge. Executive functions allow the older child to use what (s)he already has.

As an example, Kagan analyzes Piaget's stage of "concrete operations" in this way. In this stage younger children are presumably more influenced than are older ones in their reasoning by the more superficial and apparent aspects of a situation. Thus, pouring a pint of water from a low, round dish into a tall, slender beaker influences the child into thinking that there is more water in the beaker. Kagan suggests that coming to understand, as older children do, that the quantity of liquid remains identical, *does* involve cognitive maturation. But perhaps what changes is the executive process of understanding the nature of the problem and the nature of the question being asked. So, for example, a 5-year-old, when asked a class-inclusion question related to this stage such as, "There are ten red beads and four green beads here. Are there more red beads or more *beads*?" responds typically "more red beads." It may be that he understands the question to be: "Are there more red beads or *green* beads?" It doesn't occur to him that the examiner would ask the question that he does. Important to rising above an apparently concrete response is the growing ability of the child to understand what adults are after. "As with answers on intelligence tests and the replies of schizophrenics, very few answers to examiners' questions are irrational, although they are scored as incorrect if they are not the answer intended by the questioner. What happens in cognitive growth, in large measure, is coming to appreciate the mind of the questioner and knowing at once the [meaning] implicated in the question [Kagan, 1976, p. 28]."

Now, the particular point for our consideration is that children achieve executive processes at different speeds depending partly on the history of their experiences with the environment. These are probably associated with social class to some degree and possibly with ethnic group differences. Kagan cites research to suggest that exposure to varied stimulation enhances the development of these processes. It may well be that inner-city children do use such processes in contexts outside of the school. We shall have more to say about this idea later in this chapter and in the next one.

8. This, of course, bears directly on Sandra Scarr's point that some black children may learn different language rules and thought styles at home. Earlier (p. 54) we cited Feuerstein's conception that some children learn to adopt a passive approach to intellectual problem solving which makes them seem to be limited solely to a reproductive way of interacting with stimuli. Perhaps there is something about certain kinds of communication styles within the family that fosters this passivity. We will have more to say about this in Chapter 4.

9. This mode of intervention is treatment-oriented, that is, it seeks to identify and begin to repair faulty learning patterns. Heber's program on the other hand is prevention-oriented. Both methods obviously can be quite expensive and lengthy. Whether or not society wants to spend money on such remedial efforts is an ethical and social policy question. However, the cost of perpetuating an underclass by not spending money on social rehabilitation may in the long run be an even more expensive and ultimately self-destructive luxury.

10. It is of interest to note how these ideas regarding the importance to cognitive development of mediated learning fit with certain psychoanalytic ideas. Psychoanalysis places particular importance on the effects of the mother-child relationship on personality development. In one sense what Feuerstein postulates reflects Rudolf Ekstein's notion that development proceeds from "learning for love to love of learning [Ekstein & Motto, 1969]." In other words, from early on the child begins to learn in order to gain the love and acceptance of the adult, acting as mediator, and then the child proceeds in its growth to the love and active pursuit of learning on his or her own.

Other data bear on this. Blatt et al. (1975) cite data that the quality and speed of early cognitive development depends to an important degree on the quality of the early mother-child relationship. For example, more rapid development of conceptions about the physical object world occurred where mothers had a more accepting relationship toward their babies and expressed more availability to their child. This supports the idea that the quality of the interpersonal mediation experience between parent and child affects the quality of cognitive development.

Some even more dramatic results have been reported recently using a method developed by Silverman for investigating unconscious ideation (1976; in press). In this method a number of carefully controlled experimental studies have shown that one can influence behavior by showing subjects particular messages subliminally. This involves showing subjects messages at speeds faster than they can register them consciously. All that subjects are aware of seeing as they look into the machine showing them the messages are flashes of light. However, there is considerable experimental evidence from Silverman's research that subjects do respond in predictable ways to the presented messages. The theory is that this is so because the messages do register at subconscious levels. The studies that are particularly relevant to our concerns have to do with the use of the stimulus "Mommy and I are one." This stimulus is designed to evoke fantasies of being united in a "symbiotic-like" relationship with a loving and all-providing mother, fantasies that derive from the normal psychological situation in the early months of life, according to psychoanalytic theory (Mahler, 1974).

Silverman's research has shown that the "Mommy and I are one" stimulus has had an adaptation-enhancing effect on various kinds of behavior, presumably because residues of these yearnings remain in the unconscious fantasy of all people. It is as if stimulating the symbiotic fantasy decreases an individual's customary levels of anxiety, making better psychological functioning more possible. In one study using this paradigm, Parker (1977) found that subliminal presentations of the symbiotic stimulus over a several-week period to a group of students were associated with better grades in a college course. This was in comparison to a control group in the class who received a neutral stimulus. Even more relevant to our discussion in this chapter, Tuckett (1980) found that the symbiotic stimulus was associated with improved school performance (reading and math scores) for emotionally disturbed adolescents with learning problems. Almost all of these subjects were black and Hispanic. Thus, from a different vantage point these studies seem to bear on the quality of the mediation experience. The results suggest that stimulating the fantasy of closeness with a maternal (mediator) figure enhances learning. We only have theoretical speculations as to the exact way in which this works, but for one thing it does indicate that while cognitive and affective factors can be differentiated in principle they are very much related in actual learning situations. We shall have more to say about this later when we discuss affective assessment as a factor in learning.

11. The individually tailored administration is of course an expensive process. Feuerstein and his co-workers have devised group procedures for administering the LPAD (1979, Chap. 5). In those procedures, typically two examiners, possibly with an assistant or two, work with a group in a modification of the "test-train-test" situation. The test materials provide the gradual modification in the test stimuli from simple to more complex which assess the child's ability to be modified. Some children are able to show learning potential in the group situation where the individual interpersonal feedback from the examiner is minimal. Such children are good candidates for being placed in school settings. Other children who have more serious problems in cognitive ability and lowered motivation often need the support of one-to-one interaction with an examiner. The group procedure can be something of a screening device to find those who do not need close personal attention in the training process. This implies that the children able to profit from the group administration are more developmentally advanced than children unable to profit. To go back to the Scrofani et al. study (1973), this may be something like the difference between the category B and C children. Perhaps the category C children, although not retarded, need more individually tailored assessments of their learning ability. The group procedures are used when, for example, people want to know about the learning capacities of homogeneous groups of children in order to make educational decisions.

12. Just how much of the performance difficulties of Afro-American children represent "cultural difference" and how much represent "cultural deprivation" is an issue of considerable debate among black social scientists. Black children are undoubtedly a heterogeneous group. Some children who have performance problems on IQ tests may be sufficiently different in their background to be inefficient in carrying over skills that they actually possess to particular situations with which they are confronted. This might be something like Scrofani et al.'s category B children. Others may well have some degree of deprivation with respect to requisite skills also. They may actually not have had certain skills passed on by their own family environment. Category C children might fit this description more closely. An alternate hypothesis would be that category B and C children differ in the degree of "deprivation" they experience—the latter group experiencing more but probably not nearly as much as a group as some of those that Feuerstein has worked with. Seen this way it may very well be that all children suffer some degree of deficit in that probably few families of any class have a perfect mediated learning process for their children. In other words, possibly not even middle-class children achieve the ceiling of their abilities in school as much as they would if each child's learning style were addressed individually by an attentive evaluator assessing each child's learning potential.

13. In one test example subjects are asked to find which pair of pictures out of a set of three pictures of objects belong together. Two answers are possible for different reasons. One picture is of a simple wood chair with one leg missing; the second is of a plain wood table with a leg missing; the third is a picture of an intact, overstuffed arm chair. The relational subject with a more global style is presumably more likely to pick the chairs as belonging together. The analytic subject with a "parts-specific" style is more likely to pick the chair and table as going together—because each has a leg missing (see Cohen's appendices, 1969, for detailed comparisons from the measures used in research in this area). There is considerable overlap among tests of cognitive style (Rice, 1979), and research has not gotten a clear handle on these issues. Yet it is interesting that personality theorists have observed for some time that people tend to adapt to the world by emphasizing thinking and ideation on the one hand or by responding to a situation in terms of the emotions aroused about it on the other. Thorough personality description is much more complicated than this, of course. However, such styles, which we might loosely call thinking and feeling types, adopting terms used by Carl Jung, seem to correspond loosely with Cohen's analytic and relational types. (See also Harrison, 1979, for a recent study of cognitive style in black children.)

14. Cohen (1969) notes further that the studies from her laboratory raise questions about the rationale for "culture-free" tests. Such tests presumably reduce the culture-bound characteristics of assessment procedures by reducing the verbal and informational aspects of such tests that are felt to carry much of the cultural loading. Cohen suggests, however, that the resultant "culture-free" tests require the use of an analytic conceptual style. In the effort to emphasize reasoning skill in the nonverbal sphere, she notes that such tests are composed of items requiring a parts-specific, stimulus-centered mode of abstraction. Bright students who achieve higher levels of abstraction through relational means are particularly penalized by these higher level analytic tests. Cohen found that on concrete tasks bright relational and bright analytic students do equally well. It is only when high-level analytic abstraction is involved that the former pupils are no longer competitive. Thus, not only the mode of conceptual organization but also level of abstraction is a factor in performance. It is in this sense that nonverbal tests have not freed themselves from their culture-bound features.

15. Observing low-income groups from a variety of ethnic backgrounds, Cohen concluded that the two conceptual styles are related to an important degree to experiences in different primary socialization groups. Relational modes of conceptual organization are derived from socialization experiences in "shared function" groups and analytic modes of conceptual organization derive from "formally" organized primary groups. As compared with the latter kinds of groups, in shared function groups

> critical functions such as leadership, child care, and the discretionary use of group funds are not assigned to status-roles within the group. Instead, critical functions are periodically performed or widely shared by all members of the group . . . [p. 831].

(See the Cohen article for a detailed comparison of formally organized and shared function groups and a further discussion of exclusive and mixed use of the two conceptual styles.)

16. There were four types of tasks and five tasks in each type, making 20 tasks in all. Presenting all five tasks of one type to the subjects and going on to all five of those of the next type, and so on, represented an unvaried format. Mixing the four types of tasks across the 20 presentations represented a varied format.

17. The test items are in a multiple-choice format; the subject's task is to choose the one alternative for each item that represents the "correct definition as Black people use the words and expressions." Among examples that Williams gives are the following (1975, p. 124):

1. *Black Draught*
   (a) Winter's coldwind
   (b) Laxative
   (c) Black soldier
   (d) Dark beer

2. *Blood*
   (a) tire
   (b) worthless
   (c) an injured person
   (d) a brother of color

18. Some black psychologists criticize Mercer's approach because a standard IQ test is still a central part of the intellectual evaluation. The core culture is still the standard against which deviation is judged. Furthermore, the need for some correction of WISC-R norms is underscored by Hanley and Barclay's findings (1979) of lower scores for black children on that test than on the WISC. Mercer acknowledges that the factors that she finds as influencing IQ performance are not necessarily the only ones or even necessarily the best ones to select out. They seem to be reasonable ones and empirically they seem to work in greatly narrowing the gap between black and white IQ performance when used, without, we might note, calling for any intervention in the family to change their cultural style. In fact an Estimated Learning Potential that shows a child able to perform better than his or her School Functioning Level puts the burden on the school system to adapt to the child's abilities. It is of interest to note, too, that Mercer's work carries forward the

themes expressed in the Society for the Psychological Study of Social Issues (SPSSI) "Guidelines for Testing Minority Group Children [1964]."

19. Zigler and his group (1974) feel that the IQ as the prime index of problem-solving ability is greatly overemphasized in our society. Others, of course, have a similar view; see, for example, Jencks, 1969; Kagan, 1973; McClelland, 1973; Samuda, 1975). Zigler and Trickett (1978) feel that we should be educating and assessing for "social competence"—how well an individual uses his or her abilities to live a productive life. We all know from our own experience of very "bright" persons unable to do this. Social competence, though not easily defined, is seen as comprising a number of facets. In addition to the three factors of cognition, achievement, and motivation, some index of a child's physical health and well-being should be included and some index of how well a child is meeting societal expectancies. Seen from a different perspective this is very much like what Mercer (1979) attempts to accomplish in the SOMPA.

20. The idea that lower-class black children are able to express intellectual ability when freed from the constraints of the standard IQ situation is illustrated in an interesting study by Gerstein et al. (1976). They administered the Rorschach ink blot test to children being seen for emotional and learning disorders in their outpatient clinic. The Rorschach stimuli are ambiguous in shape and force the subject to structure the material visually in answering the question, "What does this (blot) look like?" (A similar job of imaginative structuring is involved in the game we have all played of finding shapes of real things—animals, ships, faces—in clouds passing overhead.) The Rorschach is used to assess the unconscious strivings and thought styles that make up personality structure. One way of scoring responses yields an approximate measure of how mature a child's perceptual style is. It is one way of getting at formal cognitive ability and similar to the developmental approaches to intellectual assessment.

Low IQ black children were found to be developmentally more mature in cognitive ability with this measure than were low IQ white children. These authors took their results to mean that "standard IQ tests may not adequately tap the cognitive capacity of some Black children and that use of the Rorschach from a developmental-structural perspective may provide a useful adjunctive measure of intelligence that would more realistically assess children's cognitive competence [1976, p. 760]."

21. In a large number of carefully controlled experiments Rychlak and his co-workers (1977, Chap. 9) have shown that the reinforcement value—the subject's reliable rating of liking or disliking the sound—of so-called "nonsense syllables" (consonant-vowel-consonant trigrams such as SAJ, COV, BIK, etc.) influences the learning of such syllables. Subjects tended on the average to learn more readily the trigrams they had independently rated as liking than those they did not like. (Similar results have been obtained when the stimulus material was words, abstract designs, and names to faces.) He and his co-workers have shown that reinforcement value defined in this way is independent of the "association value" (AV) of the trigrams in two ways. It is independent of the number of familiar associations for the subject aroused by the trigram, and it is independent of the general familiarity of the syllable in terms of the number of people who recognize the trigram as being wordlike. The particular RV choices an individual makes are probably related to his or her personal history. In this sense they are mediated by experience. However, Rychlak posits that the propensity for making affective assessments of *some* sort is native to the individual.

22. Rychlak hypothesizes that the influence of affective assessment on learning is a broadly human characteristic and is particularly prominent early in life. The tendency to learn along AV dimensions is more likely to be a function of sociocultural issues. "That is, a word is only 'wordlike' because of the culture that sustains this particular referent as a collection of letters having a consensual meaning [1977, p. 453]."

23. We noted earlier in passing that personality factors influence the RV effect. Specifically, research has shown that persons with certain severe emotional disorders and persons with measurably low self-esteem reverse the RV-positive effect. In one study, persons with low self-esteem tended to learn *disliked* trigrams more readily than liked ones. By contrast, persons with

high self-concept showed the usual RV-positive effect. From the perspective of logical learning theory this is seen as reflecting the way in which persons extend their conception of self into a learning situation such that they are more receptive to material consistent with their premises about themselves.

However, August (reported in Rychlak, 1977) found that high self-concept black fifth-graders learned trigrams they *disliked* better than ones they liked. High self-concept white children were considerably more efficient with liked trigrams than low-concept white children. This unexpected finding led the researchers to consider retrospectively the factors that could have influenced subjects' attitudes. As it happened, in this study all of the experimenters were white. Furthermore, there had recently been some interracial conflict in the community where this study was conducted. It seemed plausible that the black subjects' attitude toward the task (and the researchers) per se had influenced the affective assessment process that they brought into the learning situation. More specifically, the black subjects' dislike of this situation may have been carried forward or expressed in greater learning of their disliked trigrams.

To test this possibility more directly Marceil (reported in Rychlak, 1977, Chap. 10) asked a group of white high school students to rate how much they would like being in a paired-associates memory task demonstrated to them. In the experiment that followed those who indicated they would like such a task showed the usual positive RV effect; those who expressed in advance their *dislike* for such a task showed as much learning for disliked trigrams as for liked ones. (Further research has indicated that such results are not simply an artifact, a function of manipulation by the subjects of RV-learning factors.)

Chapter 4
The Black Speaker: Cherishing Pluralism

This story bout three lil pigs. One day, the lil pigs went out to play. They made lil house. One made a dog house an one made a hog house. One made a pen. . . .

[The wolf] came to the big house. And the wolf say, "Let me in!" And [the pig] say, "No, no, no, my shinny shin shin!" He huff, and he puff, and he tough, and he rough, but he couldn't knock the house down. . . .

And ol wolf say, "I'm a jump down you chimney!" And that ol pig put some water on the fire till when you could jump in it, and the lil pig had cook [some] greens. Yeah, he fool him! He jump in the hot water, and the pig, he had greens and wolf! Greens and wolf! [Houston, 1973, p. 46].

The above is an excerpt from an 11-year-old southern black child's oral rendition of the familiar story of the "Three Little Pigs." It is told in a vernacular form of the English language called the Black English Vernacular (BEV) which this boy probably speaks much of the time. Many lower- and working-class black Americans frequently use this style of speech or variants of it. It could even be said that such speech represents one distinctly observable way in which some black Americans are different from many white Americans, and this in turn reflects some of the differences in cultural history between Euro- and Afro-American peoples. To some extent the consistent and unique features in the language of some Afro-Americans provides evidence of the existence of cultural pluralism in America. In the case of the language spoken by black Americans it not only can be distinguished from the so-called standard American English spoken by many white Americans, but black Americans themselves speak the language in various forms. In other words blacks as a group represent a pluralistic speech community. They differ, for example, by region and by social class in terms of the styles of speech that they use. Whereas the speech of some blacks is indistinguishable from that of white people living in the same region, other blacks, particularly in the northern United States are clearly identifiable as being Afro-American by their speech patterns. Since differences are so frequently viewed with hostility in America it is important to understand what some of the implications of using "nonstandard" speech styles are for black Americans.

BLACK ENGLISH: WHAT KIND OF DIALECT?

The fact that there is considerable overlap between black and white individuals in speech styles raises the question of just how different black and white speech variations really are. After all, these speech styles are forms of the English language spoken by people living in the same nation. Actually there is difference of opinion among linguists as to how similar or how different "Black English" is with respect to the other dialects of the English language spoken in the United States. "The term *dialect* refers, strictly speaking, to differences between kinds of language which are differences of vocabulary and grammar as well as pronunciation [Trudgill, 1974, p. 17]." From this perspective, because "standard" English differs lexically and grammatically from other forms of English, it can be considered to be a dialect, too. The reason we think of it as being standard is that it is "that variety of English which is usually used in print, and which is normally taught in schools and to non-native speakers learning the language. It is also the variety which is normally spoken by educated people and used in news broadcasts and other similar situations [p. 17]." Nonstandard forms of English do not differ from standard English along the dimension of formal versus colloquial. Standard English has colloquial variants as well as formal ones. Nor does more "bad language" appear in nonstandard dialects: "standard English speakers swear as much as others [p. 17]."

The definition of "standard English" is what could be called a "stipulated" definition rather than an operational or factual definition arrived at by observation. In other words, the definition of standard English is an arbitrary one that a group of people (educated speakers of English in this case) agree is an acceptable range of styles for speaking the English language. It is not "standard" in the sense of being purer or better than nonstandard versions in any absolute or factual sense. It follows then that "nonstandard" English refers to those dialects that are not the (arbitrary) standard of English. Nonstandard means different from standard—not worse than standard. What used to be called Nonstandard Negro English, what we are referring to here as the Black English Vernacular, is not sloppy English. It is another dialect form of the English language.

Some linguists argue that the separate history of Afro-American people has made a unique contribution to black language forms. William Stewart (1970) is one of a number of scholars who advance the idea that the distinctiveness of Black English stems from its African origins. This view proposes that Black English derives from a creolized English that drew partly on West African pidgin forms historically and thus is different from other English dialects. (When a linguist refers to a "creole" language he refers to a dialect that derives from a "pidgin" language—a simplified form of a complex base language by which nonspeakers of the language communicate with the speakers of the language and other nonspeakers with whom they do not share a common language. Over the years a language may develop from the pidginized language, a "creole," which becomes the native tongue for the group in question. The creole may become as complex grammatically as an unpidginized language over time.) Although Black English has lexical and structural similarities to the dialects used by both uneducated and educated whites, in the vernacular form in particular there are syntactical differences between British-derived dialects and those dialects deriving from speakers of West African tongues. What needs to be noted, Stewart suggests, is that Black English is a language form governed by rules, that it has a specific historical derivation, and that it has been passed on within a subculture through legitimate processes of socialization. Above all, it is not just sloppy or ungrammatical English, as it is so often regarded, but it has separate origins in Africa for some of its roots and a grammar and syntax of its own as well.

Other social scientists disagree with the claim that Black English is a dialect separate and distinct from those spoken by other Americans. They argue that black speech patterns have resulted from a blending with other "nonstandard" English speech patterns. For these writers whatever African linguistic influences there may have been, and these are not always granted, they have not survived sufficiently to make for any real distinctiveness of the black dialect (see Trudgill, 1974, pp. 73–76, for a brief summary of these opposing views). Rather than using a single dialect of their own, it is argued, blacks speak a variety of forms of the American language, the dialect used depending on the region of the country they come from and the social situation in which they find themselves (Williamson, 1975). In both the past and the present, so this argument goes, there has been and still is a great deal of borrowing of speech patterns cross-ethnically. Thus, blacks and whites actually speak variants of a common American language rather than, to any significant degree, distinctly separate ethnic dialects. Based on this interpretation Black English is more accurately viewed as any language form which black Americans speak according to where they live and what social class they belong to.

While it is still possible to debate the origins of black speech forms a number of social scientists find it meaningful to identify Black English, particularly in its vernacular form, as a distinct linguistic entity, which while sharing characteristics with other American English language forms also has a "core of linguistic features . . . which are found in none of the American or other language systems . . . [and] which . . . are sufficient to make most black speakers ethnically identifiable [Taylor, 1975, p. 35]." Other linguists seem to agree (for example, Hall & Freedle, 1975; Labov, 1972; Trudgill, 1974).

Among the frequently cited features of Black English Vernacular (BEV) that differ from standard Anglo English are its phonological characteristics (pronunciation) and its grammar. Although many features of BEV are shared by speakers of British-derived nonstandard styles, some linguists argue that these forms occur with greater frequency among black speakers (Smitherman & McGinnis, 1980) or that there are fairly exclusive variants in BEV. For example while the deletion of "r" in such words as "car" and "cart" is common in many English dialects, the deletion of "r" after initial consonants—as, for example, "p'otect" = "protect," "f'om" = "from"—may be restricted to BEV (Trudgill, 1974). In respect to differences in grammar, a frequently cited form in BEV is the use of "invariant be" to indicate "habitual aspect"—referring to an event that is repeated but which is not continuous, as in, "Sometimes she be late," which in standard English would be, "Sometimes she's late." Trudgill suggests that this is strongly reminiscent of creole language: "In Caribbean creoles, verb aspect—the distribution of an event through time (whether it is repeated, continuous, completed, and so on)—tends to be of greater importance than tense—the actual location of an event in time [p. 72]."

VARIETIES OF BLACK ENGLISH

It is typical to equate all Black English with the vernacular form. Since the varied and distinct speech forms of black people are identified exclusively with the vernacular, there is a tendency for the public to regard all deviations from standard Anglo English by black people as lower class and uneducated. This view stems from an ignorance of the variety and complexity of Black English forms and the wide range in the verbal repertoires of Afro-Americans (Hoover, 1978; Wright, 1975).

As Claudia Kernan notes in her ethnographic study of speech within a West Coast Afro-American community, even among vernacular speakers, "As one moves from household to household and indeed within households one is impressed by the amount of individual variation among speakers with regard to the use of non-standard variants [1971, p. 36]." Moreover, many blacks who are relatively better educated and/or who maintain contacts outside as well as within the black community speak what could be called a standard Black English (Taylor, 1975) which is like standard Anglo English in certain characteristics and different in others. The speaker of standard Black English unlike the vernacular speaker uses standard English syntax; however, in vocabulary, phonetics and intonation his or her speech contains features similar in varying degrees to vernacular Black English. "The speaker of standard Black English will tend to weaken final consonants, simplify consonant cluster, and exhibit general *l*-lessness and *r*-lessness; where the weakening of final consonants affects grammar, however, as in lack of possessive *s* or loss of *l* in the future, or the *ed* past tense, standard Black English speakers will retain the ending [Hoover, 1978, p. 69]." In other words, Black English is far from a monolithic entity.

SOCIOLINGUISTIC ISSUES

The use of particular Black English forms has social as well as linguistic significance. To give just one illustration of this, the speech employed by black Americans affects the way they are allowed to function as workers in the white society. How a person speaks also has meaning within the black community. Standard Black English, for example, tends to be seen as good English when it is used in appropriate settings and when discussing certain topics. These "good" speakers are distinguished from what some would call the "ultra proper talking" black speakers who characteristically strain to adopt the Anglo dialect in phonetics and vocabulary. (Of course there are many black speakers whose standard English style has practically no detectable vernacular features. This is characteristic of their normal, unaffected speech.) When they are in the presence of black listeners they may be ridiculed for their attempts to make an impression by creating social distance from their black listeners (Hoover, 1978; Kernan, 1971). Sometimes, of course, a black speaker will switch into such "proper" talk as a way of teasing or "sounding on" a friend about, for example, his unusually neat attire, as in, "My goodness, Mr. Jones, don't you look elegant today!"

For black speakers, then, whether they use a nonstandard vernacular form of the language, standard Black English or any one of the other linguistic categories that a black speaker may fall into, there are social consequences resulting from how they speak. Two of these consequences are, first, how language functions in establishing social relationships, and, second, what role language plays in conveying information about the speaker (Trudgill, 1974). To say that people in a national society speak different dialects of the national language, or even different languages, is a statement of linguistic fact. But the fact itself has the potential for eliciting value dispositions or affective assessments about the speaker.

People use information they get from others' language styles to make social judgments about them. Cataloguing people by their speech is a way of expressing social preference of either a positive or negative kind. On the one hand people can feel pleased and intrigued to hear the different variations of language in their society and feel that they live in a richer cultural milieu on account of it. On the other hand such differences from established speech can elicit negative affective assessments. One's habitual use of one or another speech form can open or close doors to privileged society, as Shaw pointed out so masterfully in "Pygmalion." This phenomenon has operated with telling effect not only in societies in which the British influence is strong but in every culture. Speaking of the relationship between the French and their colonies, Fanon (1967) wrote:

> The colonized is elevated above his jungle status in proportion to his adoption of the mother country's cultural standards. He becomes whiter as he renounces his blackness, his jungle. . . .
>
> The Negro of the Antilles will be proportionately whiter—that is, he will come closer to being a real human being—in direct ratio to his mastery of the French language [p. 18].
>
> Yes, I must take great pains with my speech, because I shall be more or less judged by it. With great contempt they will say of me, "He doesn't even know how to speak French" [p. 20].

This tendency to stigmatize the speech of conquered people has probably characterized most historical instances of one society imposing its culture on another. As with many other aspects of their differences from Euro-Americans, many Afro-Americans have reacted to the stigma attached to the Black English Vernacular by feeling a considerable ambivalence toward the way they speak. Even though black speech styles derive from a legitimate linguistic form, many black people feel that the Black English Vernacular represents "incorrect" and deviant speech rather than different and legitimate speech (Smitherman & McGinnis, 1980; Taylor, 1975). The negative evaluations given their speech styles illustrate the difficulties created for black Americans in various aspects of their lives as they try to sustain positive racial self-concepts. Thus speech style becomes one of the dimensions on which blacks may experience conflict about themselves.

Simply put, speaking involves using a certain syntax; but it also entails considerably more: "It means above all to assume a culture [Fanon, 1967, p. 17]." People who assume the culture that is involved in black speech styles not only communicate with words but also use the gestures, vocal intonations, postural adjustments, and facial expressions that go along with the words. These accompanying features provide a context for and augment the meaning of the communication. In addition to the formal grammatical distinctions from textbook English, black speech styles are rich in the structured use of nonverbal communications to convey specific social meanings. One recent effort to classify some of these "kinesic" or gestural and postural styles (Cooke, 1980) identifies various modes of greeting—for example, "giving and getting skin" and the Black Power handshake—as well as styles of standing and walking that men and women use to communicate various messages. A people's speech and communication style are ways they express and develop their conceptualization of the world.[1]

On an individual level when the person achieves the capacity for language in the course of psychological development (s)he has a powerful way of shaping a sense of self by applying tentative labels to aspects of self and using these labels and a myriad of other ideas to guide action in the world. Language is a powerful tool for framing and carrying out intentions. Language gives an important boost to the process of developing a sense of identity. In logical learning theory terms, it is a way of giving expression to developing conceptualizations and a way of extending meaning about oneself—in one's cultural context as well as in wider arenas of activity. Trying to do away with children's cultural language variations—as opposed to simply teaching them additional language styles—tends to stifle the way they are extending the meaning of themselves. It is like saying this (ethnic) part of yourself expressed through your language is not acceptable. By using the language—assuming the culture—of a particular group, an individual can also solidify his or her group membership, which is an aspect of identity. However, having to confront a dominant norm in this society that says that the only respectable language style is a narrowly defined Anglo American one, some Afro-Americans are confronted with a challenge to one aspect of how they define cultural identity.

BLACK ENGLISH VERNACULAR: DIFFERENCE OR DEFICIT?

Some psychologists and educators have assumed that failure to use language in the standard grammatical way implies the presence of cognitive deficits in the user. According to this traditional view, speakers of Black English Vernacular (BEV) are speaking English *badly* rather than simply speaking it *differently*. The difference is considered negative because it is interpreted as evidence of deficiencies in the overall language development of speakers of BEV. It follows, according to this assessment, that a change of language habits is required before intellectual skills can be taught to users of BEV. Remedial measures are essential because, it is maintained, speakers of BEV are linguistically and hence cognitively deficient.

A trenchant critique of this position is made by William Labov in a classic essay entitled "The Logic of Nonstandard English" (included in his 1972 volume) in which he counters in several ways the notion that BEV puts limits on the intellectual development of the speaker. Differences in grammatical expression of an idea, that is, in the "superficial structure" of a language, says Labov, do not imply differences in meaning or "deep structure" of a language form. There is, according to Labov, more than just *one* grammatical way to express a concept. When a person learns a grammatical form (s)he uses it to communicate in a particular cultural context, but it is not necessarily the best way or the only logical way of expressing an idea. The French are not illogical for expressing the negative in a double form (*ne . . . pas*); by the same token neither is the speaker of Black English illogical when (s)he uses the double negative. Thus, the sentence, "Don't nobody here have any common sense," communicates the speaker's scorn quite clearly, and the addition of a triple negative—"Don't nobody here have *no* common sense"—makes it even more emphatic, without any loss of logic.

An incident from a language session will further illustrate the point:

Student: (*reading from an autobiographical essay*): This lady didn't have no sense.

Teacher: What would be a standard English alternate for this sentence?

Student: She didn't have any sense. But not this lady: *she didn't have no sense* [Gumperz & Hernandez-Chavez, 1972, p. 102].

This student had an understanding of differences in superficial structure but still had a preferred way of expressing the deep structure—meaning. Whether to use or not to use such forms is governed by arbitrary conventions which have linguistic and historical derivations. Speakers of the regularized BEV dialect are therefore not conceptually weak because they use conventions that are different from "standard" English usage.

Because learning standard grammatical form is necessary for functioning in a complex technological society, Labov thinks it is important for inner-city children to acquire some of the language characteristics that are often associated with middle-class speakers. This will allow the children to communicate adequately in more formal public settings when they need to, but it does not mean that middle-class speech patterns are necessarily better ones than their own. There are, in fact, qualities of middle-class speech, such as verbosity and circumlocution, which are nonfunctional for clear expression. To illustrate this point, Labov compares the transcript of a lower-class inner-city adolescent's discussion of his conception of God with that of a college-educated, middle-class black speaker's presentation of his views on witchcraft. For example, in the former instance, in the course of the discussion with the inner-city resident, the interviewer (JL) poses a hypothetical question:

JL: No, I was jus' sayin' jus' suppose there is a God, would he be white or black?

Larry: . . . He'd be white, man.

JL: Why?

Larry: Why? I'll tell you why. Cause the average whitey out here got every-
thing, you dig? And the nigger ain't got shit, y'know? Y'unnerstan'?
So—um—for in order for *that* to happen, you know it ain't no black
God that's doin' that bullshit. [Labov, 1972, p. 217].

Though ungrammatical by standard English canons, the lower-class speaker's
discussion is direct and shows sophisticated logic in grappling with the problem.

The middle-class speaker (Charles M.) presents a contrast:

CR: Do you know of anything that someone can do, to have someone who
has passed on visit him in a dream?

Charles: Well, I even heard my parents say that there is such a thing as something
in dreams, some things like that, and sometimes dreams do come true.
. . . I don't particularly believe in that, I don't think it's true. I do feel,
though, that there is such a thing as—ah—witchcraft. I do feel that in
certain cultures there is such a thing as witchcraft, or some sort of
science of witchcraft. . . . I do believe that there is such a thing that a
person can put himself in a state of *mind* (Mhm), or that—er—something could be given to them to intoxicate them in a certain—to a certain
frame of mind—that—could actually be considered witchcraft [Labov,
1972, p. 218].

This middle-class speaker is vague, rambling, and repetitive. Familiar stylistic
devices in the latter's speech mark him as an educated person but, in fact, he
does not necessarily think through the problem presented him any more
effectively or deal better with abstractions than the speaker of Black English
Vernacular.

The comparison of the two speakers illustrates the need for more careful
study of linguistic behaviors in the speaker's cultural context before making
generalizations about the relative merits of language employed. In fact, Labov
found in his studies that a majority of people used well-formed, complete
sentences in their everyday speech, but, surprisingly, working-class speakers
did this more frequently than middle-class ones. The precision of expression
associated with technical and scientific writing is not so frequently found
among middle-class speakers whose "accumulating flow of words buries
rather than strikes the target. It is this verbosity which is most easily taught and
most easily learned, so that words take the place of thoughts, and nothing can
be found behind them [Labov, 1972, p. 222]." Actually the explicitness attributed to middle-class forms is often a function of the test situation and limited to
it. Indeed, contrary to what might be expected, Labov found that not all
aspects of the middle-class style are optimal for communication. He suggests
that ideally what we should do is discover the features of middle-class speaking
style that actually help us express ideas clearly and separate them from those

that do not. This will then let us say which standard grammatical rules should be taught to young nonstandard speakers.

BLACK ENGLISH IN THE CLASSROOM

The implication of the Stewart and the Labov work is that Black English has legitimate status as a language form. It is a position that supports a pluralistic view of American society. It implies that we should, as Mao-Tse-Tung urged the Chinese some years ago, "Let a hundred flowers bloom." But such a perspective does not resolve some central educational and political issues. The problem is that children from lower- and working-class backgrounds who speak the Black English Vernacular are usually not skilled in the language of instruction used in the schools. However, they are skilled and efficient speakers of the language they bring to the school.[2] Granted the linguistic legitimacy of Black English, what should the educational system's attitude toward this speech be? Attempts to deal with the answer to this question have generated a good deal of controversy in the Black community.

Everyone recognizes that the language function is a central one for human beings. The command of language skills is essential for people to be able to achieve the full potential of their humanity. Some black parents and educators relate this fact directly to its presumed effect on academic achievement, feeling that language styles used by some black children are a detriment to their educational progress. They emphasize that children must learn to speak "properly" to succeed in American society. These critics argue that giving legitimacy to Black English speech styles is just another way that white society has of keeping black children from attaining competence in the standard language forms necessary for achieving in America. They emphasize the fact that if the children don't master standard speech forms they will not be able to read, will consequently fall behind or drop out of school, and will be unfit to be hired in good jobs. In short, these critics continue, the promotion of Black English in the classroom is just another racist ploy for keeping blacks out of the competition for the good things in this society.

Acting on another aspect of this issue, a group of black parents brought suit in 1979 against the public school system of Ann Arbor, Michigan, for what they alleged were the teachers' pejorative attitudes toward the children's Black English and the school's attempt to obliterate their ways of speaking. The purpose of the suit was to have their children's speech styles recognized as legitimate ways of talking rather than being interpreted as indicators of subnormal academic ability. Although the parents very much wanted their children to learn to read, write, and speak the standard English taught in school, they did not want it to be carried out at the expense of the children's self-image and the language spoken by their own people. A sympathetic court ordered the school system to accommodate to the children's Black English while it taught them the standard curriculum.

Those who would celebrate the kind of diversity represented by black speech patterns have to deal with the possibility that the use of Black English forms may actually interfere with learning classroom English.[3] This possibility has arisen not only with respect to the linguistic format of educational tests, but perhaps even more important with regard to learning to read.

BEV and Learning to Read

Some linguists have suggested that the children who speak nonstandard dialects may have difficulties learning to read in school systems that provide instruction in standard English. This may be an explanation for an important part of the low reading achievement found in inner-city schools. Most of the research on this issue of dialect interference in reading is directed at questions of phonological or grammatical interference (Hall & Guthrie, 1979a; Simons, 1976). Phonological interference would arise presumably because certain written words are pronounced differently by black dialect speakers than by standard English speakers:

> The results of these differences are words that have a pronunciation unique to Black dialect, e.g., "ness" for "nest," "ress" for "rest," and "han" for "hand." In addition, there are words whose Black dialect pronunciation results in a different word, e.g.; "tess" for "test," "men" for "mend," "walk" for "walked," "coal" for "cold," etc. The latter result in an extra set of homophones for Black dialect speakers. These differences in pronunciation presumably could interfere with the acquisition of word recognition skills even though the precise way they interfere has never been spelled out [Simons, 1976, p. 6].

However, in a variety of studies using different kinds of designs, Simons notes that black dialect phonology was not found to hamper the reading of standard English passages by black elementary school children.

Regarding grammatical interference it has been advanced that the mismatch between the black child's syntax of standard English texts would produce greater difficulty in reading passages in standard English. For example, the form of standard sentences would not be equivalent in the black dialect. The sentence, "He will be working," might be interpreted by the black dialect speaker as habitual action because of the meaning in dialect of the word "be." Or the reader might fail to interpret "ed" as a past tense marker because it is not pronounced in BEV. But on testing this hypothesis, Marwit and Neumann (1974) found that presentation of passages of the reading comprehension section of the California Reading Test in standard or dialect form did not change the comprehension of them by black children. However, according to Simons, there is evidence that the failure to pronounce "ed" in singly presented sentences can often lead to failure to recognize the past tense. Thus, in the sentence, "When I passed by, I read the posters," the word "read" is pronounced in the present tense because the "ed" is dropped from the pronunciation of "passed" by the BEV speaker (Labov, 1972, p. 30–31). In contrast with single sentences presented out of context, reading passages composed of several sentences probably provides sufficient cues to the intended meaning and thus offsets the possibility of interference due to differences in pronunciation.

The Sociolinguistic Hypothesis

All in all, the research does not give strong support to the idea that structural linguistic interference alone is the primary place to look for the reading problems of inner-city children (Hall & Guthrie, 1979a). What seems to be a more fruitful source of hypotheses has to do with the sociolinguistic factors in the reading instruction or talking situation. For example, educators have reported that many black children in inner-city schools do not speak fluently in the classroom in relating to educational materials. Rather than using this as an indication of a lack of verbal abilities in the child, such a fact may be attributable to the way the social situation is structured. Labov (1972) notes that much of the sampling of the verbal facility of inner-city children has failed to take into account how much the response of the subjects was affected by the circumstances and surroundings they were in when tested. The result is that the testing situation has contaminated the results. Attacking the notion that the inner-city child's language capacity can be adequately measured in the typical testing situation, Labov cites the meagre output of speech often secured from the children by researchers. However, when the language assessment situation is changed from a "vertical" one (in terms of the structure of the status relationship between the examiner and child) to a "horizontal" one in which the social situation is more egalitarian, the verbal abilities of these children are abundantly demonstrated. For example, in a testing situation a research associate of Labov's was unable to get black lower-class children to say much to him even though he was from Harlem, spoke BEV, and was from a working-class background. But when he altered the situation by getting down on the floor with his young subjects, encouraging them to speak about taboo topics, and bringing them party snacks to eat, their reticence changed into a verbal flood.

The work of other scholars supports the idea that a speaker's fluency changes according to the situation (Cazden, 1970; Houston, 1971, 1973). Houston suggests that lower-class black children actually have two speech "registers" available to them. There is one register that they use in the formal classroom situation and perhaps other situations with unfamiliar adults. In this mode their speech is likely to be sparse and rather inhibited. There is the other they use at home and in surroundings that they experience as being friendly and socially gratifying. Speech in this latter context, which may be filled with Black English forms for children who have them available, is likely to have a great deal of what Houston calls "flair"; that is, it shows originality and liveliness while at the same time being quite communicative of meaning and logic. The speech of children using the more informal register definitely "makes sense." One can see all of these things in the "Three Little Pigs" excerpt.

The operation of flair can be seen in the kind of storytelling tasks that Houston has presented to black and white children. Middle-class and white children tend to report details more accurately than poor black children, but the latter children as a group insert more original elements into their stories without losing the overall theme of the story. If the task had been considered a test of memory the black children would have failed. But if it were an index of active conceptualizing ability, they came off quite well.

These children heard and understood the directions clearly but they took "the given instructions as a base line upon which to demonstrate individual imagination and creativity [Houston, 1973, p. 48]." They responded differently in other ways too.

> They generally interacted with other children far more often than did the other groups. . . . They frequently attempted to help their partners, prompting them nearly twice as often as the other groups did. They also made greater use of nonverbal behavior, and their gestures often involved the whole body, unlike the more confined gestures of the white children [p. 48].

They tended to do this whether their partner was white or black. The picture that Houston draws is one that sounds very much like Boykin's (1979) concept of "verve" discussed in Chapter 3. Again there is the implication that the standard school setting is not geared to helping lower-class children capitalize educationally on what they bring to the learning task.

But the disjointedness between child and school may have to do even more with the dynamics of teacher-pupil relationships. With respect to the question of reading failure in particular, some sociolinguists have suggested that there are additional social consequences of speaking the black vernacular. One thing about "nonstandard" speech is that it signals that the speaker is different. Research has been reported which indicates that teachers from inner-city schools are sensitive to deviations from what they consider correct English and they sometimes respond negatively in their evaluations of it (Williams, 1970). For some teachers it is sufficient to hear a child speak Black English to assume that (s)he will be a low achiever. Teachers have been observed to structure the seating arrangements in their classrooms to distance themselves from these kinds of students insuring that the children, who probably need *more* attention, in fact get less of the teacher's time (Gouldner, 1978). While this is a rather straightforward expression of bias, culture clash in the schoolroom is often more subtle than this, though just as telling. Teachers and students may "turn off" to one another to the detriment of the learning process, because of the different ways they use language even when they *are* trying to talk to one another. This may stem partly from the fact that people from different cultural groups use language and accompanying nonverbal cues of gesture, intonation, and facial expression differently to express themselves. People may misunderstand each other because of these differences.

While dialect interference may not be involved when a child is reading to him- or herself, it may occur when the teacher is giving instructions in reading (Simons, 1976). For a listener to understand a speaker, the listener must understand the speaker's specific intent in the context of that particular social situation. Calling this the "situated meaning" of an utterance, Gumperz suggests that the parties in the situation must share an interpretive framework regarding the meaning of the cues emitted, both linguistic and nonverbal (Gumperz, 1974; Gumperz & Herasimchuk, 1972). But differences in cultural background can lead to differences in the ways people will understand and interpret the cues in a communication context and may lead to a breakdown in communication.

Unfortunately there are not many studies of what actually transpires in the classroom during reading instruction in inner-city schools. One study that does describe teachers and their pupils working together on reading exercises exemplifies some of the potential pitfalls in communication (Piestrup, 1973). In one instance a teacher is trying without success to get a pupil to pronounce the word "they" in the standard fashion, instead of as "dey." Analyzing this interaction, Simons (1976) hypothesizes that the teacher's failure to change the student's pronunciation is at least partially due to the fact that (1) the participants do not share background information about standard and dialect pronunciation, and (2) the teacher uses only indirect cues to communicate her disapproval of the child's pronunciation (e.g., by getting him to start the sentence over repeatedly and by pointing to the incorrectly pronounced word without being specific as to what is wrong). Commenting on the interaction, Simons notes:

Indirectness is an effective strategy when there is a great deal of shared background knowledge. In the case of Black children there is probably less shared background knowledge than teachers assume, because, in addition to adult-child differences, there are cultural differences in communicative background experiences. . . . Also in everyday conversation where there is a great deal of indirectness when someone does not understand the meaning of an indirect speech act s/he can ask the speaker to explain in a more direct way. In the tapes under study this does not happen very often. It may be that it is not encouraged or accepted in school discourse. If this is the case, then the child is put at a further disadvantage in interpreting indirectness than s/he would be in everyday conversation because s/he cannot use his/her normal repair strategies when s/he does not understand something [p. 25].

Of course such an inappropriate communication strategy is not the only factor affecting the success of reading instruction. There are many other conditions in the students' lives such as peer group relations and verbal play styles that are significant. However, it is agreed that one of the most critical factors is the teacher's belief in the child's ability to learn. What the teacher's attitudes are and how the teacher communicates with the child are particularly important.

Noting that talking is a fundamental activity in teaching, Amidon and Hunter (1966) developed a system for helping teachers change their way of talking to pupils so as to increase the pupil's motivation to learn and to enhance their self-esteem. The "Verbal Interaction Category System" is a relatively simple system designed by Amidon and Hunter for use in the classroom. It is organized in ways that help distinguish between talking behaviors that enhance the interaction between child and teacher and those that stifle it. Indeed, as we have seen, one of the problems encountered by the child speaking a nonstandard dialect is the negative reaction it elicits from teachers.

The study of Ann Piestrup (1973) just referred to sheds further light on sociolinguistic issues involved in the language used by teachers and pupils in the classroom. The subjects of the classroom observation were 14 1st-grade teachers and their approximately 200 pupils selected randomly from predominantly black inner-city schools. Under investigation were the effects of the teacher's classroom style on children's reading performance and on their tendency to use various amounts of BEV in the classroom.[4] The researchers identified six different styles used by the teachers during reading instruction. These were called the Vocabulary Approach, the Decoding Approach, the Standard Pronunciation Approach, the Interrupting Approach, the White Liberal Approach, and the Black Artful Approach, each of which was characteristic of no less than two and no more than three of the teachers.

The Vocabulary Approach teachers focused on explaining the meanings of unfamiliar words, emphasizing especially the distinctions in meanings between homonyms. Teachers who used a decoding emphasis spent time helping children sound out words, often at the expense of meaningful reading. However, these children did less wild guessing at words than children in other groups. The teachers employing the Standard Pronunciation Approach insisted that the children always employ formal standard English during reading classes. These teachers would sometimes stop a child who was reading aloud and instruct the class to repeat the correct sounds—a practice that the researchers thought was quite distracting for the children. In the interrupting groups there was an even greater emphasis on stopping children to correct their Black English, and although the standard pronunciation was presented to the children, the teachers did not necessarily see to it that the children repeated the correct forms accurately. The teachers using the Interrupting Approach used a good deal of unfamiliar materials without explaining the content.

The White Liberal teachers accepted the use of Black dialect by their pupils in their writing and speech, and they used it occasionally themselves in communicating with the children. Although they seemed to engage the children's interest in reading more successfully than teachers using some of the other styles, their emphasis seemed to be more on friendly communication than on the task of learning to read.

Black Artful teachers used Black English during reading instruction and spoke it fluently in class. While they accepted use of dialect by their pupils they also made sure that the children learned standard English forms as well. While making use of the vernacular to establish good rapport with the children, the Black Artful teachers also set high learning standards for them. These teachers appeared to be the most successful at involving the greatest number of children in the reading task.

> The label Black Artful is used to describe teaching which incorporates a form of rhythmic play unique with Black dialect speakers. It is not the surface features of phonology or grammar that are important, but the rapid interplay with intonation and gesture familiar to Black children as one of the art forms of Black culture (Piestrup, 1973, p. 103).

> Unlike the White Liberal teacher's brief, imitative phrases, the Black Artful teacher's dialect seemed familiar and comfortable [p. 105].

In comparing the effects of these teaching styles on the children's reading performance and dialect usage, Piestrup's results seem to show that the Black Artful teachers had the most positive effect. Children exposed to this approach had the highest mean reading scores of any group—significantly higher than those exposed either to the White Liberal Approach or the Interrupting Approach. The latter group had the lowest reading scores. Children experiencing the Black Artful style also had the lowest dialect usage scores on the sentence repetition task, significantly lower than the Vocabulary or the Interrupting groups. In fact, there was a tendency overall for those children with higher reading scores to have lower dialect usage scores. It appeared that the adeptness in the vernacular of the Black Artful teachers added to their success in involving the children in the reading instruction, whereas the Interrupting teachers created just the opposite effect on their pupils:

> Some children from this group tediously worked alone at decoding without reading as if they understood; others seemed to guess at almost as many words as they were able to read. Some children withdrew from participation in reading, speaking softly and as seldom as possible; others engaged in ritual insult and other forms of verbal play apart from the teacher [pp. 131–132].

Since an exploratory observational study of this kind could not account for the many factors contributing to the outcomes it would be premature to jump to any firm conclusion about effects of the six teaching styles on reading achievement. At the least, however, it appeared that the use of Black English Vernacular in certain classroom contests did not hamper learning standard reading skills. In fact it turned out that the use of dialect by students was lowest in those classes in which the teachers not only emphasized the vernacular while giving reading instruction but also permitted their students to use it without interrupting them. In these classes the children learned how to switch from the vernacular to the more standard form as the situation warranted and in the process gradually became able to use less of the vernacular. It may have been that the pupils paid better attention to the reading instruction because they felt more at home in the classroom in which their speech was not constantly under criticism. According to Piestrup there was good reason to believe that it was not the structural conflict between the vernacular and standard dialect forms that interfered with the learning in these classrooms. Rather she thought a functional conflict was primarily responsible for the deterioration of the communication between some of the teachers and pupils to the point that they no longer tried to "reach" each other when they talked. This occurred

> when teachers did not listen carefully to children, as if they were interested only in a correct answer and did not expect to hear it, or when children did not attend to the lesson, as if they gave up on its making sense or being of interest [p. 65].

Labov makes a similar point regarding functional conflict in the classroom. Among the inner-city youth whose language he studied, those youngsters who were most alienated and frequently truant from school were the purest speakers of the Black English Vernacular. Some of them were quite bright and verbal with good learning potential. Although they were most intensely involved in gangs and the peer group culture, they not only understood the values of the mainstream society but also had a good grasp of how the system operated. It was Labov's (1972) conclusion that reading failure among this group of boys was to a large measure a consequence of political and cultural conflict in the classroom rather than linguistic difference as such [p. 35].[5]

Although accepting BEV in the classroom may be one method of improving the communication between teachers and students, it is evident that it does not in itself substitute for teaching the standard dialect features in reading instruction. It was possible to be a reasonably effective teacher of students speaking BEV without using the vernacular in the classroom. Students of some of the teachers who used no Black English had scores which, though not equal to, were not significantly worse than those in the Black Artful groups.

CHERISHING PLURALISM

Why then accept the use of vernacular forms by children whom we want to teach to read the standard form of written English? One value of sustaining the active use of black language forms in school may be to provide institutional support outside of the home for an aspect of self associated with ethnic identity. It is a way that young people can strengthen and enrich the positive affective assessments about themselves and their cultural identity. This need not be done at the expense of membership in the larger "American" culture; rather it is possible to conceive of it as being concomitant with such participation. In a study of attitudes toward Black English, Hoover (1978) found that black parents in two West Coast communities wanted the schools to teach their children to master standard English—standard Black English was preferred (standard Anglo English was not presented as a comparison to the Black English forms in this study.) At the same time they wanted their children to be able to speak or at least understand the vernacular so that they could maintain contact with black culture and feel comfortable with black people of all social strata and varying age groups.

In a society still hostile to cultural differences the use of the vernacular may also promote a tie with positive memories and supportive relationships (Smitherman & McGinnis, 1980). Black vernacular forms are rich in the ways they are used to define and carry on social intercourse—in conveying a particular relationship between the dialect users. In informal circumstances, with family and friends who are black, vernacular forms tend to be used by those Afro-Americans who have some command of them. The use of the vernacular is a way of signaling a greater sense of intimacy and camaraderie in these close social relationships. In addition, the dialect serves as a connection to sources of creative vision or at least to alternate and meaningful perceptions about experiences that might otherwise be lost—perceptions that allow a storyteller, for example, to savor a meal of wolf and greens in fantasy. Perpetuating these forms has a self-preservative potential for the Afro-American culture.

The majority of Afro-Americans grow up familiar with the vernacular from early childhood. This is particularly true of persons from lower- and working-class backgrounds, some of whom have achieved middle-class, professional status in adulthood. The latter group are still familiar with the vernacular even though their daily work situations may demand that they communicate in the more standard language forms. If more standard and "proper" forms are used in the home most blacks still have some exposure to relatives and neighbors who speak the vernacular. For those Afro-Americans who were surrounded by a good deal of Black English during their formative years the vernacular is a kind of "mother tongue." These vernacular forms have mediated social experiences that have become a part of the self. For some Afro-Americans, having Black English language forms available enables them to "come home" psychologically and culturally. The ability to use different language forms for different social situations allows for the bipolar or multipolar (dialectical) definition of self that we have been discussing in this book.

Yet we have to recognize that there are costs as well as benefits for Afro-Americans trying to maintain speech pluralism. Although preserving the language forms of the Black English Vernacular strengthens ties with the racial group, the use of it also meets up with the bias in the mainstream society against cultural differences associated with blackness (Jones, 1972; Kovel, 1970). For all its liberal veneer the Establishment does not take kindly to reminders that its participants have backgrounds different from the European and especially the "Anglo" norm in cultural style. Consequently Afro-Americans live with the psychological dilemma of trying to sustain an aspect of self, their racial linguistic style, in the face of the disapproval of the dominant society. Although this may be somewhat easier to handle for those blacks who have relatively little contact with whites, others in both middle-class and working-class jobs must make the decision to keep their language style within a standard range, at least some of the time, if they expect to advance within white institutional structures. In his critical appraisal of the black middle-class, Frazier (1962) argued that the typical members of the "black bourgeoisie" attempted to model their behavior and institutions as much as possible after the white norm. But having expunged as many of the vestiges of cultural blackness and lower socioeconomic status from themselves as they could, they found they were not fully admitted into white society. Since in fact whites were not prepared to accept blacks as equals on any terms, middle-class blacks, according to this analysis, had worked themselves into a cultural "no man's land." The moral of the Frazier analysis would seem to be that blacks will have to sustain a dialectical relationship with the Anglo-American cultural standard, because whites by and large are still not ready to join in a truly integrated effort to create a cultural mosaic for the American society.

Let us return to the metaphor used earlier—that dialectal pluralism allows a person to "come home" culturally. A majority of blacks learn to function relatively well on the job even though this involves being away from "home" in certain aspects. (This is so even though blacks have made continual contributions to American culture historically which have been woven into the fabric of the society. Whites take such contributions to speech and various aspects of popular entertainment and art so much for granted that they are oblivious to the sources.) Maintaining black communicative styles side by side with using standard forms permits them to commute psychologically from a personal-cultural home to the common world of work and culture shared with other ethnic groups in America. For them switching codes may be a useful way of sustaining multipolar aspects of their identity. There are other blacks who are not comfortable commuting linguistically and prefer to remain in one cultural setting or the other; that is, their speech styles are geared either to an Americanized or Afro-American orientation. Among the former are some black Americans who grow up in social class or geographical settings where they speak only "standard" English forms in all speech contexts and consequently never feel homesick. Another large group never leaves home at all. As Kernan (1971) notes:

The bi-cultural status of Black Americans makes the socialization process a time when each individual attempts to find some viable personal reconciliation to cultural patterns, values and attitudes which do not cohere or intersect in any consistent fashion. Some solutions find individuals essentially submerged in things Black, rejecting outside standards and valuations across the board. Others look outward toward the wider culture and still others straddle the two, selecting from either as the needs of the moment require. Language is an important reflector of these various positions [p. 83].

The thrust of this chapter points toward a particular ideal regarding the cherishing of pluralism in speech styles. Pluralism should imply that people will feel free to retain a variety of options and will learn to fit them to various occasions. Between blacks and whites this ideal implies that although blacks learn to handle standard speech forms competently—and it is essential that blacks have that skill in this society—they should be able to feel comfortable using black forms as well for the psychological and cultural gratifications that come with such usage. By the same token blacks should be able to feel perfectly at ease about never using Black English forms and associated communicative styles if they choose. But when opting for one or another stance toward their own use of speech, blacks should not disparage other blacks for making different choices.

NOTES

1. This way of phrasing things touches on an issue raised in the so-called "Sapir-Whorf hypothesis [Cole & Scribner, 1974; Trudgill, 1974]." This view states that a person's native language constrains how (s)he perceives the world and contributes greatly to differences in world view between speakers of different languages. The direction of influence in this view is from language to society. The alternative directional view is that language and thinking reflect the structure of the physical and social environment. Differing from both these perspectives on language and society, the logical learning theory point of view would be that language reflects the ordering activity of mind. Words give expression to conceptualizations.

2. In fact, what research shows is that black children who are dialect speakers tend to switch standard English sentences read to them into dialect form when repeating them to the experimenter (Baratz, 1970) and even tend to use dialect forms consistently in sentences containing nonsense syllables (Marwit et al., 1973). Story recall has been found to be better in the preferred dialect form, too (Hall, Reder, & Cole, 1975).

3. The British sociolinguist Basil Bernstein (1970) has described another set of differences that affect educational performance. Arguing that language development is related to social class, he has described language styles in terms of two different "codes"—"restricted" and "elaborated." Very briefly, a restricted code comes into being in more intimate or familiar social relations where there are "closely shared identifications . . . [and] a range of common assumptions [p. 32]." Understanding one another rather readily, people in such social relations do not feel the need to depend on precisely delineated verbal forms to spell out their intentions. As a result, they tend to rely more on implicit and nonverbal modes of communication. An elaborated code, by contrast, arises in social relationships where it is not easy to take others' intentions for granted. In elaborated codes, speech forms are more differentiated and precise presumably permitting expression of a

wider and more complex range of thought. There is greater extensity and explicitness of meaning with an emphasis on objective intelligibility.

In his studies of some speakers of British English, Bernstein sought to demonstrate a relationship between social class membership and the use of the two codes. His findings seemed to show that the middle-class children in his samples used both elaborated and restricted codes whereas the children from working-class backgrounds tended to use only the restricted code. Parenthetically, it should be mentioned that this relationship did not have to do with social class differences in dialect. Since some of these findings have been used by others to support positions that Bernstein felt the need to disavow, he has taken pains to say that elaborated codes should not be seen as inherently and in all ways better than restricted codes. Nor did he think that the restricted code implied either linguistic deprivation or an innate tendency: "What we have here are differences in the use of language arising out of a specific context [1970, p. 27]." Restricted code users were not nonverbal, Bernstein went on to say; rather the speech that they used was "of a different order from that controlled by an elaborated code [p. 33]." In fact, the restricted code, he pointed out, was more suited for communicating the affective meanings that enriched human life and promoted group solidarity, while elaborated codes, however affectively barren, were necessary for acquiring the educational and technological skills needed to participate in a complex industrial society. Those who brought elaborated code skills with them to school had a head start on educational achievement because the schools prized such skills.

Although it was not clear to Bernstein exactly how the association between language style and social class came about, he proposed that the language codes developed at least partly from different styles of family structure and family social control. Distinguishing between family structures that are "person-oriented" and "positional," Bernstein proposed that in person-oriented families decisions and judgments are based on the person's individual psychological characteristics rather than on their formal status. These person-oriented structures encourage open communication systems. In positional families, decision making rests on the person's formal status in the family according to age or sex, for example, making for a more "closed" communication. "In person-oriented families social control is likely to be realized through verbally elaborated means oriented to the person, while in positional families social control is likely to be realized through less elaborated verbal means, less oriented to the person but more oriented toward the formal status of the regulated (i.e. the child) [Bernstein, 1970, p. 41]." Such habitual interactions within the family presumably contribute strongly to the verbal style the child adopts.

Some British and American educators have been impressed with this kind of sociolinguistic view as an explanation for some of the academic difficulties of the lower- and working-class child (Olim, 1970). Research has been somewhat supportive of the usefulness of these categories (Cook-Gumperz, 1973; Ward, 1971). But there has also been considerable criticism of Bernstein's conceptualization (Rosen, 1974).

Trudgill (1974), for example, has suggested that some interpretations of Bernstein's work have led to biased views of lower-class children—from which Bernstein has explicitly dissociated himself in his recent writing. If one does not take the two proposed language codes as hard and fast social class distinctions and if one recognizes that language performance is a function of the context in which language behaviors occur, then according to Trudgill the following reinterpretation of Bernstein's findings might be in order:

> In many contexts some working-class children are less willing or less used to employing a more formal style than are middle-class children. This, of course, by no means suggests that they are in any way linguistically deprived . . . although it may mean that working-class children have a narrower range of stylistic options open to them. (This . . . may well be compensated for by the fact that in many working-class groups verbal skills of particular types, such as joke-telling, narrating and insulting are very highly valued: there are probably certain options open to them which are not available to middle-class children.) [p. 56].

Of course this interpretation of Bernstein still leaves open the question of exactly how social class differences have contributed to the development of restricted and elaborated styles. As we have mentioned earlier, other researchers have also come across class differences in language behavior and cognitive performance. In Chapter 3 we noted Golden's finding that children of different socioeconomic status demonstrated a differential readiness to use specific verbal labeling skills in problem-solving tests. Although performance in structured experimental situations was not a foolproof measure of capacity, nevertheless schools tended to seize upon and augment these different initial levels of performance. The Golden work suggested that there was indeed something about the preschool child's normal home experience that led to differential readiness to use certain verbal styles. Although we are a long way from being certain about what specific mechanisms influence these developments, the area of the child's interaction with mother and probably with other family members appears to be important. The work of William Hall and his colleagues, which includes observations of speech behavior of young children in a variety of naturalistic settings, is attempting to elucidate some of these issues further (for example, Hall & Dore, 1980; Hall & Guthrie, 1979b; Hall & Tirre, 1979).

4. A standard reading test was used to measure reading performance and a sentence repetition exercise was used as a measure of the amount of dialect a child was prone to use. This latter task presented the subject with Standard English sentences they had to listen to and then repeat aloud. The sentences contained words that had a high potential for eliciting black dialect forms. For example, one sentence was, "My brother is five years old because his birthday passed [Piestrup, 1973, p. 179]." The underlined portions represent parts of words where omissions might be expected in the vernacular.

5. Labov's observations shed some light on data reported by Robins (1968). Her studies indicated that black adolescent youngsters who had a history of school problems and truancy were highly likely to become involved in violence leading to their deaths at an early age. Dropping out of school based on such school problems was a better predictor of later violence than was socioeconomic status or having come from a broken home. In fact, low-income black youths who finished high school had a *lower* chance than equivalent whites of suffering early and violent death. It seems quite possible that the truancy of these lower-class youths is a result of the kind of cultural and political conflict in the classroom to which Labov refers.

Chapter 5
The Assertive Self: Emerging of a New Identity

In the late fifties and early sixties, Afro-Americans began to make changes in their style of public demeanor. Individuals became more assertive in stating forthrightly their own sense of self-worth. As a group, black Americans became more aggressive in opposing discrimination through organized militant action. Many white people, startled by this straightforward behavior, saw blacks as simply becoming more hostile towards members of the white society (Cheek, 1976). But this view on the part of whites missed the point. In the long run the primary goal of the changed behavior of blacks was not so much to put other groups down as it was to try to move to a new plane of identity development for black Americans. This was to be achieved not only by acting less conforming and submissive to the expectations of the white society, but also by putting forward their own intentions boldly and insistently. A particular hallmark of this new assertiveness, as we shall see in this chapter, was a deliberate effort on the part of Afro-Americans to link a good personal sense of self with a prideful sense of racial identity.[1]

ASSERTION AND AGGRESSION

Assertion, like affirmation, involves an *active* structuring of the world—an active "coming at" the world. In this sense the concept of assertion can be taken as another perspective on effectance and competence strivings. But assertive behavior is also related to aggressive behavior, the wish not simply to act on and change an object, but to actually destroy or harm something or someone.[2] When people are blocked from being normally assertive, they frequently respond with angry feelings and angry behavior. It is a common clinical observation that persons who feel neurotically conflicted about expressing aggressive feelings not only inhibit direct expression of hostile behavior but also restrain appropriately assertive behavior, too.

Angry feelings—rage, in fact—have been a continuing issue for blacks since being in America (Grier & Cobbs, 1968; Lester, 1968). Historically, whites have tried to suppress blacks' rebellious anger as well as assertive (and possibly competitive) self-expressions. As we have seen earlier whites have done this by being extremely punishing towards blacks. This has led partly to responses of adaptive inferiority (Pugh, 1972) a term that is also encompassed by the notion of psychological "defense."[3] In a hostile, white-controlled society, then, one of the major adaptations blacks were forced to make was controlling the overt manifestations of their aggression.

Defenses are ways of responding to and viewing the world that reduce a sense of psychological threat and allow a person to proceed with the task of living with a sense of relative inner security. Blacks have had to defend against direct expression of anger against whites. Since aggression is such a ready response in human beings, such feelings could not have disappeared from within black persons, although they were not frequently manifested in frank and overt ways. Forced to minimize direct hostile expressions toward whites, blacks have for one thing frequently directed aggression at one another using the defensive operation of "displacement" (displacement refers to unconsciously shifting the expression of a troublesome impulse to an object [person] other than the one originally intended). In some instances, of course, overt hostility and destructiveness did emerge. Riots in twentieth-century urban black communities are examples of such aggressive discharges.[4]

Aggression in Blacks: Selected Studies

There have been a number of efforts to study the effect of bottling up aggression on the personality functioning of blacks. In one often cited study, the psychiatrists Kardiner and Ovesey (1962), using a small sample of subjects, most of whom were patients in psychotherapy, concluded that blacks in general were hampered in their personality functioning (for criticism of this study, see, for example, Thomas and Sillen [1972]). Their view was that the anger aroused by the discrimination and hostility of whites was often handled in a variety of maladaptive ways. Thus, some of the anger not directed against whites was directed at themselves, leading to self-hatred and low self-esteem, and hostility toward other black people. Another effect was that, while holding white middle-class aspirations, they blocked the assertive behavior that would have enabled them to be successful in the white-dominated society. Laboratory studies have demonstrated that blacks did not express hostility toward whites where frustration was induced experimentally. But in the same laboratory situation they expressed their hostile feelings towards other black participants (Winslow & Brainerd, 1950).

The hypothesis that the segregated American society has inhibited effective personality functioning and thereby reduced social achievement in Afro-

Americans was tested in a large sample of northern urban blacks (Crain & Weisman, 1972). One of the important consequences of segregation and racial oppression, it is suggested by Crain and Weisman, has been the loss of the capacity by Afro-Americans to express assertion and legitimate anger effectively.[5] They note, "We see the beginning of a theory of black poverty which argues that in some way segregation robs the black of some vital aspect of his personality, which in turn prevents him from realizing his ambitions [p. 26]." Some of the data that illuminate this issue comes from their analysis of responses to a brief form of the Internal-External Locus of Control (LOC) Scale (Rotter, 1966) in combination with a short measure of self-esteem that they developed. Briefly, the LOC Scale describes people's perceptions about the degree of control they have over that part of the world they are trying to master. Those who have a low sense of Internal Control feel that planning and hard work are of little use since what one gets in life is determined by chance or luck. The person with a high sense of Internal Control tends to feel that diligence and personal effort mark the road to success.[6]

With respect to the handling of aggression, Crain and Weisman found that persons high in Internal Control tended to inhibit their aggression more. ("Inhibition" was defined in this study by whether or not individuals could recall being angry recently and whether reading or hearing about discrimination made them angry as opposed to sad. Those persons who could not remember a recent incident and who reported becoming sad rather than angry were seen as being inhibited in expression of aggression.) Of those men who were better educated (high school graduates), the ones who expressed a high sense of Internal Control were less likely to have been arrested or to have been in fights. Although it is a problematic measure in a number of ways, lack of arrests or a history of fighting were the authors' measures of ability to control overt hostility. In this sample, being high on Internal Control was also strongly related to expressing a relatively small amount of antiwhite sentiment, for both men and women, especially those women who were employed.

The self-esteem measure used was one that asked respondents to rate themselves as to whether they were "above average, about average, or below average on some things that you do and some things that you are" as compared to other people (Crain & Weisman, 1972, p. 71).[7] They view their measure as being one of "self-pride," not primarily one that gets at the reflected view of oneself in the eyes of "significant others." "Self-esteem, as we have measured it, has a tone of competing against others, rather than merely accepting the views of others toward oneself [p. 76]." Thus, this measure seems clearly slanted towards personal self-concept rather than racial self-concept. Further, the implied meaning was that this measure of self-esteem taps assertiveness, a kind of "neutralized" or "sublimated" aggression. "Assertiveness refers to competitiveness and the tendency to manipulate the environment to one's advantage. Assertive people are socially aggressive: they seek self-improvement and actively take steps to assure their well-being [p. 77]." Their data show that this index of self-esteem was correlated with various reports by respondents of being more socially assertive and upwardly mobile: oriented toward looking for a better job, having participated in civil rights demonstrations, being better prepared educationally, and the like. However, high self-esteem as measured here was also found to be associated with "dysfunctional" expression of aggression too; that is, with a higher incidence of getting into fights, being arrested more, and being separated or divorced.

Now, when the subjects' orientation on the Internal Control Scale was combined with their level of self-esteem, four different reaction styles emerged: "drifters," "militants," "accepters," and "achievers" (see table 5.1). "The different combinations of self-esteem and internal control represent alternative strategies in two ways: (1) they depict a choice between externalizing anger (system-blaming) and internalizing anger (self-blaming), and (2) they represent a choice between assertive behavior and deferential or passive behavior [p. 81]." The situations of persons in groups A and D were realtively straight-forward. The so-called "drifters" in group A had a sense of low personal control over their lives and low self-esteem, seemed to be non-assertive and less

Table 5.1

	Internal Control	
	Low	High
Low Self-Esteem	A ("drifters")	C ("accepters")
High Self-Esteem	B ("militants")	D ("achievers")

Source: adapted from Crain and Weisman, 1972, p. 81.*

*The four groups are identified by letters here with Crain and Weisman's descriptive terms being put in parentheses to help minimize the tendency to take the labels as being real entities rather than suggestions as to what the data may mean. Reported relationships involving these variables are low, accounting for small amounts of variance and hence any conceptual characterization would best be an approximation of the richness of the actuality of the respondents' lives. For example the characterization, "drifter," for group A does not necessarily imply marital instability for this group, although this is not an infrequent connotation of the term. Group A's reports of their divorce and separation history is essentially no different than that of persons in Group D ("achievers").

effective in the larger world, and expressed a good deal of hostility. The group D subjects, the "achievers," were both quite assertive and tended to act as if they believed they could control their destinies. (These are the two categories—Groups A and D—that have typically been found for whites according to Crain and Weisman and they are usually positively associated with socioeconomic status, group D being middle class and group A being lower class.) Persons who were in group B, the "militants," and those in group C, the "accepters," are particularly illustrative of the personality dilemma that racism has imposed on blacks. While persons in group B were assertive, they had less of a feeling that they could control their lives and so they were presumably less inclined to rein in their hostile behavior. Group C persons, being high on the Internal

Control variable, were quite "responsible" and muted in their expression of aggression. But, lacking the buffer of a sense of self-worth, they were self-blaming and nonassertive.

Crain and Weisman's depiction of the group B person (the "militant") is somewhat similar to the descriptions of those persons found more likely to be actively involved in ghetto riots of the 1960s. Caplan (1970) and Forward and Williams (1970) characterized these individuals as seeing themselves as capable but blocked by racism and the faults of the social structure rather than feeling alienated and hopeless (Caplan's review of the studies which paint this picture are in an article he entitles "The New Ghetto Man"). The group C person (the "accepter") has behavioral qualities reminiscent of Grier and Cobbs' (1968) description of the person who fits the "postal clerk syndrome": "This man is always described as 'nice' by white people. . . . He is passive, nonassertive, and nonaggressive. He has made a virtue of identification with the aggressor, and he has adopted an ingratiating and compliant manner. . . . This man renounces gratifications that are available to others. He assumes a deferential mask. He is always submissive. He must figure out 'the man' but keep 'the man' from deciphering him [p. 66]."

In the Crain and Weisman study, there were mixed consequences of being in groups B and C. Of the two, those in group B, who were higher in self-esteem, tended to have somewhat higher incomes than those in group C. However, the latter group described themselves as being generally more content with their lives. Thus, higher self-esteem, assertiveness as defined here, did not necessarily bring "happiness." Which of these choices was more dysfunctional—"over-externalization" or "over-internalization"—was partly a matter of the observer's political values. There clearly were personal costs and gains in both styles. For those blacks able to combine assertiveness and control of hostility, that is, group D subjects (the "achievers"), the highest degree of social achievement was possible. So lack of aggressiveness on the surface was not always accompanied by low self-esteem and a diminution of assertiveness.

The complex ways that blacks have handled their aggression historically was analyzed by Powdermaker (1943). She pointed out that, although victimized by certain aspects of the culture, blacks have also found subtle ways to resist, and were able to ventilate otherwise problematic aggressive feelings. Blacks displaced angry feelings onto safer targets (other blacks, for example) and also dealt with aggressive feelings by attempting to withdraw socially from or deny the impact of contact with whites ("I just don't let it bother me"). In some cases, they defended themselves by attempting to identify with and become like whites in order to minimize persecution.[8]

Much of Powdermaker's article was devoted to trying to understand how the great majority of black people remained meek and unaggressive and at the same time were able to maintain sufficient identity and dignity to survive as human beings. She suggested that the superficial meekness dating back to slavery helped first to defend against conscious and perhaps less conscious awareness of anger at whites. Being meek and "turning the other cheek" helped appease the guilt feelings of persons who believed with Christian conviction that it was wrong to hate. In the racial situation that constantly stirred their rage and consequent guilt, presumably meekness helped them atone. But equally as important, she argued, meekness achieved a moral victory as well in which blacks could experience feeling more righteous in their forbearance than racist whites and thus earning a place for themselves in heaven. They even contributed to their oppressors' eventual punishment by "heaping coals of fire" on their heads; that is, by returning good for evil, they magnified even more the moral affront of the oppressors' crime.

Furthermore, there was the continuing moral victory in this world of fooling whites by making them think that they (the blacks) *believed* the role they were playing. As noted earlier, many blacks were probably never fully identified with the racial role assigned to them by whites. Blacks had the intention of using the disguise of meekness to assert themselves covertly. As the old folk song says, "Got one mind for white folks to see, got 'nother for what I know is me [Ames, 1950]."⁹ The victories they gained of course helped to ensure the status quo to some extent by helping blacks maintain some psychological balance in an oppressive situation and at the same time not threaten whites. But while not provoking retaliation, it also tended not to promote social change because blacks maintained outwardly subservient roles.

With respect to overt expression of aggression, Powdermaker predicted that as blacks became increasingly urban they would be less willing to deal with their anger in the traditional ways. The historical events of the 1960s have of course borne her out. The recent mood in the black community seems to have moved more toward approval of Crain and Weisman's pattern B, the "militants," over pattern C, the "accepters." Group B persons were more openly antiwhite on interview items than either group C or D people. Other survey data (Schuman, 1974) and experimental data indicate that such inhibition and displacement of aggression away from whites have been changing. As we saw earlier, experimental work demonstrated that blacks were reluctant to express hostility toward whites (Winslow & Brainerd, 1950). More recently, by contrast, Wilson and Rogers (1975) found in an interracial laboratory situation that black subjects were quite retaliatory towards whites who were perceived by them as insulting. The measure of hostility used was the intensity of shock that subjects thought they were delivering to a "victim." While their reactions toward other black subjects showed a considerable residue of the traditional in-group hostility, it was the overt expression of anger toward whites that had changed in character. However, even prior to such changes there have always been persons who represented militancy (group B) in the black community, and a large number of persons who silently identified with them, at least in part.

Assertion: An Individual and Collective Voice

The research we just discussed focused on the emergence of a more forthright assertiveness and aggressiveness in the black community. The Crain and Weisman study in particular primarily looked at factors that influenced *individual* achievement. The perspective seemed to be the traditional one, namely, that social advancement for Afro-Americans as a group would come from the aggregate effect of individuals having bettered themselves as individuals.

But even as Crain and Weisman were collecting their data, changed notions were surfacing about the route to group advancement for blacks. On college campuses, for example, some black young people were beginning to join with other blacks to promote the advancement of Afro-Americans through assertive group action. (This is not to say that no other blacks had been involved in collective social action before the 1960s, but rather that these trends, which had existed before, were carried to a new plane and into a different mode of expression.)

This changing perspective comes to life more clearly in the work of Patricia Gurin and her colleagues. In *Black Consciousness, Identity and Achievement,* Gurin and Epps (1975) described some of the factors that contributed to some students putting together a positive sense of personal competence with a positive sense of racial (group) identity. Their study was done at ten historically black colleges in the South during the 1964–1970 period of ideological ferment on campuses (on southern campuses, the activity involved participation in the civil rights movement in local communities and later is shifted to activism for changes on the campuses themselves.)[10] This generation of college students, like many before them, had frequently come from families that had had to struggle to get these youth to college in order to give them a better chance for personal status in the American society. This has been the time-honored way of advancing "the race." In the first set of data collected, students tended overwhelmingly to believe that good academic preparation by individuals was the best strategy for breaking down the barriers of discrimination for blacks as a group. But during their college years many of them were also beginning to believe in the need for a different route to group achievement as a way of supplementing individual effort. Students sampled in their senior year in 1968 and 1970 had come to the view that collective action was the way of furthering progress for Afro-Americans.

Some of them took on the task of trying to combine individual achievement with collective action for group advancement. In essence these modes of behavior represented two different avenues for the expression of assertion. However, the job of balancing these dimensions was not an easy one. Some were successful at doing this while others couldn't do both at the same time. Of those who were most involved with social activism, particularly early in their college careers, a greater proportion had difficulty keeping up their motivation to study and dropped out of school. (They may have attended other colleges later on.)

Those who remained did not differ much in their academic performance during college—their grades and standard test scores were, more or less, equivalent. However, they employed a variety of ways of using (or not using) the opportunities for personal achievement and group action. In order to sharpen some of the issues these students struggled with, Gurin and Epps (1975) described their data in a kind of typology based on whether students were high or low in their commitment to group action[11] and high or low in personal achievement aspirations. (Data for this part of the study came from two sources: [1] a follow-up investigation of seniors at one college who had been in the research as freshmen; and [2] a body of data collected from a sample of seniors at six of the originally participating colleges.) Four groups emerged in this typology: "Committed Achievers," "Individualistic Achievers," "Activists," and the "Unengaged" [Gurin & Epps, 1975, p. 356] (see table 5.2).

The students who were able to put together a high sense of personal efficacy with a strong positive sense of commitment to group identity were the "Committed Achievers." They were the ones who expressed occupational aspirations for high professional and/or academic status and were "committed" to action, i.e., had engaged in social action throughout their four years of college. It was this group that was most successful in blending individual and group modes of assertion. Other groups in one way or another were less oriented toward combining these two dimensions. (More specifically, the criteria for high individual aspiration were: [1] intent to pursue the Ph.D. or a graduate professional degree; and [2] holding aspirations for jobs whose nontraditionality for blacks or ability demands were in the top 25% for this student population. This last was determined for each occupation by asking a random sample of students to judge "what percent of their college class, ranging from only the top 1% to almost everyone would have the requisite ability for the job [Gurin & Epps, 1976, p. 47].")

Table 5.2

| | | Individual Achievement | |
		High	Low
Commitment to Action	High	Committed Achievers	Activists
	Low	Individualistic Achievers	Unengaged

"Individualistic Achievers" were those who had personal goals for achievement that were as strong as those of the Committed Achievers but had not participated in collective action at all during their college years. The "Activists" were differentiated from the Committed Achievers on the other pole. They had been just as involved in group participation as the Committed Achievers during college but they had low occupational goals for themselves at graduation. The "Unengaged" had taken part in no collective social action during college and did not have particularly high personal achievement goals either.

There were some further specific differences in postcollege plans among these groups of students that set them off from one another. Committed Achievers more than any other group spontaneously expressed the intention of choosing an occupation that would directly benefit black people. In joining their high personal aspirations with their commitments to collective action, the Committed Achievers were overwhelmingly headed toward professional schools. They seemed to focus themselves rather narrowly on a small range of occupations—predominantly law and medicine—as ways of trying to carry out their social action goals. Individualistic Achievers had career goals that were not tied to engaging in social action particularly. They were planning to turn their high aspirations into a broader range of options spanning the spectrum of academic and research degrees. Most of them had the aim of pursuing the Ph.D. degree in various fields (see Table 5.3).

The Activists, who had been just as involved with group strategies as the Committed Achievers, also aspired to jobs that might provide them outlets for their social idealism, but at a lower prestige level. The Activists in many instances did not expect to go beyond the B.A. degree. If so, they had rather remote plans to get Master's level training in such areas as social work, guidance and counseling, public administration, and the like—in areas related to human service.

Motivational and ideological differences between the groups were particularly illuminating. Over their college careers the Committed Achievers developed more of a feeling of academic self-confidence, a greater expectation of being able to succeed in their chosen occupations, and a greater sense of personal efficacy than any of the other three groups.[12] None of the others gained in these areas by the time of their senior year. And this gain occurred even though the four groups had not differed on those variables as freshmen; only the Committed Achievers made such gains. (The groups also had a similar mixture of precollege social backgrounds and levels of occupational aspiration in the first year.)

A particularly interesting set of group differences was that between the Committed Achievers and the Activists. As we have seen, these two groups were similar in having been actively involved in promoting collective strategies for black advancement. They were also similar not only in activity but also in their ideologies concerning the black situation. They both espoused a "System Blame" point of view—a belief that factors in the social system rather than in

Table 5.3   Career Aspirations of Committed and Individualistic Achievers in 1970

Committed Achievers	Individualistic Achievers
33 Lawyers	8 Lawyers
17 Doctors	10 Doctors
3 Pharmacists	4 Pharmacists
3 Public Health Nursing administrators	14 Engineers
	10 Biologists
4 Researchers in natural science	8 Mathematicians
1 Writer	2 Physicists
61	2 Chemists
	2 Biochemists
	4 Pharmacological researchers
	1 College professor: Romance language
	1 College professor: English
	1 Artist
	2 Sociologists
	9 Psychologists
	2 Economists
	4 Business administrators
	1 Educational administrator
	86
58 Professional degrees	20 Professional degrees
1 Ph.D.	62 Ph.D.'s
2 Master's degrees	4 Master's degrees

Source: Gurin & Epps, 1975, p. 359.

blacks as individuals were primarily responsible for blacks' social plight.[13] Committed Achievers and Activists also tended to agree with one another more than with other groups in holding politically nationalist views—for example, favoring political self-determination, community control, and the use of violence if necessary to attain political ends. But, and this is of particular interest, the differences between Committed Achievers and Activists on the self-confidence and efficacy measures was as great or greater than between any other group. In fact, the Activists *decreased* the level of their occupational aspiration more than any other group through their college years. In other words, in gaining a greater sense of competence through their college years, the Committed Achievers left their compatriots in the struggle far behind with respect to the dimension of self-confidence.

How did this come about? The Activists as a group seemed to come to the conclusion that they had no right to pursue high personal goals once they were acquainted with the hardship and poverty of the lower-class black community. The idea was almost that individual and group ambitions don't mix. As one female Activist put it: "I've come to feel that you can't think about what's best for you and ever make the choices that help other people. If you think about personal advancement, there'll always come a time when you rationalize taking a better job that makes you leave the people you've been working with. It just always happens [Gurin & Epps, 1975, p. 376]."

But were the Committed Achievers somehow "selling out" by sustaining high personal ambitions? The data did not support this. In fact of all four groups the Committed Achievers seemed to have a particularly sensitive "race consciousness"—even somewhat more so than the Activists. They felt more than any other group that discrimination affected blacks in all occupational and status levels—that no blacks were exempt. But their strong views about the nature of the racial situation led them to be even more demanding of themselves with respect to the occupational level at which they planned to enter the struggle for human rights.

It is interesting to note that, while most of the students in the overall sample became more system blaming and external in their Control Ideology, the Activist group changed along these lines most of all. Recall that this group dropped the most in their level of occupational aspiration. Their differences from the Committed Achievers may be accounted for by the different ways in which they used their college experience. For example, commitment to action had to be embedded in a broader set of positive campus experiences for the student to sustain high individual aspiration. There were specific dimensions on which the Committed Achievers could be differentiated from the Activists:

> The Committed Achievers, but not the Activists, stood out for having had contact with more faculty outside the classroom, turning to faculty specifically for help in planning their future careers, finding these faculty contacts more helpful, belonging to more campus groups, holding more leadership positions on the campus, having had more experience in campus governance committees and groups concerned with educational policies, and having taken advantage of more campus events with a distinctively Black political perspective. Activism alone did not promote the integration of collective and individual achievement. Activism in a particular context did [Gurin & Epps, 1975, p. 389].

Many of the same kinds of issues separated the Individualistic Achievers from the Committed Achievers. They had tended not to form supportive relationships with the faculty as the Committed Achievers had. They had not been particularly active, even in the more conventional kinds of collegiate activities. In terms of friendship patterns, they seemed more to be loners. "Overall, they seemed less integrated into campus life, less touched by the experience of going to college [p. 390]." While the Committed Achievers were most sensitive to racial issues, the Individualistic Achievers were least sensitive to such concerns. The latter group tended most of all to hold to the belief that race was irrelevant to blacks getting ahead; they believed talent and effort alone would carry the day. The Individualistic Achievers were the group that remained outside of the trend of the total sample away from Individual Blame toward external explanations regarding the racial situation. Thus, they remained where they had come in as freshmen, both ideologically (conservative) and in aspirations (high). "What they did in atypical numbers reinforced their conventionality rather than shaking them up. They needed what colleges ideally can do best: they needed to be challenged, personally and ideologically [p. 390]."[14]

In ending this brief discussion of the Gurin and Epps material, it is possible for us to draw some parallels between their Committed Achiever, who was a college student, and the black youth seen as "the New Ghetto Man [Caplan, 1970]," who participated in ghetto riots. Basing their protest on a system-blame perspective, these young rioters had a sense of being blocked from achieving what they could in a fairer society. They were a group that decided that they were not willing to give in to a sense of hopelessness and simply take discrimination "lying down." The Committed Achievers embody a similar feeling of personal worth and system-blame, but with the opportunity to get to college they made use of these opportunities to try to achieve things for the group as well as themselves. In Caplan's idiom they perhaps represented a "new college man and woman" in the black community, persons who came out of the turbulent years of the civil rights and student activist movement of the South.[15]

For our second metaphor, we can draw on an older and more deep-rooted aspect of American cultural mythology. It has been fashionable in the lore of the American professional prizefighting game to label an especially promising white boxer as "the great White hope"—a man who might be able to wrest the crown away from the black champion of that particular division. This notion obviously exemplifies the racism that pervades the symbols in this culture. However, we can paraphrase this particular label for our own purposes. The Committed Achievers, in one sense, represent a "great Black hope"—not primarily because of wanting to conquer white people in physical combat, but because of having demonstrated that a firm sense of self as a person need not be at the expense of a continuing commitment to group action and ideology. However, this group of Committed Achievers was not necessarily perfect. They restricted themselves by electing to become lawyers or doctors in the effort to carry out their sense of social mission. It was as if they failed to appreciate that they could contribute by training in other professions. Researchers trained with Ph.D. degrees in the social sciences, for example, can be in the vanguard of knowledge and action about the racial scene. Even if a black person's choice seems to be unrelated to Afro-American issues, such as in natural science or humanities careers, there are a variety of ways that one can be of use. The individual can take direct action within the profession and be a visible role model in nontraditional (for blacks) occupational areas. The problem for the Activists was that many of them lowered their goals below what they might have accomplished had more support been given to sense of self-esteem and other achievement values. To the extent that a "less prestigious" career is chosen with a genuine sense of potential fulfillment and as offering opportunities for self-development, then there could be little quarrel with the choice. The point in this study was that the drop in aspiration was accompanied by a drop in self-confidence. That should be the alerting cue for the educator's and counselor's concern.

Nigrescence

There have been other approaches to describing the ways blacks have come to assert pride in group identity. Over the past decade some writers have characterized some of the identity changes in Afro-Americans from the perspective of what Cross (1978b) has called "psychological nigrescence," the process of becoming "Black." This involves developing a sense of self and personal worth that explicitly takes its reference points from a perspective of Afro-American history and consciousness, rather than primarily from the frame of reference toward oneself and blacks dictated by white society. Charles Thomas (1970; Thomas & Thomas, 1971) and William Cross (1978b), working independently, have constructed models describing the specific steps that blacks may go through in the conversion from Negro to "Black."

Comparing his model with that of Thomas, Cross describes five stages of the conversion process. The first stage is that of "Pre-encounter" in which the "person's world view is dominated by Euro-American determinants [1978b, p. 17]." In this stage those features of the individual that characterize his or her black racial identity are denied or downgraded in the interest of accepting the Euro-American view. Such a person's cultural orientation is a "deracinated" one. The stage of "Encounter" follows next and consists of a disrupting confrontation with a new way of viewing the Afro-American situation. "The 'Encounter stage' describes a shocking personal or social event that temporarily dislodges the person from his old worldview, making the person receptive (vulnerable) to a new interpretation of his identity and his condition [p. 17]." This stage ends when the person becomes convinced that a change of perspective is in order and (s)he makes the decision to "become Black." This involves a highly motivated—what Cross calls a "frantic and obsessive"—search for black identity.

In the "Immersion-Emersion" stage the individual works to get rid of all traces of the Pre-encounter frame of reference in the self and explores the implications for him- or herself of the new point of view. The person acts the way most converts to emotionally involving ideologies do. There may be "glorification of African heritage, dichotomous ('either-or') thinking, Blacker-than-thou attitudes, unrealistic expectations concerning the efficacy of Black Power, and the tendency to denigrate White people and White culture while simultaneously deifying Black people and Black culture [p. 17]."

As an individual emerges from the emotional heat of this period, (s)he begins to be able to step back and look more critically at the strengths and weaknesses of his/her new identity and be less intensely involved in the search. The person then enters a phase of "Internalization" in which (s)he had made the new values his/her own. There is less need for rhetorical posturing as a way of impressing others but rather a "calm, secure demeanor" characterized by "ideological flexibility, psychological openness, and self-confidence about one's Blackness. . . . While still using Blacks as a primary reference group, the person moves toward a pluralistic nonracist perspective [p. 18]." As Thomas puts it, "You lose your hangups about race, age, sex and social class and see yourself as a part of humanity in all its flavors [1970, p. 78]." Hopefully, when this has been accomplished, the individual moves on to the fifth stage, "Internalization-Commitment" in which (s)he finds activities through which to manifest the new identity in ways that will further the progress of the group. "This 'ideal person' has not only incorporated the new identity but is struggling to translate personal identity into activities that are meaningful to the group [Cross, 1978b, p. 18]." Cross notes that his model is not explicit as to whether or not one can go from Stage III directly into Stage V. We will have something to say in a moment about the Gurin and Epps research in the context of this scheme.

Clearly, the description embodied in the Cross model is one of identity movement that shows activity and self-creation as we have been defining these concepts in this book. Now, how valid is this framework when viewed from the perspective of research? Cross (1978b) reports eight studies, including some of his own, that have attempted to answer this question. The research that Cross cites, which has been inspired by his and to some extent Thomas' model, has been of two sorts. There have been studies that have elicited introspective data—that is, subjects' perceptions of how they have changed in their sense of racial identity—and there have been studies that have gotten at more "extraspective" kinds of data, correlating a person's status in this model with other measures of attitude to try and get a more objective index as to whether or not the individual has changed. Both kinds of studies seem to have confirmed that identity for some black subjects has changed in the directions depicted by the Cross model; that is, the studies support the order of stages that the model has proposed.

Cross notes that he is not describing a total personality style in this model of racial identity issues. While he proposes that important values are represented in these stages and these values have changed in some black people—permanently, in many cases, he believes—many other features of personal style may very well remain the same. As he suggests, it is likely that "people who began the conversion as 'neurotic Negroes' emerged from the experience as 'neurotic blacks'; likewise, fairly well adjusted nonneurotic Negroes were well adjusted nonneurotic people with a new Black worldview at the completion of their conversion [1978b, p. 29]." Similarly, a fairly well-adjusted person—who before the conversion approaches the world through modes of emotion and action rather than primarily through thinking and ideation—will respond in similar ways afterwards. What some personality theorists would call "basic personality structure" is not postulated to change necessarily in this "process of becoming Black."

An important additional caution is in order about the applicability of the Cross stages to members of the wider black community. Although we can identify certain descriptive trends in the attitudes of black Americans in this research, we must continue to remember that Afro-Americans are not a monolithic group in their attitudes or in the way they express them. Black people have a variety of ways of adapting to the American situation. Many of the studies using the Cross model have included college students in samples that were modest in size. In one such study in which the results were related to socioeconomic status, a disproportionate number of persons at the Internalization stage tended to be college students. Pre-encounter subjects, on the other hand, had less education as a group than subjects at any of the other stages. It may be that the kinds of experiences the students had in college made the difference. Key to this experience, perhaps, is the opportunity college provides to have close interaction with peers in the concentrated intellectual situation of the campus. This possibility, along with the fact that the stages do not necessarily imply changes in basic personality style, suggests that ideological, not personality, changes are involved here. College can have profound effect on ideological beliefs, and such beliefs can have important consequences for behavior, without altering all aspects of an individual's personality.

Malcolm X

Although the measurable changes in ideology are perhaps more apparent among higher status persons, there are clear examples of how this model does apply to persons of working- and lower-class background too, notably in the case of such leaders of the Black Revolution as Malcolm X. His life can be seen to reflect many of the issues that have been discussed in this chapter. Any conceptualization about a personal history or biography is somewhat arbitrary. But for our purposes here, I think we can see five periods in Malcolm's life from the perspective of a struggle to achieve greater self-realization. In the first period during his days as a youngster in Michigan, although wanting to achieve and be accepted by whites, he was aware of racial conflict and the need to maintain color consciousness. This was brought home to him not only by his experiences in school but by the activities and eventual lynching of his father, an outspoken follower of Marcus Garvey's movement for Afro-American liberation. Racial identity was further emphasized through his mother's open ambivalence towards him because of his light skin color. He felt the racially tinged derision of the welfare worker toward his poverty-stricken family. But his sense of self was never so flattened that he could not see the anomaly of having achieved in school only to have his teacher counsel him out of aspiring to a high occupational level. When his 8th-grade teacher told him that his ambition to become a lawyer was "no realistic goal for a nigger," he noted, "It was a surprising thing that I had never thought of it that way before, but I realized that whatever I wasn't, I *was* smarter than nearly all of those white kids. But apparently I was still not intelligent enough, in their eyes, to become whatever *I* wanted to be. It was then that I began to change—inside [Malcolm X, 1965, p. 37]."

In response to the bruises he received from trying to integrate, Malcolm withdrew from whites and went to the East Coast where he immersed himself in the world of lower-class Negro culture. In this second phase of his life, he became part of an underworld culture and also made contact with a large segment of much of the vitality of black culture, some of it outside the law and some not. The thread of identity here was still one of assertive "resistance," in Lester's terms (1968), resistance to working a "slave"—a menial job with meager material returns—and accepting the white society's definition of him as being second class. He bent all his effort toward becoming a successful hustler partly because he found a subculture that supported his sense of competence as a black and as a person. Being outside the "law" was irrelevant; Malcolm could see that the law operated primarily to support white upper- and middle-class privileges. "I have no mercy or compassion in me for a society that will crush people, and then penalize them for not being able to stand up under the weight [p. 22]." He came to see the humanity of the outcast and saw that many of the pimps, hustlers, and prostitutes he encountered were intelligent, spirited men and women like himself who had been defined out of the human race before having had a chance to develop and prove themselves. His rejection of a "dignified" menial job within the system was his recognition that he, like many other blacks, was potentially far more competent than such work implied. He chose one of the few avenues of exceptional individual achievement available to him. This phase does correspond to the Pre-encounter stage in the Cross model from a black consciousness political perspective. But from a perspective of active self-creation, Malcolm was even during this period busily working on the process of self-definition.

The third phase that I am positing was a transitional one that corresponds to Cross' Encounter stage and the beginning of the Immersion-Emersion phase. In the first part of his prison career, with his customary assertive avenues in society blocked, his rage mounted and his negativism toward white society reached what he himself described as its peak. He spent considerable time in solitary confinement because of his rebelliousness to the prison system (which had put him there not only for burglary but probably even more, he felt, because he had involved white women in his illegal activities). Even though he was in some ways like a dangerous, caged animal, his aim was a very human one—to resist the prison's effort to subjugate him and rob him of an identity. He expressed his selfhood in the only way he knew how at the time.

In the fourth phase, beginning in prison and extending through most of the rest of his life, he turned to Elijah Muhammad's definition of the religion of Islam. He described his conversion as being fueled by his sense of guilt and his recognition of the errors of his past life, but it is likely that his willingness to submit to the Black Muslim discipline stemmed to a significant degree from its allowing him to continue his development of himself through the avenue of assertive resistance to racist America. As a disciple of the religion he could turn his intellectual talents and both hostile and assertive energies not only to individual achievement but also toward group advancement. In terms of personal dynamics, it seems quite plausible to postulate further that Elijah Muhammad also represented a paternal figure for Malcolm, perhaps allowing him to reunite symbolically with his beloved father who had also preached both the dignity of blacks and the necessity of a separatist solution to the racial situation.

In a last phase before his death, after his trips to Mecca, it seems as if he was taking further steps toward self-development by narrowing his scorn to certain segments of white society rather than the white race as a whole and concomitantly broadening his concept of brotherhood. At the time of his death, he seemed clearly to be manifesting Cross' fourth and fifth stages.

A central theme illustrated by Malcolm's life is that of dogged self-creation, constantly moving toward greater competence, frequently in dialectical opposition to an oppressive "Other's" definition of him—a white "Other" and sometimes a black "Other." This sometimes led him into the position of being an "outlaw" in white society's eyes or a dissident in the view of his black colleagues in Islam. Malcolm did not change his personality style. He remained a forcefully assertive and often an aggressive person trying to persuade people to his point of view and standing up to his antagonists. His effort at self-development did not begin with what Cross would call the Encounter phase. An active orientation toward self-realization marked his entire life—from his days in Michigan up to his final hours—notwithstanding that some phases of his development were destructive to himself and to his race. To some extent his life illustrates my earlier statement that self-contributions to behavior, the choice processes that one brings to the world, are not always positive from a socioethical or a personal point of view. Yet they are an expression of a person's effort to take hold of life, have an impact on it, and make something of oneself and the world. (Milliones [1980] interprets Malcolm's life more strictly in accordance with the Cross stages.) In the eventual overall thrust of his life, in spite of negative periods in it, Malcolm wedded his striving for individual development to a drive for group advancement, and in the merger a new sense of identity emerged not unlike that of the Committed Achievers that Gurin and Epps talked about.

Malcolm said that he laid bare the intimate details of his life not to titillate but as a guide to others and an illustration of a central problem in American society—its treatment of its colored minorities. In doing so he made clearer how many adequately competent blacks, though perhaps less talented than he, turned to socially marginal and less productive activities because they were not able to express and develop a sense of competence within established American social structural boundaries. The point being made here is that much creative energy is and has been available in the black community for generations and generations. Much of it has been suppressed or forced into other channels. The need for social change among minorities is not just that of teaching blacks how to make use of opportunity and engage in self-development, but rather making available to them in the first place the same range of social opportunities that have been provided for whites of upper socioeconomic stratas. Given this, many blacks will "take it from there." Indeed, in some cases—for example, for the so-called "underclass"—there *is* a need for special training to participate in the technological aspects of society. And these needs must be addressed fully— in technical detail. However, it is equally important to realize that blacks in general have the wish to be competent and infinitely self-developing and they have continually expressed this striving against great odds with sometimes remarkable results.[16]

While it is possible to see this kind of ideological development in the lives of some blacks, Harrell (1979) rejects the idea of using a sequential-stage approach as a way of characterizing the adjustment of most blacks to the racial situation. He feels that postulating stages through which people pass to reach an endpoint necessarily applies value judgments about the status of the various points along the continuum. In other words, the criticism here is of the implicit idea that there is a single albeit broad psychological process through which blacks *should* be moving, with the presumption that the last stage is the most mature and desirable. He argues that different circumstances for Afro-Americans have led to different ways of adapting to racism and that blacks have not simply chosen one way to respond, even though they have had similar perceptions about the fact of social oppression. Harrell proposes six "coping styles" that blacks have developed in recent decades in response to their situation. He derives his framework from the analysis of the contemporaneous black situation done by historian Vincent Harding (1975). An important aspect of each style is that it is seen as having both positive and negative possibilities for personal and social adjustment; that is, no style is seen as being without its problematic aspects. There is no optimal endpoint for Harrell. His six styles are labeled "continued apathy," "seeking a piece of the action," "obsession with counter-culture alternative," "the black nationalist alternative," "identification with an authoritarian solution," and "historically aware cognitive flexibility."

The person living with "continued apathy" regarding the racial situation may acknowledge the damaging effects of racism but manifests little or no coping strategy for responding to it. "A passive or reactive posture underlies [this] approach to life [Harrell, 1979, p. 101]." However, there can be positive as well as negative aspects of such passivity from an individualistic point of view. The person living in this style perhaps does not succumb to some of the more damaging kinds of symptoms such as severe psychosomatic reactions (for example, ulcers or hypertension) that might well result from a highly emotional response and an active struggle with racism. A major negative consequence is that in the characteristic tendency of this style to blame the "man" for all troubles, the person develops a strongly dependent attitude in which (s)he looks to this same "man," an external source rather than to the resourcefulness of self, to provide the benefits of life and for relief from difficulties.

The "counterculture" solution represents a mode of living in which the individual engages in what may be very active but quite personalized efforts to avoid or transcend the entire black struggle. "The solution may take the form of heavy drug usage, involvement in exotic religious or art forms, or the frequent use of any number of consciousness altering techniques [p. 103]." The positive side of this is that an individual "involved in a complex dialogue with 'self' " may be very creative as a result of the unorthodox activities (s)he may commit him- or herself to. The negative side is that the individual, even if living in a creative fantasy world, no longer maintains touch with the practical reality of racism. Harrell believes that total loss of awareness of the kind of threat that racism represents is pathological.

Regarding some of the other styles, in "seeking a piece of the action," an individual may be highly motivated toward achieving competence in certain skills but pay little attention to the effects of his or her drive for personal gain on other blacks. The "Black Nationalist" orientation promotes a positive view of black people and black culture but, as in the Immersion phase, it may become too narrow and rigid in its approach to white institutions. In "identifying with an authoritarian solution" such as Marxism or the Nation of Islam the individual gains direction and discipline in his or her behavior but may lose contact with personal perspectives in the overdependence on the authority. Drawing on Fanon, Harrell argues in critique of this position: "The oppressed must always question . . . the oppressed must be creative [p. 105]."

Finally, the "aware cognitive flexibility" style is one that is not as sharply defined as some of the others. It is a position in which the black person is aware of the ambiguities and complexities of the racial situation. This fits our humanistic definition of awareness—a consciousness of alternatives (see Chapter 2). This orientation to life recognizes that "the struggle against racism is not over, and indeed, there are presently no comforting or even familiar answers to the issues facing Black people today. This individual stands poised and processing—creating new theory, practice, ideology, and consequently, new hope [Harrell, 1979, p. 105]." This position sounds very much like the final stages of the Cross and the Thomas models. However, Harrell sees this style, though embodying maturity—relative openmindedness, nondefensiveness, and a readiness to generate creative strategies for dealing with racism—as also potentially having pathological effects. Psychological awareness leaves one open to pessimism and despair: "This emotional state is not inconsistent with the recognition that after protracted struggle an unfamiliar and uncertain road lies ahead [p. 105]."

It is likely that most Afro-Americans would be best described by several of these categories at once. For any style to be sustained, it has to have some features that the individual feels are positive even though there are also imperfections and personal costs in the way the adaptation works. It is quite conceivable, for example, that a person might show the achievement orientation of the "piece of the action" style in a competitive interracial work situation and at the same time support organizations that have a black nationalist ideology, and have an aware cognitive flexibility about the position of the Afro-American in this society. As we have been saying, people use more than one frame of reference to structure the world for themselves. The styles that Harrell describes in many instances are probably modes that an individual may call upon at different times depending on the situation (s)he is in or at various points in his or her life. Furthermore, and this is an important point, it is quite likely that people develop a number of such simultaneous facets in their coping style during the course of their lives. Combining Harrell's notions with the Cross-Thomas kind of model, it may be that development from Pre-encounter to Internalization kinds of phases corresponds to a person's opening up a wider range of options for conceptualizing and coping with the world, not just the change from one single stage to another.

In this chapter I have developed the point that one of the hallmarks of the assertiveness that has characterized the psychology of the Black Revolution is the unabashed linking of sense of self as a person with the sense of oneself as being black. Throughout their history in the United States, Afro-Americans have had to struggle with the angry feelings stirred by the "obstacles and meannesses imposed on them." This struggle has been made particularly difficult by the limited opportunities for giving vent to their hostile impulses. While becoming more frank about their hostility towards whites in recent times, many Afro-Americans have not let themselves simply be consumed by the fires of their own rage. They have continued to turn much of their energy into efforts at more effective expression of assertion and competence strivings. In the words of a song: "I've been treated like a mule and I've turned [myself] into a human being." And the "continuing set of unending . . . mutually modifying long-range enterprises" that Chein (1972, p. 289) attributes to the human being has involved for blacks an increasingly self-conscious effort to assert both individual and group pride.

NOTES

1. The insistence in recent years by many Afro-Americans that they be called "black" rather than "Negro" was an angry and defiant insistence that *they* decide what to be called, that is, that they define their own identity. It involved taking a word that white culture had attached primarily negative connotations to and (dialectically) focusing on the contexts in which black is "beautiful" (black is the color of rich, fertile earth; precious oil; valued ebony; etc.). Further, blacks insist that because dark-skinned people are fully human they are by definition beautiful—like all human beings they are the "chosen ones."

2. Psychoanalytic theorists have argued that aggression is innate, an instinctual force that must be channeled properly to insure the individual's survival (and ultimately that of the human species, of course). A differing classical position regarding the source of aggression is that it is the result of the *frustration* or blocking of some goal the person is striving for at the moment. The instinctual theory would not preclude frustration as a source of aggression, but the frustration-aggression theory does intend to exclude the innate drive notion. A modern psychoanalytic position that is quite consonant with the ideas we are developing in this book is expressed by Kovel. He suggests that aggression is best conceived as

> a raw striving, relatively undifferentiated, able to undergo any number of transmutations, and able to direct itself to any number of objects . . . aggression is in the most basic sense an impulsion to *act* upon an object, and to alter the object of its activity. Thus its range of expression extends from a "healthy" sense of mastery to the most unbridled and seemingly gratuitous aim of destruction. Seen in this light, aggression loses its connotation of badness and becomes instead a basic propulsion to act upon the world. What is "bad"—i.e., destructive—is reserved to a particular outcome of aggression, one all too universal, to be sure, but not so much a biological given as it is the consequence of the human situation [1970, p. 257–258].

Aggression expressed as mastery is similar to assertion as we have described it here. (Classic psychoanalytic theorists would probably account for "mastery" as a "neutralized" expression of the aggressive drive, that is, a drive that has the same source but aims that are not associated with destructiveness.) Robert White indicates his belief that the problems with the usual drive notion, some of which we discussed in Chapter 1, make it unwise to put mastery components, those conceived as competence at least, under the umbrella of the aggressive drive (1963). It does seem plausible that an impulse to act on and change the world, as Kovel conceives it, might contribute to many constructive kinds of acts. This would not preclude effectance behavior from emerging independent of a more traditionally acting drive such as aggression in its various forms. This is not the place to try and resolve the longstanding controversies regarding the origin and nature of aggressive behavior. I will assume that assertion and mastery in some forms can conceivably be expressed in part through the aggressive drive as it is more broadly formulated by Kovel, for example, and that some efforts to act on and change the environment stem from the independent competence motive.

3. Although competence strivings are ubiquitous in all groups, it can't be denied that Afro-American individuals have developed some chronically self-defeating behavioral styles. Many of the behavioral attributes that Pugh (1972) refers to as "adaptive inferiority" are descriptive of such styles. Rainwater (1966) makes a similar point. In his investigation of life in an urban slum, he suggests that the suffering of lower-class blacks in such settings is not only a function of oppression by whites and their institutions but also is a function of the personal adjustments and adaptations to such situations that blacks have made. For example, the pressures on the lower-class family are such that interaction patterns develop among family members that limit the performance of emotionally supportive functions in the family. This leads to negative impacts on the socialization of children.

Rainwater expresses this as a kind of paradigm. He argues that it is an oversimplification to see the suffering in Afro-American inner-city communities as coming about only from white oppression. He suggests that such suffering comes about also because white oppression leads to chronic personal reactions on the part of blacks that keep them from advancing socially. This is the traditional view of problems in the inner cities. Breaking the equipment and disregarding the punctual starting time are ways of actively expressing "resistance" but they also get the worker fired and keep him from advancing economically. Rainwater argues that blacks' behaviors—perhaps most importantly those toward one another in their families and communities—do the work of caste victimization for the white society. The specific misfortunes of a black person are, then, not necessarily the direct result in every case of a racist act.

Now, not only does this kind of emphasis overlook the continuing positive features of a great many blacks—the loving sacrifices made for their children's benefit, the work at more than one low-paying job in order to make ends meet, the sustaining of an essentially humanitarian perspective toward the world—it tends to blame the victims for their plight, a tendency to which social science is prone (Caplan & Nelson, 1974). While cataloguing the kinds of maladaptive reactions that can legitimately be seen among blacks and in their families we must also keep a clear focus on the overbearing social context in which these behaviors occur. If this pathological institutional and cultural context were corrected, in some cases behavior would change, and in the other cases the effort to correct the chronic self-defeating habits would be an easier task.

4. Are blacks more aggressive than whites? This is a question that some have felt deserves serious consideration (Baughman, 1971). The longstanding evidence of intragroup hostility and crime within black communities and the rioting that has erupted with some frequency in the last 15 years seem to make this a legitimate query. Some white people may see hostility in blacks where none is intended due to failure to understand black cultural styles (Cheek, 1976). However, beyond such considerations, one cannot look at the history of some 400 to 500 years of colonialist and racist exploitation of native populations in Africa and North and South America and justify the contention that blacks are more aggressive than whites. In fact, there seems to be considerable *projection* (the defense of unconsciously attributing to others the unacceptable impulses that exist in oneself) by whites involved in such an indictment of Afro-Americans.

5. Related to the issue of unique effects on blacks, Crain and Weisman (1972) wrote: "We have argued that blacks have more personal problems than whites [p. 26]." The ethnocentric bias in this statement is striking. To the extent that "more personal problems" refers to the fact that blacks proportionate to their numbers in the population suffer more effects of poverty, there could be some merit to the statement. But the fact is that it has been the white mentality and personality that have created the conditions from which blacks suffer. This implies a striking number of problems in white people. A statement such as Crain and Weisman's does not address this issue. At best, then, it could only be said that whites have different personality problems from blacks—certainly not *fewer* personal problems than blacks (Kovel, 1970).

6. The scale used by Crain and Weisman consisted of five items, three used by Coleman et al. (1966) and two from Rotter's original 23-item scale. On the Coleman items, the subject was asked to express agreement or disagreement with a statement; for example, "People like me don't have a very good chance to be really successful in life." On the Rotter (1966) scale, a person is to select one of a pair of statements that (s)he agrees with: "Being a success is mainly a matter of hard work, and luck has little or nothing to do with it" (Internal) versus "Getting a good job depends mainly upon being in the right place at the right time" (External). Blacks have been found to be more externally oriented generally—that is, low in Internal Control, and in this study this was true on three of the five items according to Crain and Weisman. We shall look at other interpretations of blacks' performance on this scale later in the chapter.

Of particular interest to us, too, is the notion that Internal-External Control can also be related to Rychlak's causal constructs which we discussed in Chapter 1. Having a sense that one is the master of one's fate involves confidence about being able to impose one's own intentions as a frame or pattern on events in one's life and thus be able to determine the direction of things. Rychlak (1977; Rychlak & Barna, 1971) has developed a Causal Construct Scale (CCS) that attempts to operationalize some of the implications of the causal principles and show their impact in human functioning. The scale consists of 72 statements, each of which attempts to express the sense of one causal idea. Thus the statement "A man is about as good as the stock he comes from" expresses a

Substance construct. "The great minds of all time have risen above misfortune to shoot for better things in the future" expresses an Intention construct. The scale consists of 36 items that pair the various statments with each other requiring the subject to choose the one (s)he prefers. As predicted, Rychlak and Barna found in one study (1971) that preference for Intention constructs tended to be associated with emphasizing Internal control statements; Impetus meanings were associated with External Control. This picture was clearer for men.

7. A list of ten items was read to the respondent covering three areas. The first dealt with the roles related to being a family member—as child, parent, and spouse. The second group dealt with aspects of character—"trustworthiness" and "willingness to work hard." The last few items tapped the subject's assessment of his or her ability in five areas such as intelligence, mechanical ability, and athletics. The same scale had been given in a different study to a large national sample of white men and women and so comparison data were available. Results indicated that overall the black sample rated themselves as above average on fewer items than did the white sample thus presumably indicating lower self-esteem. However, when results were considered by region of birth it was found that southern-born blacks (raised in the North) scored considerably lower than whites, but northern-born blacks scored at least as high and in some cases higher than whites. It's not clear what the reference group for comparison here was for the black sample but it is again in opposition to the Kardiner and Ovesey notion of uniform low self-esteem in the black population. In her dissertation, K. White (1977), using a semantic evaluation measure, also found that the self-esteem ratings were equivalent in degree of positiveness in a sample of northern urban black and white adults.

8. Pettigrew (1964) postulated similar styles of responding. He drew on Karen Horney's tripartite description of human personality to propose abstractions about historical reaction tendencies among Afro-Americans, recognizing that no such conceptualization does full justice to the complexity of individual human behavior. He proposed that general tendencies can be identified for (1) "moving toward the oppressor," that is, seeking acceptance through integration; (2) "moving against the oppressor," conscious experiencing and open expression of hostility toward whites at an individual or group level; and (3) "moving away from the oppressor," ranging from avoidance of contact with whites to avoidance of contact with problematic racial situations.

Taking off from Pettigrew's perspective, Gibbs (1974) identified four styles of adaptation of black students to predominantly white universities based on her counseling contacts with a sample of students at the Stanford University mental health service. The modes of relating are called "assimilation," "separation," "withdrawal," and "affirmation." Assimilation corresponded to moving toward the oppressor in which the student was conforming and was desirous of acceptance and approval by the dominant group and tended to be an overachiever to prove his/her worth. These persons tended to be anxious socially and quite sensitive to ethnic references and cues. The mode of separation, corresponding to moving against the oppressor, was characterized by hostility, anger, interpersonal conflicts, and rejection of white middle-class values. Such persons tended to be active protestors against white institutions and customs. In the withdrawal mode, moving away from the oppressors, apathy, depression, and alienation were some of the primary feelings leading to the students wanting to pull away from contact with troubling academic and social situations. Gibbs suggested that a fourth adaptive mode could be seen among black students also, an affirmative mode. This designation refers to those oriented toward moving *with* the dominant culture not simply toward it or against it; that is, such black students accepted their own culture and were trying to "merge [their] minority identity with the broader American identity [1974, p. 731]." Gibbs described the students operating within this mode as showing "self-acceptance, positive ethnic identity, hyperactivity, high achievement motivation, and autonomous self-actualizing behavior [p. 736]." They tended to run into trouble when they were unable to live up to their own standards because of conflicting pressures from blacks and whites. Gibbs discussed the incidence of these patterns in terms of their relative frequency, especially as related to class backgrounds. Although statistical analysis of results was not performed and although this was an analysis of behavior of students presenting themselves for counseling, suggestive trends seemed to emerge. The withdrawal mode, which seemed to be accompanied by the most serious psychological symptoms, was the most frequent one regardless of class and it was characteristic of those who rated themselves as feeling inadequate. A large percentage of those who rated themselves as feeling adequate were in the affirmation cateogory. Among results related to socioeconomic status there were no separationists among the upper middle-class students and no assimilationists or affirmationists among the students in the lowest of the socioeconomic backgrounds. Further whether or not the student had attended an integrated high school seemed to have a bearing on the mode of adjustment to college: "Twice as many students who attended integrated high schools compared to those attending predominantly black schools developed the mode of affirmation, while four times as many were assimilationists and one-fourth as many were separationists [p. 738]."

9. These role behaviors in interracial settings can be seen to be an aspect of the "persona" of black individuals in Jungian terminology. The persona is a concept Carl Jung used to describe the fact that we all have a social facade which we adopt in playing our socially prescribed roles. While this may be a consistent way of being in certain situations and hence a part of personality, a person is usually aware of this aspect of him- or herself as being different from other aspects of self. The danger to the individual comes when (s)he comes to accept the persona as the real personality. It may be possible to see the Group D persons in the Crain and Weisman analysis as persons able to maintain a distinction between certain role behaviors and self, whereas the accepters, with low self-esteem (Group C persons) may have come to believe in the role imposed on them. For them, the mask had come to stick to the face.

10. This study yielded considerable data about patterns of student achievement and motivation in college, students' precollege backgrounds, and development of their ideologies and political action during college years. There were findings discussing characteristics of the various college institutions as learning environments and information on the different kinds of contexts the campuses provided for students' social action interests. This provided a representative picture of the heterogeneity of these black colleges. There is a far larger body of data here than can adequately be reported or than is relevant to our main theme. We will select for discussion that relatively circumscribed though central set of findings that discusses how students linked aspects of individual and group identity.

11. Students varied in the amount they participated in activity. Gurin and Epps divided their involvement into joining in on only one demonstration during the year on the one hand as against sustaining activity through the year by frequently taking part in demonstrations and working with a group that was actually coordinating local activities. The latter group was more external on Control Ideology items and had a highly system-blaming orientation as compared to the former group. The point is that people who were more critical of the system were not "alienated" from it and feeling helpless. They were the ones most engaged in trying to take action upon it in order to change it for the betterment of black people.

12. Gurin and her co-workers have made use of the Internal-External Control variable as a measure of personal efficacy and competence. As we have seen, Internal Control refers to the degree to which an individual believes that his/her own efforts are the determining factors in gaining rewards in life. The thinking about this variable has traditionally placed a strong positive value on the Internal end of this dimension and tended to associate that pole with a masterful conception of the self. However, in their extended program of research (e.g., Gurin et al, 1969) the Gurin team found that for blacks only *some* of the Rotter items get at the individual's belief that (s)he can control factors directly affecting his or her life. They have identified these five items as a "Personal Control" factor; all five of them are phrased in the first person. An example of the Internal end is, "What happens to me is my own doing"; at the External pole would be, "Sometimes I don't feel I have enough control over the direction my life is taking [Gurin et al., 1969, p. 37]."

Other items in the scale, only one of which is worded in first-person terms, are seen to refer to the respondents' belief in the Protestant work ethic as a general social value irrespective of their application to the individual him- or herself. This factor has been labeled Control Ideology. An example of the Internal orientation on this variable is, "Some people just don't use the breaks that come their way. If they don't do well, it's their own fault" (as opposed to the External version: "People who don't do well in life often work hard but the breaks just don't come their way"). The reasoning behind the distinction is that Afro-Americans may grow up accepting the value of hard work in general, but their experience in American society is that hard work does *not* pay off in their lives, because factors in the social system keep them from reaping the benefits of hard work. Thus, many Americans have worked their way to the top of the economic ladder. But a disproportionately large number of blacks have been kept on lower rungs, no matter how hard they have worked. It was the belief in one's personal efficacy (high on Personal Control) not a belief in the general work ethic alone (Control Ideology) that was associated with higher academic performance and aspiration variables in the black college student sample (Gurin & Epps, 1975).

Gurin and Epps (1975, p. 73) and Gurin, Gurin, and Morrison (undated) in a more recent, unpublished paper, note the finding from their studies and those of other workers that the distinction between Personal Control and Control Ideology holds also for whites who are highly liberal. Thus for many such persons and many blacks, it is the first-person (Personal Control) items that carry the weight of sense of personal effectiveness. Third-person items (Control Ideology) are interpreted in political terms; these people tend to take an external orientation on these items indicating their recognition that the system doesn't always work for people, even when they do work hard. Gurin, Gurin, and Morrison assert that an important point for prediction with black and liberal white populations especially is that the Personal Control items reflect sense of efficacy in those arenas in which these individuals actually feel they can have an influence. Their political ideology, however, leads them to feel that the individual alone cannot have an influence on social system issues, and hence collective action is necessary. For politically conservative people the distinction is not made between Personal Control and Control Ideology.

13. While it is supposedly good to be Internal, it is presumably not so good to be External in one's Locus of Control orientation. In other words, the Locus of Control theorist looks with a jaundiced eye on one who believes that random luck or chance rather than effort are what pay off in life. However, again Gurin et al. (1969) point out that the racial situation forces a different view of life on blacks: "The operation of the labor market which can lead to layoffs over which individuals have no control, poor transportation facilities which reduce their possibilities in the job hunt, the tendency of employers to hire within the social network of those already on the payroll, etc. [p. 33]" operate quite systematically and reliably in the lives of the poor and nonwhite minorities. For persons experiencing such events an external orientation is not just a belief; it fits the facts of their lives all too well. In their research with the Internal Control variable Gurin administered items worded to get at how blacks might view the way the racial situation affects opportunity. They derived an Individual vs. System Blame factor indicating people's feeling about the extent to which factors external to the individual are responsible for blacks' racial plight as opposed to the degree to which the failure of individual blacks to work hard enough to prepare themselves accounts for their situation.

For example, the statement "The problem for many Negroes is that they aren't really acceptable by American standards. Any Negro who is educated and does what is considered proper will be accepted and get ahead" represents an Individual Blame response—an internalization of responsibility by directing blame back at the group (and by implication, at the self). The alternative choice, "The attempt to 'fit in' and do what's proper hasn't paid off for Negroes. It doesn't matter how 'proper' you are, you'll still meet serious discrimination if you're Negro," rests responsibility on factors outside the individual (Gurin et al., 1969, p. 49). It blames the system and is an externalizing response. For most black people and for the group as a whole, taking an "external" stance on this scale squares with the facts of life in America and therefore would seem a more realistic response. Of particular interest here is the fact that in their college student sample Gurin & Epps (1975) found that men who took a System Blame stance ranked higher on some performance and aspiration variables than men who took an Individual Blame perspective. This was true even among men with an equally high sense of personal efficacy (high Personal Control).

14. The value of having counselors and faculty attuned to the need for supportive contact with

students is apparent. These data also make clear that having meaningful opportunities on campus to take leadership and planning roles is a requisite for students. Such values are not newly discovered in this study, of course. However, these authors do see their data as supporting the value of the black college for some black youth, especially those from rural and poverty backgrounds, who often thrive socially and intellectually in the more compatible milieu they find there.

15. Recent research from a junior college campus in the San Francisco Bay Area provides information about a later generation of black students, this time comparing them with their white classmates (Jones, 1978a). One of the measures used in this study was the California Psychological Inventory (CPI), a paper-and-pencil test of personality. Jones analyzed differences between black and white students in terms of different responses to the 361 items, rather than differences in the scale scores of this inventory. The more global scale scores derived from summing responses to different clusters of items are invariably standardized on predominantly white samples. Because he wanted information about blacks as well as whites, Jones felt it would be a more fruitful approach to analyze the more specific (item) responses from his own sample in order to arrive at more meaningful conclusions about personality differences. Previous research had shown that item differences are more sensitive than scale scores to black-white disparities.

He found that about 80% of the items on the CPI differentiated significantly between black and white respondents, a magnitude of differences that had not been previously reported in the personality literature. He noted that, as compared to white subjects:

> The young Black subject emerges in this investigation as assertive, poised, outspoken, tough-minded, power-oriented, and somewhat skeptical and cynical; [the picture is of] a person who is determined to get ahead, values action, tends not to show emotions, and is not easily hurt or readily put down. This particular psychological stance does seem, however, to extract a price in the form of a certain lack of flexibility, cautiousness, and a tendency not to take risks, as well as a proclivity toward self-criticism and feelings of guilt. To this description can be added traditionalism in matters of religious belief, conventionality in moral attitudes, and conformity to social mores [p. 250].

These similarities do not mean that blacks are homogeneous as a group. Jones cautions that characterizations about Afro-Americans must be made with the relevant socioeconomic, regional, and generational features kept firmly in mind. But there is the indication in these data that, although campus political activity seems to have quieted down in recent years, the evolution of assertive behavior continues among black students—a development that was accelerated by the civil rights activities in the black community during the late fifties and the sixties.

16. The linking of individual and group identity as seen in the Gurin and Epps and the Malcolm X material touches on an issue raised by Nobles (1973). He has suggested that Afro-Americans come from a historical tradition in which the emphasis is not so much on individual self, the "I," as in Western society, but on a group self, the "we." He suggests, "The African world-view suggests that 'I am because *we* are, and because we are therefore I am.' In so emphasizing, this view makes no real distinction between self and others [p. 23–24]." He goes on to argue that in Western thought self is defined in terms of the separateness and distinctness of the individual from others—in *opposition* to rather than in *apposition* to the group. The sense of "we" added to the "I" and "me" contributes a sense of "extended self" which is needed to fully describe the experience of the Afro-American. What needs to be made clear in this analysis, it seems to me, is that a sense of "we" does not obliterate a sense of "I." To take the tribal society as an example, even within the "we" there were different "me's." Some group members were men with their prescribed roles and tasks; some were women with their particular roles. Though all were competent, some warriors were more expert at running, some at using specific weapons, and the society probably took note of this and made use of different warriors in different ways. The individual and the group maintain a dialectic relationship. The black person can be seen in bipolar (or multipolar) terms as a unique individual who also takes important meaning from group definition. While "group mentalities" may be said to exist, "We must recognize that group intellects . . . occur because of the *conformity* of human intelligence to the premises which all individuals in a given group take to be collectively advantageous or the 'right way' to look at things [Rychlak, 1977, p. 306]." Conformity in this sense represents the individual act of taking the group norm as the guide for the person's behavior. "The

social norm is a mutual 'that for the sake of which' (premise) employed in common affirmation by all members of a discernible group . . . lending them a common sense of identity and commitment in life [pp. 305-306]."

Gurin and Epps indicate that the Committed Achievers were able to blend elements of individualized striving with a strong sense of commitment to group action. They pointed themselves toward occupations that they experienced as rewarding and that could potentially make significant contributions to the community such as in law and medicine. These would seem to be the people who blended a clear sense of "I" with a sense of "we." Those who were "activist," who had an equally strong sense of "we," but who had developed less of a sense of personal competence were less effective in college and not prepared to move on to more influential professional positions. These data support the idea that for group advancement an emphasis on "we" can usefully be a strong supplement to, but not necessarily a replacement for, a clear sense of self that guides personally meaningful life choices.

In addition, the Cross and Thomas kind of model suggests that too narrow a definition of "we" is also not necessarily the most desirable solution. The final stages desribe a sense of "we" that is more broadly defined. Malcolm came to a sense of "we" that included people who were not of black African heritage.

Chapter 6
The Wayward Self: Distortion and Repair

Some argue, and with good reason, that much of the personal stress for people in modern times can be attributed to societal disorder and social pressures. An unstable peace in an age of nuclear arms; racial strife in beleaguered cities; job scarcity for the unemployed and job dissatisfaction for many of the employed; declining certainty about ethical standards, these among other things—symptoms perhaps of a "sick" society (Fromm, 1955)—contribute to chronic tensions that can be the seedbed for severe emotional upset. With problems such as these surrounding us it would seem we don't need to look within the individual for explanation of mental disorder. But not everyone thrown out of work becomes unusually morose and begins to hear voices telling him he is bad, or withdraws from and neglects her children, refusing to talk to anyone. While many of our formulations about mental disorder must take the external conditions of living into account, concepts of disordered *personal* reactions cannot be eliminated.[1]

As we look at the psychological problems that black people may have, it is tempting to rest all the blame on the oppressive social conditions to which blacks are exposed. And this is an understandable and sometimes quite justifiable perspective. Racism does put an added burden on the psychological adaptation of blacks by presenting direct assaults on the sense of self and the self-activity of Afro-Americans. Since the earliest days of slavery, racist practices and ideology, extending beyond the individual behavior of white persons into the institutional structure and cultural mores of the United States, have had as their goal the dehumanization of black people (Kovel, 1970). Dehumanization involves first forming an idea of another living person as a "thing" and then acting on that person "so as to sustain one's dehumanized conception of him [p. 36]."

Although slavery as such is long gone, many of the attitudes toward blacks that grew out of that period of American history remain. Developing the belief out of their own psychological and economic needs that blacks are "no better than animals," white people have treated black people in ways that make it harder for the latter to develop their humanity (in fact whites also stunt their own growth by the efforts they sustain to keep black people down). In the terms of this book a dehumanized view implies that blacks are seen as not being capable of or entitled to a full sense of self-worth and competence or to an independent sense of agency that would help promote a sense of self-esteem.

Our concern here is particularly with some of the issues involved when the conceptualizing process goes so much awry that people find themselves unable to decide on or make satisfying and effective choices about which road of self-development to take, and experience along with this considerable anxiety, despair, and confused, sometimes strikingly bizarre thinking. Obviously there are many ways of looking at the facts and theories about mental and emotional disorder. Our goal here is not to catalogue disorders and their treatment in the fashion of an abnormal psychology text. Rather our purpose is to speak to issues of abnormal personality functioning from our humanistic perspective as these issues pertain particularly to racial group membership for Afro-Americans. (In this chapter we will use such terms as "mental/emotional disorder" instead of the more familiar term "mental illness" for disturbed psychological reactions. I have long been persuaded of the soundness of Thomas Szasz' argument that the use of the term "mental illness" has had some damaging consequences [1961]. Szasz rejects a "medical model" that the word "illness" suggests as the appropriate framework for conceptualizing the events of emotional disorder. Szasz' ideas agree with our basic humanistic position that behavior is guided by the person's conscious and sometimes unconscious *intentions*. This places responsibility primarily on the person rather than on some factor of sickness which overtakes the individual.)[2]

There is a legitimate call in recent years for innovations in mental health service delivery that is geared to taking account of the cultural diversity of people in minority communities (Smith et al., 1978). Jackson (1980) has suggested the need for being prepared to deal with the extended family system that a black client may live in as a way of dealing with the mental health problems of some blacks. The task of helping people to choose more effective paths of self development in life involves making available to people a variety of techniques and even different conceptual viewpoints. Fitting such techniques and perspectives to the individual client involves a clinical approach, the recognition of the uniqueness of the individual that exists along with the similarities of that person to other people. In other words, besides cultural diversity there is also a considerable degree of individual diversity among peoples of the same cultural background. A clinical approach is tailored to the individual's needs and uses theory and research about human personality generally, along with data about cultural group membership as an orienting point from which to reach out to understand the particular person. We shall be concerned in this chapter with some of the implications for emotional disorder and its amelioration that derive from the humanistic view we have adopted here. I will argue that humanistic perspectives in some of the traditional clinical approaches are a necessary though not sufficient part of understanding disturbed psychological behavior in Afro-Americans. In discussing psychopathology, traditional terms will be used as a way of raising issues that are consonant with our humanistically oriented discussion here. Although there are codified ways about how to categorize people's behavioral difficulties, culminating recently in the third edition of the *Diagnostic and Statistical Manual of Mental Disorders* of the American Psychiatric Association (1980), there is considerable controversy about the adequacy of such categories for *anyone,* let alone for minority group persons (Menninger et al., 1963; Schact & Nathan, 1977; Smith et al., 1978).[3]

ANXIETY AND DEFENSE

The process of daily living involves harmonizing needs and intentions with the limitations and opportunities posed by "reality." Defenses, what the noted psychiatrist Harry Stack Sullivan called "security operations," are of particular use in preserving a sense of equilibrium in one's life. When a person's personality organization seems to be threatened, for example, when a cherished aspect of a person's view of self seems to be under attack or is being called into question, that person is likely to experience "anxiety" at some level of awareness. Anxiety is the "state of apprehension and dread cued by threat to essential personal values, [to] the integrity of the personality, or to life itself [Korchin, 1976, p. 57]." At such a point the individual may resort to a psychological defense. As we noted earlier defenses operate to change one's awareness of a disquieting external stimulus or of a troublesome thought or feeling so that a person no longer experiences the anxiety.

Let's take as an example a man who, since early childhood, rather than become aware of forbidden angry thoughts at his younger brother, has come to *repress* such thoughts—keep them out of consciousness—and unconsciously to replace them with kindly, friendly thoughts and actions toward his brother and *all* men younger than himself all of the time. Adopting his parents' prohibitions in this regard he has developed his personality in this way so as not to run the risk of tarnishing his sense of self with fratricidal fantasies. Or, to take another example, suppose that a policeman speaks to a black man in what the latter perceives as a racially demeaning way. The man has a choice of retaliating directly or, for example, suppressing his anger and perhaps even forgetting for a while that the event had ever taken place. Taking one or another of the latter courses makes it more likely that he will be able to get on with other important tasks in his day and allows him to perhaps direct his simmering anger into social action groups working to improve police-community relations.

From one perspective defensive activity of this sort is another example of the kind of dialectical activity that is inherent to the human individual. We have described the dialectical mode, the capacity to consider a variety of other options in a given situation, as a part of human creative potential and an important mode by which blacks have sustained their sense of competence in a racist milieu. Through the act of defense an individual tries to reduce the sense of threat to manageable proportions by acting as if certain impulses did not exist or that they have other sources than their true ones, for example. In essence the individual imposes a (dialectical) alternative on the situation that attempts to resolve it, at least temporarily. This too is a part of the everyday creative activity of the human being. (Freud had many case examples and theoretical formulations illustrating the ingeniousness of people's defensive compromises. See G. Mahl [1969] for a thorough discussion of the classic psychoanalytic ideas about defense.)

However, this capacity can be a mixed blessing. The trouble with defenses is that their primary function is to blot out anxiety. If they work too well they tend to make a person's behavior in the world less flexible and adaptive. For example, it might be appropriate sometimes for the above-mentioned man to be stern and irritable with his younger brother's not infrequent cheekiness—both for his own and his brother's good. But his defenses won't allow that, and so his interpersonal relations and his personal development are less effective than they might be. Regarding the man who walked away from the policeman, because of the strength of his personal character overall (what psychologists call "ego strength"), he may well be able to function effectively on his job and be amiable with family and friends. On the other hand it may be that his anger is so great that although he did not show it very much to the policeman he "displaces" the expression of the anger to the form of irritableness and hostility towards his boss and family. Or perhaps although he "forgets" about the incident (represses it) his encounter adds to the general level of tension he feels about the racial and social class conditions that affect him, and his propensity for psychosomatic reaction—perhaps hypertension or an ulcer—may be aggravated significantly.

Sometimes a person's energies are so caught up in trying to keep anxiety out of awareness that adaptive efforts are noticeably strained or even distorted. Then we are talking about psychological disorder. The particular behavior patterns manifested are a result of a person's life history combined with the particular set of stressful circumstances. Different people would respond differently to the same stress; one person often responds differently to different kinds of stress. One might ask why a person would use behavior patterns that are socially maladaptive or seemingly personally distressing, patterns that don't seem to work adaptively. The answer is that such patterns usually *do* work, at least temporarily, in shutting off the experience of potentially severe anxiety—and that is what is crucial. In a choice between not being obviously socially awkward or not being so anxious, not being anxious usually wins, even at the expense of, for example, crippling phobias or time-consuming obsessive-compulsive rituals. Psychopathology or mental disorder, then, can be defined as disproportionate or inappropriate reactions to anxiety.

Throughout the book we have described the person as being active in creating the conceptual frames that are crucial to determining the understanding of experience. From the perspective here the same is true for psychopathology. Mental and emotional disorder also stems from an active conceptual structuring of events. However, when it is designed primarily to ward off anxiety at all costs, it becomes maladaptive. The point here is that the mentally disturbed individual is still actively trying to cope even though caught up in the tangle of disturbance. From one view the individual's behavior, even though objectively we call it "disturbed," seems to him or her to represent the best choice (s)he can make under the conditions as (s)he sees them, that is, as (s)he (actively) conceptualizes them. (Compare the discussion of this point in Chap. 2, p. 35.)[4]

MENTAL DISORDER AS DISTURBED SELF ACTIVITY

People in need of psychological help are not always the first to know it. However, when the individual does have insight into the need for assistance, the psychological state experienced is one that Jerome Frank calls "demoralization." Persons in such a state are

conscious of having failed to meet their own expectations or those of others, or of being unable to cope with some pressing problem. They feel powerless to change the situation or themselves. In severe cases they fear that they cannot even control their own feelings, giving rise to the fear of going crazy [1973, p. 314].

In previous chapters we have proposed that people have as a basic goal the maintenance of a positive self-esteem, a feeling about themselves that the organization of attitudes and strivings called self is in good order. Another way of putting the term "demoralization" is to say that people in a state of demoralization have exhausted the options they can see for sustaining a positive sense of self-esteem—or at least they feel they have exhausted such options.[5] Racism certainly operates to make it harder to find such options.

This characterization is like saying that people experiencing emotional disorder have a diminished sense of being able to meet their intended goals. Rychlak has applied his Causal Construct Scale to the analysis of such issues. In an earlier study Rychlak and Barna (1971) had shown that scores indicating emotional abnormality on the Minnesota Multiphasic Personality Inventory (MMPI) were strongly associated in a positive direction with endorsement of "substance" and "impetus" constructs. "Pattern" and "intention" constructs tended to be associated negatively with abnormality, that is, the more the endorsement of such proverbs the less abnormality in the personality test scores.

In another study he and a colleague found that a sample of men hospitalized with the diagnosis of schizophrenia tended more often to endorse proverbs representing "material-cause" themes than did a group of men hospitalized for nonpsychiatric disorders (Rychlak & Ingwell, 1977). This latter group tended to endorse "final-cause" proverbs. The greater preference for the intention-oriented proverbs among the nonpsychiatric subjects was taken to reflect their greater sense of being agents—active in their own lives, more in control of their affairs. The schizophrenic subjects on the other hand expressed a sense of being constrained by the nature of things around them with little sense of a reciprocal influence on the world.

This supports Frank's description of the demoralized person as one experiencing a sense of powerlessness. It is not so much that people suffering from various degrees of disturbance do not have intentions. From a psychodynamic view it is that important and pressing intentions, some held at unconscious levels, are in conflict with one another. The individual is not able to impose a kind of order and harmony on conflicting tensions for the purpose of achieving adaptive goals. All of us experience conflicts among our strivings; "ego strength" partly involves the capacity to concentrate our energies on a select set of goals and keep others subordinate. Such an organizing focus, embodied in a person's experience as a sense of self, is either missing or not in effective control in psychopathology. Perhaps another way of describing psychological disorders from our perspective here is to say that the individual has lost the capacity to generate adaptive alternative modes of handling the problems (s)he experiences.

RACIAL DIFFERENCES IN MENTAL DISORDER

To an important degree these issues are relevant to both black and white people; American blacks are prone to the same disorders that other groups are. What does their special racial situation add to this? It is conceivable that some kinds of disorders will be more emphasized than others among black Americans as a result of their collective cultural experience. Although the striving for some more effective level of self-expression exists everywhere in the black community, there is no question that this flame burns lower, and sometimes flickers out, for persons trapped in degrading social circumstances or victimized over generations by social and family pathology.

If there are special stresses such as racism that have an impact on black Americans it is reasonable to wonder whether or not blacks, especially working- and lower-class blacks, are more susceptible to mental/emotional disorder than whites. Are the rates of serious psychopathology different across racial groups? Although this sounds like a straightforward question, the answer is not so simple. Such kinds of queries are the province of "epidemiology," which is the discipline concerned with whether or not certain aspects of the population are more prone to certain diseases because, for example, of their gender, their occupation, their social grouping, or their geographic location. Having established such descriptive differences, one must then analyze the patterns to determine the often multiple causal factors involved. For example, the historically greater appearance of chest diseases (heart and lung disorders) in men can be associated with differential smoking rates and probably the stresses associated with differential occupational pressures. The increasing rates of such disease for women are being associated with increases in smoking and their increased entry into hitherto exclusively male executive professions. The epidemiologist seeks to establish the "incidence rate" of a disorder, that is, the number of new cases in a specified time, and the "prevalence rate" of the disorder, the number of cases present over a specific interval of time.

The reasons for asking questions about the incidence and prevalence of mental disorder ought to be to find out where mental health services are most needed, for one thing. Also such information could presumably be useful in identifying ways in which cultural groups respond differently to life situations and thus contribute to our knowledge of the human condition. However, another possibility is that establishing differences can contribute primarily to stigmatizing black people. For example, some writers have noted the contradictions in epidemiological descriptions of Afro-Americans (Thomas & Sillen, 1972). Some studies have found blacks as having more disorder than whites; others as having *less* mental disorder than whites. In either case a pejorative inference is drawn. In the former instance Afro-Americans are seen as having inferior ego strength; in the latter blacks are seen as being too simple to appreciate and be bothered by the stresses of life in a technological society: "In short, you're damned if you're ill, and you're damned if you aren't [Thomas & Sillen, 1972, p. 124]." Some prominent psychiatrists stated their belief that slavery, and later segregation, provided a stable situation for blacks. Desegregation and the consequent competition with whites, according to this notion, led to greater stress and mental illness. The fact that blacks streamed out of the "happy" South of the early twentieth century was explained by these being the "unstable" Negroes.

Even if one tries to do unbiased epidemiological studies the task is not an easy one (Kramer et al., 1973). One major problem has been that epidemiological studies were based on state mental hospital records, and people in different social groups have different access to the different kinds of treatments available in society. Thus, if there are more blacks in a given state hospital population over a period of time, that doesn't necessarily mean that more black people were seriously disturbed than whites. Lower class blacks ordinarily do not have as many other treatment alternatives to state institutions as whites do. It's likely then that illness rates based on state hospital data are spuriously inflated.

Further issues cloud the process of identifying the incidence and prevalence of mental disorder among blacks. Racial stereotypes on the part of community officials and even misunderstanding on the part of a person's peers and family can determine who gets counted in the mental illness census. For example, Brody and his colleagues (1967) investigated the case histories of a sample of 38 young black men, first admissions to a Maryland State Hospital. It became clear that many of these people had been candidates for psychiatric treatment—psychotic or chronically antisocial—for several years prior to contact. One of the principal agencies that had previous and often repeated contacts with them was the police. Even their families, confronted by frightening and aggressive behavior, often saw them as being more in need of control or needing discipline of their withdrawn and "lazy" behavior than in need of psychological help. At times the family and friends aware of the realities of prejudice were inclined to accept the complaints of the troubled person when he spoke of specific social injustices done to him. To the extent that socially striking symptomatology is an aspect of a cry for help, this delayed identification of mental disturbance typically required that black males had to "shout" louder and longer than did a white person.

> In a crude sense it seems likely that the police (as do other social institutions, e.g., schools, hospitals, employers, etc.) applied different standards to the behavior of middle class whites than of lower class Negroes. . . . The apparent tolerance of the urban policeman to psychiatrically disturbed behavior in lower class Negro men may also be coupled with a tendency to view it as the naturally expected consequence of the "lack of responsibility" of members of a simple or inferior race [Brody et al., 1967, p. 215].

Thus, accurately determining the presence of mental disorder among black people in white society is a complex matter. All the evidence may not be in but there seems to be good reason to think that actual mental health differences between "advantaged" and "disadvantaged" groups reflect differences in socioeconomic status rather than racial group membership (Robins et al., 1971; See & Miller, 1973; Warheit et al., 1975). Research studies on severe clinical depression, specifically, come to similar conclusions (Steele, 1977; Tonks et al., 1970; Warheit et al., 1973). (There are indications of qualitative differences in depressive phenomena between racial groups; we shall discuss some of these later.) In any event it does seem that a greater amount of severe psychopathology exists among the lowest social classes than among the more well-to-do.

Diagnostic Understanding

The question of the identifying of mental disorder in the black community leads naturally to the more personologically focused question of diagnosis; i.e., of how one goes about determining that a given individual is disturbed, or, granted that a person's behavior is disordered, what the nature of that disturbance is. This is the process of trying to "understand eccentric symbol performances." Diagnosis is a difficult and fallible activity. It rests on the skill and training of the diagnostician.[6] It depends on his or her ability to encourage the client to be open enough to be willing to reveal things that are painful and that indicate that (s)he can't handle life at this time, or it may involve the revelation of things that might lead to the client being hospitalized. It depends on the interviewer's empathic attitude and ability to establish rapport with the patient. (We shall have more to say about factors involved in establishing a helping relationship later in the chapter.) Under such conditions the client will begin to reveal himself or herself and allow the interviewer access to his or her mental life so that help can be given. This is difficult enough when client and mental health worker are of the same social class and ethnic background. It can be considerably more difficult when the two are of different backgrounds.

Over 20 years ago Hollingshead and Redlich (1958) pointed to the differential distribution of mental health services by social class—longer and more intensive talking therapies to the middle and upper classes, somatic and brief supportive therapies to the poor. Frequently being poor, blacks have perhaps been more likely to fall victim to this trend. But there is the added dimension of ethnic difference that many white professionals have had trouble bridging. Tomes (1976) cites various recent studies indicating differential attitudes toward blacks who present themselves for treatment. In one such study black men tended more than others to be denied access to a university-controlled inpatient treatment facility, usually a more prestigious kind of treatment unit (Weiss & Kupfer, 1974). Foremost among the reasons for their being barred were that these men were not seen as fitting the service's treatment model (for being verbal and insightful, for example), and they were also seen as being physically dangerous and sexually threatening.

While one kind of bias has been to see blacks as *more* disturbed than traditional services can handle, Lewis et al. (1979) report an opposite kind. In their clinical and epidemiological studies they found that there was a tendency to underdiagnose disturbed behavior in black delinquents, attributing aberrations to cultural factors:

Many black delinquent children referred for psychiatric evaluation to clinics, private psychiatrists and psychologists, and mental hospitals, were dismissed as characterologically [less severely] impaired in spite of what appeared to us to be clear evidence of psychotic or organic disorders. Symptoms that would have been recognized as pathological in white children or their parents, were ignored in black children [p. 54].

In one striking case a child, described as an intelligent and quite paranoid black youngster, was admitted to a private psychiatric institution where his aggressive and bizarre behavior was diagnosed to be the result of an epileptic disorder. (Paranoia is a disorder in which an individual experiences him- or herself as being victimized, persecuted, sometimes under attack from hostile outside forces or agents. The individual's response tends to be one of hostile defensiveness, vigilance, and sometimes combativeness.) However, he was transferred out of the hospital, eventually winding up in a correctional facility without clear mention of the neurologic disorder and was not given continuing therapy for that disorder or the concomitant psychological problems. It is likely that both disorders were controllable and deserved primarily a psychiatric rather than a correctional response. Thus, too often the problem for black clients experiencing severe personality difficulties is that such persons, youngsters and adults alike, are caught as it were between the Scylla of being seen as too disturbed for more prestigious interpersonally oriented therapies and the Charybdis of being seen as not really meriting psychological treatment—as simply manifesting "culturally appropriate" behavior or meriting incarceration.

These examples are raised to further the notion that if one has a clear conception of human behavior, empathic sensitivity to people, and a recognition of how cultural differences for a particular group tend to be expressed in interview or test situations, the process of coming to understand "eccentric symbol performances" can be carried on in ways that are helpful to Afro-Americans and relevant to their personal and clinical troubles.

An example of sensitivity to this issue is a study by Haimo and Holzman (1979). They used a scoring system developed for assessing the presence of "thought disorder" in the test records of a sample of persons including black and white schizophrenic patients and a psychiatrically normal control sample. The procedure involves evaluating thinking processes through the quality of the verbal productions on the Wechsler Adult Intelligence Scale (WAIS) and the Rorschach Test.[7] The authors were also especially interested in whether differences in language style of lower/working-class blacks made them more vulnerable to being diagnosed as manifesting thought disorder on these tests. They scored the protocols of black subjects in the standard way and in two other ways that explicitly took account of Afro-American speech styles. They found that there was a significant tendency for the standard scoring system to overdiagnose thought disorder on the intelligence test but not on the Rorschach. However, all measures of thought disorder, whether corrected for language style or not, significantly differentiated schizophrenic subjects from normal controls in the predicted direction—the schizophrenics showed more thought disorder. Thus the thinking disorder of the disturbed black subjects could be discerned. It indicates that relatively accurate diagnosis is not necessarily confounded by this aspect of cultural difference in blacks. Of course this does not mean that present systems do not need refining or drastic overhauling for people in general and minorities in particular.[8]

In sum, the implication of what I have been saying here is that when carefully studied there is not good evidence that the amount of mental disorder differs between blacks and whites when social class is controlled. It does suggest that the racial attitudes that poison our society in so many spheres can hamper the efforts of black clients to make themselves understood and get help in regaining a productive course of living. The tendency to see blacks as "too sick" or culturally inappropriate for talking therapies, or not really psychologically disturbed, may be a way not only of avoiding their own race and class attitudes on the part of white professionals but also of avoiding exposure to the intense feelings that black clients may want to vent toward them concerning their social and racial as well as their personal concerns. Black professionals can be as much a target for such resentment at first as white ones. But the mental health establishment must turn and face such feelings, helping clients to resolve those that are unrealistic and dealing straightforwardly in personal and in institutional practices with those that are accurate (Krebs, 1971; Waite, 1968). Actually the individual, group, or family treatment relationship and a secure well-run hospital setting when needed can be a marvelously therapeutic social and personal experience freed from the multiple pressures of the external world. This happens when the professional person makes the office or community setting a place where the minority client can feel well understood and fully able to express him- or herself. We shall look further at research bearing on this issue in our discussion of treatment.

SELF DISTURBANCES AND RACE

In this abbreviated discussion of race and mental health issues we will focus the commentary on problems in sense of self. As we have stated, the impacts of racism, though perhaps manifested somewhat differently according to social class and regions of the country, have placed a special psychological strain on the sense of self of the Afro-American as a capably active agent. Consider again the example of that psychologically normal man who had the encounter with the policeman. It may well be that this man's situation in life enables him to be a good and loving provider for his family. Yet at some level of awareness perhaps not fully conscious, perhaps within his conscious awareness for a brief period at least, he is very likely to experience a blow to self-esteem at this incident. Perhaps the history of what armed whites—whether police or not—have done to blacks, and periodically continue to do to them, momentarily becomes vivid for him. For a fleeting moment, along with his anger, he is likely to experience some self-doubt, some sense of inadequacy, some sense of vulnerability—the sense that he will be at the mercy of others and unable to exercise independent control over his own existence. From a clinical view, one that is not confined to any single racial group, the chronic intense experience of such feelings is central to pathological developments in the self (Kohut, 1977). In the extreme some of these disorders emerge in what are called narcissistic character problems.[9] In this terminology racism is an assault on the healthy egocentrism—a sturdy sense of self—in black Americans. As I have said before, doubts occasioned by the negative reflections from a racist society are usually kept in check. (Normal people experience such doubts in occasional fleeting thoughts or in dreams and nightmares giving evidence that such issues are indeed part of the psychic system.)

However, when a person's individual history has been troubled and/or when the weight of events becomes too crushing (s)he may develop clear psychological symptomatology; that is, the person becomes psychologically disordered. Then some of the things that the person ordinarily keeps out of the way come to the surface psychologically. Thus, to the extent that the psychological symptomatology of those black persons who become mentally disordered has admixtures of damaged narcissism, these may be exacerbated by racial pressures.[10]

Depression

What kinds of psychological experiences might trigger disturbances in a functional sense of self? Depression is one major source—derived from the experience of feeling in some ways unwanted and unacceptable.[11] A number of writers have suggested that along with the experience of anger and rage that we discussed last chapter, a widespread feeling of sadness, a kind of "cultural depression," is a part of the black individual's response to historical and current conditions in America (Comer, 1972; Grier & Cobbs, 1968; Poussaint, 1972). Florence Halpern, commenting on her clinical work with rural blacks in Mississippi in the late 1960s, noted that "reactive depression was almost universal [1973, p. 124]." Crain and Weisman (1972, pp. 86–87) report data from several studies that asked the question, "Taking all things together, how would you say things are these days—would you say you are very happy, or not too happy?" The indication was that blacks were twice as likely as whites to identify the category "not too happy" as applying to them.[12]

When Halpern indicated the widespreadness of "reactive" depression in her rural population she was referring to the responses of blacks to the oppressive external circumstances under which they lived. As pointed out in the last chapter, confronting such issues continually can lead to some chronic problems in personality functioning (Crain & Weisman, 1972). A particular problem that is worrisome is that of sorting out the meaning of white people's behavior. Is the white personnel officer's iciness toward the black applicant a habitual personal style? Is it due to the fact that she "got up on the wrong side of the bed" this morning—an attitude that she would display toward anyone today? Or does it reflect her racially prejudiced attitudes toward this black applicant? These kinds of issues have long been a problem for blacks living in some northern settings where racism was not always so blatantly expressed. In the South, for example, where whites pride themselves on cordiality and warmth, a harsh response towards a black had a clearly racial meaning. As the frank expression of personal racism becomes more muted in the South, perhaps the Afro-American's dilemma regarding how to interpret white behavior will apply there too. Such issues are not only depressing but can contribute to the suspicious, self-protective style in interpersonal relationships that was noted earlier and is a quite understandable stance for a person to take (Grier & Cobbs, 1968). This can be seen sometimes in the problems that a black person brings to therapy.

One 19-year-old black woman of working class background presented herself to a psychology clinic with marked feelings of depression and loneliness, continual feelings of anger toward people generally which she had trouble justifying even to herself, and problems with identity and lack of sense of purpose in life. Her personal history included strong feelings of having been neglected by her family, especially by her mother, leaving her with considerable anger and unfulfilled dependency longings. Her sense of mistrust of others and her expectation of not being treated kindly led her to look for racial insults from white co-workers where it was not really clear that such animosities existed. Being able to be clear about how much of her rage could be justifiably applied to her interracial contacts and how much was referrable to sources in her own particular family history was quite difficult and in and of itself depressing to her. The dilemma was made more difficult by the fact that it was frightening and saddening to her to acknowledge how furious she was at her mother whose approval she still craved. Further the shame she felt at revealing these things to her black female therapist made it difficult for the therapist to help her since she kept the therapist at arm's length, as it were, with her hostility, her missed appointments, and lateness to sessions, all of which helped her to avoid getting involved in psychotherapy.

Her sense of self was like a sensitive wound, bruised easily by events that had even a trace of reference to race or her personal worth, and this very problem for which she came for help kept her from letting herself get closer to her therapist. One illustration of her personality-based dilemma was that she was being seen in a clinic whose fees were extremely low. She was able to afford the fees but felt she wanted to take a vacation trip to the Carribbean soon—something she had long wanted and felt she owed herself. She couldn't afford to do this and pay for therapy and recognized a need for therapeutic help. She was angry with her therapist for not agreeing to see her for nothing. The therapist was seen by the client as not being sufficiently giving or sufficiently understanding of what she saw as real deprivations in her life (although she was earning a living wage currently). It seemed as if racial sensitivity had added to her more basic sense of fragility as a person to make her difficult to reach, even for a black therapist.

Depression as Hopelessness. Let's look further into the literature to try and understand depression and self disturbance in Afro-Americans. Classical psychoanalytic theory originally described the general psychological source of depression as stemming from anger that had been directed at a loved one seen as abandoning the subject. This anger now turned defensively against the self is the experience of depression (Freud, 1917/1957). Anger turned against the self may well be an element in many depressive episodes.[13] However, such a formulation does not seem fully relevant to the social dysphoria of the Afro-American. What is called for is a perspective that recognizes that racism represents a psychological assault on the sense of self. Another point of view, a more recent contribution to the psychoanalytic thinking about depression, is that of Edward Bibring (1953/1968). Though we do not have to be concerned about all of the implications of Bibring's formulation, it provides a more useful perspective for minorities. In discussing clinical depression as a human phenomenon he suggests that this state represents a feeling of helplessness and hopelessness with respect to achieving healthy, egocentric goals—goals that could be considered basic to human self-realization. He suggests that all persons normally strive to achieve at least three interrelated but conceptually separable aspirations in their personal growth. Expressed as central strivings or "wishes," these are:

> (1) the wish to be worthy, to be loved, to be appreciated, not to be inferior or unworthy; (2) the wish to be strong, superior, great, secure, not to be weak and insecure; and (3) the wish to be good, to be loving, not to be aggressive, hateful and destructive [p. 163].

Making progress toward such goals at least partly spells out the process of achieving competence as we have defined it in this book and it does so here in interpersonal spheres, not just in relation to the material world.

Depression in this view stems from the individual's perception that (s)he is unable, helpless, to achieve one or another of these cherished goals in psychological development. Depth of depression could be related at least partly to the degree that any of these achievements in personal living were seen by that individual to be beyond reach. (The idea that the experience of helplessness is basic to depressive conditions has received a considerable amount of supporting experimental investigation from an experimental psychology perspective [Seligman, 1975].) Now, racism in its personal and institutional forms in American society operates intentionally and perhaps sometimes unintentionally to thwart the achievement of such psychological goals for blacks where it can. In the effort to dehumanize blacks American society has portrayed blacks as being unlovable and unworthy. By intimidation and by limitation of social opportunity society has attempted to keep blacks from establishing the kinds of family and other institutional settings that would provide loving contacts and help them provide strength and security for one another. Society works directly to make blacks feel competitively inadequate by abridging educational opportunities and relegating them to dead-end menial jobs, for example. The frustrations in Afro-Americans stemming from these unfair hinderances have generated the kind of rage and despair that have made it harder for blacks to experience themselves as being good and loving. These are ways of characterizing the uphill struggle that blacks and other minorities have experienced psychologically. There are a number of variations in theory about how clinical depression comes about in general (Arieti & Bemporad, 1978; Gaylin, 1968; Scott & Senay, 1973). Some of these may apply to incapacitating clinical depression in Afro-Americans. Although greater helplessness among blacks does not show up in clinical depression, the milder, more pervasive "cultural depression" related to race may perhaps be best understood in terms of a formulation that emphasizes the degree to which society engenders a sense of helplessness and hopelessness regarding the achievement of basic human strivings. Since blacks do persist in their competence strivings, these feelings are relatively milder where personal and social circumstances allow a black person to overcome obstacles. Where circumstances are chronically defeating, the chances are that socially generated experiences of hopelessness come to be taken as meaningful at a personal level. Negative experiences that get associated with aspects of self related to racial group membership can spread to other aspects of self and one begins to believe them to apply to one's personal self. The individual then begins to develop conflicted feelings and ideas about the self and develops maladaptive reactions to protect the self.

This casts another light on the role the family has in trying to provide the black child a sense of self as agent, one who is loved, and who can find ways of making itself adequate and skilled ("strong and secure"), and thereby feel able to be worthy, loving, and giving to others. Thus, the quality of the "mediation" experiences in the family are important, to call on a term we used in Chapter 3. In this chapter the emphasis is more on emotional than on cognitive aspects of the mediating activity. The development of a cohesive core or "nuclear" self, one that provides the base for healthy personality functioning, comes about only in the context of parenting that is "empathic," that is, parenting that anticipates the child's needs and responds to them appropriately (Kohut, 1977). (We shall have more to say about empathy later.)

Typically the prototype of this kind of relationship is established in the interaction between the mother and newborn child in the feeding situation. The task of the minority mother is made more difficult because she has to help the child develop healthy facets of self and self-esteem in important areas related to racial self-evaluation as well as in broader aspects of personal self-esteem. The mother's (or parents') ability to take on these extra tasks depends on her own well-maintained sense of self. Where this is minimal or lacking the parent may feel affronted by the child's healthy efforts to establish an independent sense of itself. The family can become a punishing place where the child may have his or her sense of self torn down by the other family members (Gouldner, 1978; Rainwater, 1966). A number of writers tell of black parents feeling the need to teach children early to curb their verbal and physical assertiveness so that they will not endanger themselves in interracial situations. Often this is done out of love for the child but sometimes it may stem from a projection of the parents' own sense of worthlessness onto the child. To the extent that the black mother is aware of the potential effects of racial prejudice on her children, she can offset much of the impact of racism on healthy egocentrism. Kohut and Wolf (1978), in discussing early personality development in general, make a comment that applies to the situation for the black child and its parents coping with the racial situation. Granted that the child will be exposed to traumatic events

these events leave fewer serious disturbances in their wake than the chronic ambience created by the deep-rooted attitudes of the [parents], since even the still vulnerable self, in the process of formation, can cope with serious [traumas] if it is embedded in a healthy supportive milieu [p. 417].

When an individual's family background and early personal history have not provided a stable core of experiences from which a solid sense of self can develop, the individual frequently can with supportive experiences later in his or her development, spurred by competence strivings, compensate to some degree for early experience. Many theorists feel that early experience does set some limits to personality development, but even with such limits, many people with later remedial contacts with lay or professional people are able to do remarkable things in turning their lives into more productive channels. It is likely that sometimes, when help is not available to blacks to support their compensatory efforts, the way in which the social system routinely hinders a person's efforts at self-development may begin to reawaken in him or her the memories of a painful family setting in which that person grew up. Thus, the person may come to identify past injuries with present ones and react with psychological disorder.

Emotionality in Afro-Americans

In our consideration of disturbances in self-activity let's turn briefly to a topic that bears on our previous discussions in this book regarding affect. Halpern ventured the impression from her clinical contacts with southern rural blacks that "a tendency to hysteria was prominent" in those persons she saw with emotional problems (1973, p. 124). Hysteria is a neurotic disorder with a long and important history in psychodynamic psychology (White & Watt, 1981, Chap. 1). The most striking of the manifestations that have been focused on in hysteria have been the bodily symptoms—for example, paralyses, anesthesias—which do not seem to have somatic origins but rather appear to have origins in psychological conflict. Modern interest in hysteria has broadened beyond these kinds of "conversion" symptoms to a concern with the more pervasive style in a person's responding, the "hysterical personality." This pattern tends to be characterized by reacting to the world through emotional and impulsive responses rather than primarily by ideational or thinking responses (see Chap. 3, note 13). In its more extreme form one cluster of traits that has been identified clinically as typifying this style is that of a "fluid change in mood and emotion, excitable, episodically flooded with feelings [Horowitz, 1977, p. 5]."

It is not surprising that blacks might tend to develop a style that emphasizes emotional response to the world. Certainly much happens and has happened to them to justify sharp emotional response. (In considering Halpern's use of this category to describe black reaction styles we must remember that she worked with people from a certain geographical region—rural southern blacks. The tendency to see blacks as hyperemotional and impulsive has been used to stereotype them diagnostically. In wider samples of Afro-Americans which include urban and middle-class persons, a different picture might well be expected. Yet, without assuming that hysteria as a neurotic style characterizes blacks, her observation may be instructive.)[14]

The picture that some blacks present of emotionality and "impulsivity" may also reflect a cultural value placed on being able to manage life stresses actively. Block (1981) suggests that "the black culture stresses early in life the ability to 'do it.' Emphasis is placed on the active—managing difficult situations without showing stress [p. 179]." This observation is of course in line with the basic philosophical considerations of this book regarding active mastery strivings being present in the personality functioning of Afro-Americans. When a black person, whose circumstances over the years have taught a coping style emphasizing physical activity and intense feeling, stumbles psychologically and is at a loss as to how to proceed, the symptom picture (s)he shows may have "hysterical" (or as the current DSM-III manual phrases it, "histrionic") components.

Conversion hysteria, in which bodily or "somatic" symptoms are predominant, has been seen as a reaction pattern in lower class groups (Temoshok &

Attkisson, 1977). Such styles have been attributed not only to lower class black but also to hispanic groups. From a broader psychosocial perspective it has been suggested that conversion reactions have long been one way in which persons who experience themselves as having little social power in Western society can have influence and be attended to personally (Szasz, 1961). If hysterical disorders are somewhat more prevalent in blacks it may partly be a class-linked phenomenon.

There is an issue here that is relevant to our considerations of affective assessment. We noted in Chapter 3 that a tendency to bring personally based affective assessment to learning situations characterized black and Hispanic subject groups as compared to whites. This reflected a tendency of minorities to rely more than whites on the universal ability to conceptualize situations in terms of their positive or negative valence towards them. One is tempted to speculate that normally functioning persons with hysterical personality features, or beyond this, persons who are neurotically burdened hysterically, might be persons who rely more on responding to situations in terms of their affective assessments about them (in logical learning theory terms) and hence may have come to develop this facet of their response potential more. One implication would be then that emotionally or hysterically oriented persons in general will be more RV (reinforcement value) oriented than are "obsessive-compulsive" or ideationally oriented people. Such a notion could be tested rather straightforwardly in a research study. The implication would be, then, that blacks may carry the RV propensity with them into a number of situations as a personality style.[15]

Special Disorders in the Black Community

The group of mental disorders we have discussed are a selection from the traditional disorders and they pertain to persons in probably all ethnic groups in this country. Smith et al. (1978) call attention to special health problems that are important especially in lower/working-class black communities. They discuss briefly such disorders as drug addiction, hypertension, and alcoholism. The drug abuse subject is a quite complex one, as we all know. However, the raising of these topics of special, though certainly not exclusive, interest to Afro-Americans brings up another diagnostic issue that does not have wide discussion but is certainly of relevance to blacks. This is the notion of "masked depression" proposed by Lesse (1974). He points out that sometimes depression does not appear as an overt behavioral syndrome but appears first in other symptomatic guises, hence the term "masked." There can be various kinds of surface manifestations behind which an actual clinical depression exists, depending on the person's age, ethnic background, socioeconomic status, and hereditary and constitutional background. Of particular relevance here are drug abuse syndromes and apparent physical disorders which are among those he feels have especial frequency in adults. The fact that severe clinical depressions do not appear more among blacks than whites does not rule out the possibility that depressive response to social oppression may manifest in forms of behavior pathology other than frank clinical depression. It has long been known, for example, that alcohol is a widely used means of "self-treatment" for depression. The notion of masked depression, though not widely used, may have some value in understanding the effects of social pathology on blacks.

ISSUES IN PSYCHOTHERAPY

Let's turn now to a discussion of the repair of distortions in self-functioning, issues having to do with psychotherapy among Afro-Americans. There are many ways of conceptualizing the topic of psychotherapy. The term "therapy" is one borrowed from the medical perspective and it implies an intervention aimed at cure of an illness. Many researchers and practitioners in the field prefer to view psychological disorders and their amelioration from within the broad perspective of learning (White & Watt, 1981). In this view a disturbed individual has learned modes of behavior that get him or her through what (s)he sees as dangerous situations but at considerable cost to adaptive functioning. Psychotherapy, a "talking therapy," is aimed at helping people to be able to relax their defenses, reappraise their anxieties, and consider new options for behavior. (Of course some methods of intervening in emotional disorders *are* medical, that is, somatically oriented, such as electroconvulsive therapy for depression and drug therapy for various disorders. These are not psychotherapies. Also, in this discussion I am not including some of the methods associated with "encounter" groups that use, among other things, structured physical contacts as aids in helping people relax and reappraise defensive behaviors.)

Earlier in the chapter we noted that one aspect of emotional disorder is a diminution of the ability to bring one's intentions to bear on the world effectively. The aim of psychotherapy is to help an individual to regain a sense of being "back in the saddle" of his or her own affairs again, to borrow Gene Autry's old theme song. The goal is to restore the individual's capacity to organize intentions more effectively in guiding behavior, restoring effectiveness and competence to self-activity and at the same time enhancing the sense of competence and self-esteem. Psychotherapy is not the only way of achieving these goals, but it is one way. The terms "therapy" and "mental health," though borrowed from a medical context, are so much a part of everyday parlance that we will continue to use them here.[16]

The emphasis we are placing here continues to be on the individual and his or her symbolizing processes. Throughout this book I have focused on the importance of such a perspective. In essence what I am saying here is that psychopathology represents a derailing of symbolizing processes so that an individual goes off into unproductive or outright bizarre paths, or perhaps spends energy "spinning his wheels," as it were, going nowhere. Psychotherapy is an opportunity to help people free their symbolizing processes from unproductive and destructive ways of conceptualizing their world, so that energy can be turned to more constructive modes of living. Szasz in his continuing critique of psychiatry, *The Myth of Psychotherapy* (1979) makes a similar point about the overall meaning of this enterprise when he cites (on the fly-leaf of his book) Joseph Conrad's statement: "Strictly speaking, the question is not how to get cured, but how to live."

The focus on individual processes has come under fire in recent years from those who believe that the point of attack on mental disorder for minorities and the poor should be the community and social institutions rather than the individual. This argument has it that the pathology of oppressive social systems cause mental disorders and it is at the level of the social system that the major part of our resources should be directed. Some have even suggested that focusing on individual mental pathology and trying to ameliorate it without spending equal or greater energy on righting social conditions is a subtle form of blaming the victim (Billingsley, 1974). Further, it has been pointed out that there will not be in the near future—and may never be—enough trained human resources at the professional level to handle mental health problems on an individual or small group level. (See cogent discussions of this "community mental health" point of view in Korchin, 1976, and Smith et al., 1978.)

The need for changes in mental health delivery is real. This is partly because the poor are more at risk for severe mental disorder, and services are not reaching them effectively. However, this doesn't mean that clinical attention to the individual participants in the struggle should be abandoned. Emotional disorder is the outcome of the individual's encounter with the tasks of living. People of all classes negotiate those tasks effectively but a small segment of people of all social classes do not do so. Part of the critique calling for change in the kinds of mental health services delivered to the poor came from a view that the verbal abilities and capacity for insight into the personal styles of such persons were lacking. In response to this, Edelson's comment is appropriate:

I am reminded of the criticism . . . [leveled at] many psychiatrists for their interest in psychotherapy as a treatment modality, not only on the grounds of difficulties in making psychotherapy widely available or of our own inadequacies as psychotherapists in symbolizing and communicating with those carrying on these activities in ways different from ourselves, but rather on the grounds that psychotherapy is culturally appropriate to the verbal middle-class but inapplicable to members of the so-called lower socioeconomic class who, so it is claimed, do not value words. For them, then, pills and advice.

I wonder if it does not occur to such critics that a scarcity of language resources is not simply a preferrred life style but rather a serious handicap in living, and that an inability to symbolize emotional, physiological, and sensory experience is not incidental to psychological illness but may in fact doom an individual to it. When we psychiatrists are exhorted to use other culturally more appropriate methods than psychotherapy in treating the lower socioeconomic class citizen—to accept, to adjust, so to speak, to his level of functioning—are we being asked to abandon him to a life of sleepwalking in a twilight zone of quasi-consciousness, in which he must depend for relief of his pain solely upon the efficient manipulation of his body and his environment? [1971, pp. 118-119]

Such questions about capacity are beginning to drop away as some of the parameters become clearer about what lubricates the flow of communication between people. It is generally recognized now that verbalness depends on the situation in which people find themselves (Labov, 1972; Lerner, 1972). When lower class Afro-Americans feel comfortable and understood, they are quite expressive and reflective.

Such expressiveness can be seen in the dreams of blacks in therapy. One black man from an economically deprived childhood background, for example, dreamt of "Papa Doc," the President of Haiti at that time. His associations to the dream made it clear that he had condensed in this one symbol feelings about his father and similar ambivalent dependent feelings toward me, his therapist. I was, in one sense, a "father-figure" (a "papa") whom he usually greeted as "Doc." Another client's dream contained the image of a large dog with a grossly deformed spine lying on the floor of her childhood home looking up at her. It corresponded perfectly to her often expressed feeling during that period of being "bent out of shape," that is, quite unhappy and frustrated. In work with black clients of differing socioeconomic backgrounds and varying severity of psychopathology I have found them using beautifully expressive and apt metaphors to describe their psychological experience and using such material to make meaningful discoveries about themselves.

Psychotherapy with the Minority Poor

Are there data regarding the usefulness of psychotherapy to the minority poor? There are not many direct tests of this question but some findings are worth looking at. In one intriguing study, Barbara Lerner (1972) investigated the effectiveness of short-term, psychodynamically oriented therapy in an inner-city community mental health center. Her client group was a diverse sample. It included

a Black Muslim incapacitated by an illness that had no physical basis, a suicidal prostitute, a welfare mother who abused her children . . . a child molester fearful of the police . . . a factory worker who felt that people on television were ridiculing him and broadcasting his deficiencies, and so on [1972, p. 33].

Not all of the group were poor or black.

> The one thing all of these people had in common was a sense that something inside themselves prevented them from struggling effectively to realize their full psychosocial potential. None of them discounted real and often terrible external obstacles to such a realization, but all of them were dissatisfied with their ability to mobilize their own resources in the struggle against external obstacles [p. 33].

In her study Lerner used a variety of measures of therapy outcome and assessed a large group of client characteristics such as diagnosis, previous therapy and/ or previous hospitalizations for mental disturbance if any, race, social class, and other personality measures. She found that clients did improve with therapy and this improvement was not related to client characteristics. In other words, clients did improve in spite of factors such as class and severity of diagnosis which should have hindered them from profiting from this kind of procedure according to the typical clinical wisdom. Karon and VandenBos (1972) found that psychotherapy as compared to medication alone was an effective treatment of clients who were "primarily poor, inner-city, and black" and who were diagnosed as being schizophrenic. (This Michigan State Psychotherapy Project, as it is called, has been criticized by A. H. Tuma and P.R.A. May (1975), noted psychotherapy researchers in their own right; the critique has been rebutted by Karon and VandenBos (1975).

The Therapeutic Relationship

Granted that psychotherapy with blacks of varying classes can be effective, the question emerges as to what issues affect the therapy process favorably for the black client. To some extent that is part of the broader and longstanding question in the literature on psychotherapy as to how therapy works for anyone. The noted psychotherapy researcher Hans Strupp makes the establishment of a therapeutic relationship first of three "basic ingredients" of psychotherapy (1973).

Most people coming to therapy in a state of "demoralization," though wanting help, feel reluctant to expose to a stranger the sense of failure they feel about not being able to handle their problems independently. Part of the therapist's job is to create a relationship in which the client can dare to relax defenses so that the client can change nonproductive ways of conceptualizing and responding to life. This "helping relationship (patterned in significant respects after the parent-child relationship) [is] characterized by respect, interest, understanding, tact, maturity, and a firm belief in his ability to help [Strupp, 1973, p. 1]."

A key phrase to apply to this constellation of features would be "empathic understanding." Empathy refers to the ability to put oneself "in the other person's shoes" emotionally, while yet maintaining one's own identity and perspective. It involves trying to see another person's world, as much as one can, as that person sees it. This is an essential aspect of good parenting—being able to understand and respond to the child's sometimes inarticulately expressed needs not only for love and physical attention but also for discipline (lest the child's impulses run away with it). Thus, with respect to therapy, Kohut notes:

> Man can no more survive psychologically in a psychological milieu that does not respond empathically to him, than he can survive physically in an atmosphere that contains no oxygen. . . . The [therapist's] behavior vis-a-vis his patient should be the expected average one—i.e., the behavior of a psychologically perceptive person vis-a-vis someone who is suffering and has entrusted himself to him for help [1977, p. 253].

From the perspective adopted here the challenge to empathic understanding comes from the view that clients communicate about a number of different aspects of their strivings all at once reflecting different aspects of self being expressed. For example, a client came into my office for her session on a brisk winter's day and, spying the window open—the hospital's heating system was working overzealously—she stated emphatically: "I'm not getting *undressed* until you close that window!" At one level she meant she was not going to take off her coat in that (to her) cold office until the window was closed. At another level, less available to her awareness and reflective of her wariness about self-exploration, she was also saying: "I'm not going to reveal myself psychologically until I feel more comfortable with you." At a still "deeper," that is, more tightly defended, psychological level she was probably also making a comment that had overtones regarding sexual intimacy and nurturant physical contact consistent with hysterical character features in her personality makeup. (This does not exhaust the possible meanings in this comment, of course. Other ways of interpreting her statement are conceivable depending on one's theoretical orientation.) Thus, one sentence can be seen dialectically to have a variety of simultaneous, symbolic meanings. The tact and skill of the therapist partly involves understanding as many of them as possible to get a sense of what the client's concerns are and involves responding to the level the client is prepared to hear.

The ability to make these kinds of translations is essential to the dynamic therapies (Edelson, 1975) and one goal is to help the client do his or her own translations of thoughts and feelings so as to be able to awaken to more of what the self is about.[17] No therapist does this perfectly. Knowing what a client's words might refer to symbolically in his or her experience obviously makes this possible. When people already share this through similarity of cultural background they have a head start on the business of establishing a relationship.[18] This undoubtedly is a reason why private practitioners of psychotherapy tended to select as clients persons of their own religious-ethnic background (Catholic, Protestant, Jewish) more often than not (Henry et al., 1973). If persons do not share such potentials for communication, establishing a relationship is far less likely to go well. (This is not just a matter of cognitive familiarity. Rychlak [in press] reports a recent study by Heiskell in which the positive and negative RV [reinforcement value] ratings by subjects, who were responding as therapists might toward statements made by psychiatric patients, influenced the degree of empathy shown toward the patients.) When we add racial animosities and misunderstandings to cultural dissimilarities the potential for a widened gap between client and therapist is greater. The interracial therapy situation—and we are interested in this discussion in the black client/white therapist relationship, the most likely match-up for black clients in most sections of the country—becomes something of a microcosm of the larger society.

From the client's side it is understandable that (s)he might see the therapist as a representative of authority, the Establishment, the "Man"—more concerned about justifying society's positions than in empathic relating to the client and his or her actual troubles. The client, already reluctant to reveal him- or herself to anyone might feel especially guarded about opening up in an interracial situation to provide another example of how black folks "just can't make it." Such attitudes may not always be conscious, although for lower and working-class persons they are likely to be. Nevertheless they can be powerful determining factors in behavior.

From the therapist's side, Jones and Seagull (1977) suggest that white therapists may labor under a vareity of pressures. They may act from unresolved unconscious racial guilt feelings, making them less able to respond accurately to the needs of specific black clients. Or some therapists may unwittingly extend their wish to be helpful into needs for power and control and become paternalistic in their attitudes toward black clients. These authors do not argue that all white therapists experience such problems, any more than all white people handle the pressures toward racist expression in this society in the same way. Similarly, particular kinds of questions exist for black therapists. Racial pressures may foster unconscious attitudes in them that hinder their ability to be helpful to black clients on one hand and white clients on the other. A number of people have written about the kinds of issues that can arise in cross-racial therapies (for example, Friedman, 1966; Gardner, 1971; Jackson, 1973; Waite, 1968).[19]

Research on the Black Patient/White Therapist Interaction. Research on psychotherapy with blacks confirms the notion that "the nature and quality of therapist-patient interaction is a critical determinant in whether a black client continues psychotherapy [Griffith & Jones, 1979, p. 229]." A number of studies show that blacks drop out of therapy at a high rate quite early (see, for example, Sue et al., 1974; Sue, 1977). This is true even when at least some of the possibly relevant factors are controlled such as socioeconomic status and whether the client is seen by a professional person as opposed to a paraprofessional worker. Sattler (1970) cites studies of assessment, interview, educational, and therapeutic situations to show an inhibiting effect on the black client when the authority is white. Some research has found that "depth of self-exploration" in black clients was enhanced when those clients were seen by black interviewers (Banks, 1972; Carkhuff & Pierce, 1967). Griffith and Jones (1979) report a number of other similar studies in which clients expressed preference for black counselors or felt better understood by them. These reviewers note, however, that many of these kinds of studies have been therapy "analogue" studies (see note 19) and may well not reflect what the experience of therapy is like. They go on to point out, however, that since many black clients leave after the initial session these one-interview analogue studies may have some relevance to actual therapy situations in these kinds of instances.

When one looks at research relevant to these issues done in actual therapies, one finds that in a number of instances the white therapist-black client setting was not a hinderance to creating an effective helping relationship. In Lerner's study (1972) the therapists were white and half of the patients were black. In the Karon and VandenBos study of severely disturbed schizophrenics (1972) the therapists were white and two-thirds of the patients were black. Black patients from neurotic, middle-class populations have been shown to profit in cross-racial therapies also (Jones, 1978b; 1979). In the Jones studies there was the opportunity to compare outcome and details of therapy process in the four kinds of black-white/therapist-client matches. No differences were found in overall outcome—as a group clients in all the different therapies got better to about the same degree, as far as the measures used could tell. There were differences by racial match-up, however, in the process of the therapy relationships, that is, in the nature of the interpersonal dynamics that occurred between therapist and client.

What characteristics of the participants are necessary to the establishment of a truly helping relationship with blacks in such therapies? It has been typical, in the concept of "suitability" for psychodynamic therapy, to rest considerable responsibility on the client in principle if a helpful relationship can't be established. This criterion has by no means only been leveled at minority or lower class clients. There is some merit in this notion. If a client persists in not seeing him- or herself as a significant contributor to personal difficulties, or, while acknowledging this, does not feel sufficiently pained, or motivated, to change, such a person cannot be helped with psychotherapy—at least not while in such a frame of mind.[20]

However, Lerner designed her study to test the possibility that success in psychotherapy had as much to do with characteristics of the *therapists* as it did qualities in the clients. In addition to the considerable data that she had about clients she also got information about the therapists—amount of therapeutic experience, capacity for being empathic, their own experience of having been in therapy, and other data. Of particular interest were therapist attitudes indicating the degree to which therapists held democratic as opposed to authoritarian values toward clients.[21] Recall that she found that none of the client variables were related to psychotherapeutic outcome. People improved in therapy without regard to race, social class, previous hospitalization, and so on. To her surprise few of the therapist variables seemed to predict therapy outcome. One of those that did (as she hoped) had to do with degree of egalitarian values held toward the client. The more that therapists tended to believe in clients' right to autonomy and self-determination, that is, were free of authoritarian values, the more likely their particular clients were to improve in therapy. This effect was particularly strong for clients who were most disturbed. It makes particular sense that this latter group would be especially sensitive to such attitudes from their therapists since they are likely to be just the persons who do not get very tolerant or egalitarian treatment from society.

One of the things about an egalitarian attitude as described here is that it is one way of communicating the dialectic implication in therapy that it is appropriate to have goals different from the therapist's. The therapist is there to help the client achieve the goals that (s)he, the client, values. The effort with the black Muslim man, for example, was to help him achieve his goal of living the life of a Muslim more effectively. An egalitarian attitude respects the many approaches to effective living that individuals choose. (It is of course not being implied that this only characterizes a humanistic point of view. Behavior therapists, being humanitarian, also work to help their clients achieve their own diverse goals.)[22]

This result regarding egalitarian therapist attitudes was one of a very small number of significant trends from among a rather large number of other statistical tests that were not significant, so it requires replication. However, it calls attention to a possible factor involved in the creation of a helping relationship with minorities and the poor. Since it is likely that people will have egalitarian attitudes about groups they understand better, it is appropriate that therapists working with black clients get to know more about black people and the black community, as has been suggested by many writers (Griffith & Jones, 1979; Jones & Seagull, 1977). Smith et al. (1978) propose a "Therapist's Sensitivity and Minority Knowledge Style" which outlines ten guidelines by which white therapists can sensitize themselves to issues that can affect the way they address the "demoralization" of black clients as they come to psychotherapy.[23]

Affective Assessment and the Therapy Relationship. Speaking to the white therapist-black client relationship, Griffith and Jones (1979) note:

> The race difference appears to have its greatest impact early in treatment, particularly at the first encounter. If the white therapist can establish effective rapport at initial contact and build a therapeutic alliance in relatively rapid fashion, successful outcomes can be achieved with lower-income black clients, usually considered poor risks, and with middle-class black clients despite their initial sense of wariness and consequently slower movement in therapy [p. 230].

Perhaps logical learning theory can make a contribution to understanding how this works. Throughout this book we have discussed affective assessments as important determining factors in their behavior that people bring to situations. We have seen that the operationalized form of affective assessment, reinforcement value (RV), is a particularly important factor in the way minority group persons respond to learning situations. I suggest that such factors make a contribution to understanding the Griffith and Jones analysis. As I have suggested, the therapy situation is one naturally associated with the white "Establishment" for many blacks. This may automatically conjure up the specter of an authoritarian institution operating on the potential client to his or her detriment. The history of psychiatric treatment of blacks in this country does not refute this (Thomas & Sillen, 1972; Willie, Kramer, & Brown, 1973). But further, for many black persons when they have a problem, the consulting of psychologists and psychiatrists is not something that grows naturally out of their cultural experience. The professionals many people in the lower/working-class black community go to for problems in living are the spiritualists and astrologers, perhaps the ministers.

It is quite conceivable, then, that blacks (and probably other minorities, as well) would approach therapy situations leading, so to speak, with their affective assessment capacities. Rychlak explained the propensity of minority groups to respond with RV modes in learning situations as a way of dealing with a cultural situation they did not feel at home with. Similarly it may be that not only the defensiveness about self-revelation and self-exploration is operating for many blacks but a tendency to bring forward and be governed by their affective assessment processes as well. It may be that white clients, especially those of the middle class, are more comfortable with what they perceive initially, and, even if not, are less likely to let the negative affective assessments immediately override their faith, albeit tentative, in the therapist. It is not just that blacks, based on past experience, are expecting not to be treated well, although that is probably also a factor. This alone would only be an input from prior experience in the Lockean sense. But in addition the cultural unfamiliarity may heighten their tendency to rely more on affective assessments as a way of judging whether or not this is going to be a useful experience.

This may mean that the potential client will be more sensitive to initial difficulties in communicating that are bound to occur between strangers, especially when there are ethnic and class differences between them. And of course there will be times when the white therapist, being human, will not be sensitive to the black client. While a reliance on the affective assessment process is a natural thing, it may be detrimental in that it causes the potential client to shy away from a therapist who is well meaning and, given more of an opportunity, really could be helpful. But let's be clear here. This doesn't mean that black and other minority clients are to blame for this predicament. Falling back on the RV line of assessing comes partly from the society's having excluded these clients from a fuller feeling of being a part of the dominant culture and its institutions and practices.

It is the therapist's responsibility then to work to overcome this tendency in the therapy situation. The research we have discussed indicates that the therapist's attitudes and efforts can achieve this. While the black therapist has some advantage over the white therapist in this initial period presumably (holding constant other factors such as training and experience), (s)he still has to work hard, too, in helping the patient discover that this process can work for him or her. This conception supports the observation of some writers (Griffith & Jones, 1979; Block, 1981) that it may be important for therapists treating lower/working-class black clients to be more active than with the white middle-class client in communicating understanding in initial sessions of some of the client's pscyhological problems. Classical psychodynamic formulations on therapeutic technique have emphasized the value of minimizing early interventions by the therapist. Such a technique may lead the minority client to regard the therapist as not being sufficiently caring. And this would be consistent with the client's expectation regarding traditional authority. In addition the neutral therapist may be seen as one who has little to offer the client (Block, 1981). Similar points have been raised regarding therapy with the black students (Gibbs, 1975; G. Jackson, 1980).

In recent years, as part of community mental health approaches, the effort to reach underserved populations has involved taking the services to the clients by setting up small storefront facilities in the heart of lower class communities. To some extent this enables mental health workers to be available to help with pressing reality concerns that sometimes must be dealt with before attention can be given to underlying psychological issues. Sometimes home visits are a necessary part of the treatment approach toward severely disturbed and indigent persons.

Another way of trying to increase the client's comfort is by educating him or her to the process of psychotherapy. To some extent this is a part of the technique of psychotherapy in general. Some have proposed the use of "role induction" procedures (Frank, 1973) to give lower class clients without prior experience in therapy some sense of what to expect. In one kind of format such procedures involve one or more interviews conducted by someone other than the therapist giving the rationale of treatment, expectations about how the patient is to respond (in terms of talking about what is on his or her mind, for example), and what to expect of the therapist. Other methods have been used as well. Francois (1977/1978) reasoned that lower class black male adolescents referred to psychiatric outpatient facilities would be a particularly difficult group to keep in treatment. He devised a role induction procedure that involved showing subjects a brief film targeted, in the appearance and speech of the actors, at lower class black youth and depicting what therapy would be like. The design of this study was complicated, involving predictions about the effect of role induction, depression, and locus of control on his subject pool's response to psychotherapy. He found, as have others using some form of role induction process, that those experiencing the film continued longer in therapy than those who did not see the film. Other methods of helping blacks use therapy have been reported. The overwhelmingly larger part of psychiatric treatment of blacks goes on in settings staffed and controlled predominantly by white professionals. Some have developed group experiences for black patients led by black professionals designed to help clients express the racial feelings they have brought with them, which often do not get dealt with in these desegregated settings, and at the same time help them to disentangle racial from other personal issues with which they are having trouble. Bailey (1976) ran what she called a "Second Chance Black Family" group aimed at encouraging ward patients to deal more openly and directly with their feelings about race in the group process. The effort was to get patients to see that they did not have to run from the anxiety about their sense of self-worth into psychotic behaviors. Reports about other such efforts suggest that, though difficult to initiate and sustain, workers have had positive results in helping patients use the particular hospital's treatment resources (Davis et al., 1974; Smith & Gundlach, 1974).[24]

It is true that minorities and the poor need to have the oppressive conditions that have been fostered by social institutions lifted from them. Real and profound social change is called for—the kind that actually allows for equality of opportunity. But when people are also saddled with their own personally generated problems they are not in the best position to work for their own self-determination. The aim of therapy should not be to help people simply to get along and adjust to an unfair society, "playing more docilely and consistently with the loaded dice society hands them [Lerner, 1974, p. 52]."

What poor people reduced to a state of psychological impotence usually need is a restoration of their sense of personal power, which will ultimately allow them to join with their fellows in an organized group struggle for social change—one in which they will be less vulnerable and more effective. Generic psychotherapy is fully compatible with social change because it is an attempt to restore personal power—self-understanding, self-control, self-direction, and self-esteem— through the development of an honest, empathic, egalitarian relationship with another human being, the therapist [p. 53].

Of course individually tailored clinical approaches call not just for individual psychotherapy but for group, family, and/or vocational rehabilitation approaches among others as well that can be offered in inner-city community mental health centers (Smith et al., 1978).

In this chapter I have focused on some of the ways of describing behavior when self-activity has become distorted, self-defeating, and unproductive. The mental health service delivery system has not been very successful in meeting the needs of those Afro-Americans who could benefit from such help. Research has indicated that black clients in clinic settings are considerably more prone than are white clients to drop out of therapy early. This has not been because blacks are not potentially able to respond to the various treatment approaches available. It is partly because the mental health system has not been effective in adapting itself to the minority client. The task for mental health workers has been one of relating to Afro-American clients on their own terms, accepting their expressive styles and their special concerns and recognizing their basic human effort to free themselves of the demoralizing sense of not being able to control major aspects of their psychological life.

In general this process is easier where the cultural backgrounds of therapist and client are similar. In such cases the client more readily expects to be understood and is initially, at least, more at ease about self-disclosure. Usually, if the therapist is more familiar with the setting from which the client comes, establishing a therapeutic relationship is enhanced. However, it is clear, too, that black clients can make good use of a therapy relationship with a white therapist when in addition to being well-trained the latter is attentive to his or her own racial attitudes and makes the effort to learn about Afro-American culture and the black community. In any event, psychotherapeutic procedures can help black and other minority clients lift roadblocks to self-development by achieving a greater clarity in sense of self and enabling them to better carry out their competence strivings and intentions.

NOTES

1. In Chapter 2 we noted that in the normal course of events, in order to come to terms with the world, we create our "reality" through the exercise of our symbolizing (conceptualizing) capacities. We are all busily at work construing the import of the sensory events that confront us. As Harry Stack Sullivan noted, "From this viewpoint, it will be seen that any problem in psychopathology becomes a problem of symbol functioning, a matter of seeking to understand and interpret

eccentric symbol performances [1925–26/1962, p. 32]." Thus, as the individual fashions a sense of self by taking one "road" or another of self-development, the choices made may arise out of eccentric or unusual ways of conceptualizing things. The bases for some of the person's choices may be shut out of awareness so that (s)he comes to current situations with views influenced by unconscious conceptualizations of these events. I have suggested that racism poses special problems for Afro-Americans. I have characterized blacks as persons working hard to define themselves in ways that are dialectically different from the socially oppressive definitions applied to them. As such, Afro-Americans run a greater risk than people not under such racist pressures of straining adaptive capacities and "going off the deep end," as it were, in trying to find dialectical solutions to their societal situation. Thus from one perspective blacks have the special task of defining themselves in creative and productive ways against the odds stacked against them. But in doing so they must not allow the dialectic effort to become so intense that behavior becomes bizarre and ultimately self-defeating.

2. Although many of the persons typically identified with the modern humanistic approach to personality and psychotherapy, such as Rogers, Boss, and others (Rychlak, 1973), see themselves as being opposed to the psychoanalytic position, Rychlak has argued that the classic psychodynamic positions do have strong telic postulates central to their conceptions. Unconscious motivation, important to Freud, Jung, and Adler, represents one aspect of the individual proposing and often trying to pursue active intentions that are opposed (if the person deems it necessary) in dialectical fashion by other aspects of personality functioning (that is, for example, "defense" on the one hand vs. impulse on the other). When I use the term "humanistic" here I am referring to those aspects of theories about personality that emphasize the goal-oriented, symbolizing activities operating simultaneously at conscious and subconscious levels. For me, while this can include the self-designated "humanistic" theorists, it also includes important portions of the psychoanalytic theories (although as Rychlak points out [1973, 1977] Freud did not see particular value in dialectic descriptions of human mentality). For a summary blending of some of the more useful aspects of traditional psychodynamic notions and the phenomenological-humanistic views, see Korchin, 1976, Chapter 3.

3. The history of the study of abnormal psychology has yielded a kind of two-fold grouping of mental disorders in terms of the presumed origins of a particular disorder, namely, the psychogenic and the somatogenic. The psychogenic or functional disorders have their origin presumably in the disordered psychological processes of the individual—in a person's strivings and need patterns. A person's (learned) dread of crowded public places that restricts his or her life severely, agoraphobia, would be an example here. Somatogenic or organically based disorders have their origin in disorders of brain tissue, biochemistry, or other aspects of central nervous system physiology. The disorders of behavior stemming from poisoning the brain through alcohol abuse would be an example of a somatogenic disorder. The theories, backed up by some research evidence, that the two major psychoses, schizophrenia and affective disorder, are based in anomalies in genetic structure is an important modern somatogenic theory. The organic point of view stretched to cover all mental disorder is epitomized in the phrase attributed, I believe, to the Nobel laureate Linus Pauling, to the effect that "there is no twisted thought without a twisted molecule."

In this chapter we shall be concerned primarily with a psychogenic approach to disorder in keeping with our overall concerns with self activity which is a psychological process. However, the tendency to see two mutually exclusive domains of human behavior is consistent with Western culture's tendency to make a sharp philosophical distinction between mind and body. More and more we are coming to see that there is considerable interaction between these two aspects of human existence and a sharp distinction is not productive.

4. This is related to a fundamental point that Menninger et al. (1963) make in their book. They suggest, contrary to the standard position on psychiatric nomenclature, that all psychological disorder can be placed on a single continuum ranging from effective functioning on one end to severe psychological dysfunction on the other. In this view psychological disorders are similar in

quality but differ from each other in the quantity of disturbance, and range from relatively minor though perhaps continuing maladjustments to severely self-destructive behaviors. Each level of disorder, even a psychotic one, represents the effort to organize one's adaptive resources to maintain psychological survival and avoid the last level of disorder, that of giving up on life (examples that seem to fit this level are discussed by Seligman, 1975). Thus, one level of disintegration, let's say neurosis, while being *less* adapted than minor maladjustments (transient nervousness, irritability or bodily symptoms during a life crisis, for example) is still a *more* integrated level of functioning than explosive homicidal outbursts or psychosis. In Menninger's view, then, psychological adaptation is the active effort to maintain the best possible balance of functioning—the "vital balance"—under the given circumstances of personal intentions and environmental limitations. Such a position is in contrast to those who argue that severe mental disorder, especially, only represents the intrusion into functioning of less well-organized processes when the higher processes are disrupted. In other words, the higher order processes are unable to do the usual job of active organizing of the lower processes.

5. People may manifest a variety of degrees of personality disruption in a state of demoralization. These may range from "neurotic" to "psychotic" degrees of disorder. Historically the term neurosis has referred to a range of the less serious forms of disorder in which an individual's difficulty in balancing internal need pressures with environmental expectations is such that the person has to resort to defensive maneuvers that hamper efficiency, but that allow the person to carry on daily living fairly well. For example, a woman who harbored since childhood a fear of her aggressive and hostile impulses developed the need to wash her hands and continually check to see that the stove was out so as to be sure that she or no one else would be contaminated by germs or hurt in a gas explosion. She remained unaware of anger as the source of her compulsive behavior and generally did her clerical work on the job and her household duties adequately, although the psychological symptoms were becoming more and more of a nuisance because she had to take increasing amounts of time to go through her ritual checking and washing behaviors. All of us have areas of our lives that are less well adapted than others—so much so that in this age of super "sophistication" about psychological matters some are inclined to call the nonpsychiatrically disturbed person "normally neurotic."

There have been cogent criticisms of the term "neurotic" (see White & Watt, 1981). The latest edition of the American Psychiatric Association's diagnostic manual does not use the term "neurosis." Those disorders formerly called neuroses in the previous editions of the manual are now put under headings that are more descriptive of the major symptom features, such as "anxiety disorder" (which would fit the woman struggling with her hostility), "somatoform disorders," and "dissociative disorders." The term "neurosis" is still being used out of habit to refer to this relatively milder though personally troubling range of mental disorders and I will continue that fashion here.

The term psychosis refers to the more severe set of mental disorders marked by disruptions in the ability to appraise reality and to distinguish what is true about the world and what is a figment of one's imagination. Consider a man, generally depressed and reclusive, with longstanding deficiencies in his ability to relate to other people, who comes more and more to believe that people "have it in for him." He has always had a vivid imagination and an active fantasy life, and now he comes to the certain conclusion that the group pof people he sees on the street corner beneath his window this morning are plotting to do away with him. That they are planning to kill him is *possible*, but *improbable*. He, however, for reasons of personal psychological history and perhaps factors in his constitution, believes that the thing he had imagined has in fact come to pass. Here we can see the human dialectical thinking process having gone awry. In other words, one of the many possible alternative (and in this case unlikely) conceptualizations that one might consider about the street scene below has now become an actuality for this poor man. In the most widely accepted psychological view of schizophrenia it is the greatly unrealistic and/or bizarre thinking that primarily characterizes the break with reality. In the other major set of psychotic disorders, the "affective" disorders—the manic and depressive disorders—the individual's mood or emotional state leads him or her to think or do highly irrational and unrealistic—and sometimes very dangerous—things.

6. Some argue that diagnosis is a dangerous activity and one that should not be conducted. They argue that trying to put a label representing a diagnostic category on people's behavior limits the understanding of people and creates expectations and stereotypes based on the diagnostic abstraction rather than based on the actualities of the person's particular life and behavior. So in one frequently cited piece of research psychiatrically normal subjects who got themselves admitted to hospitals with diagnoses of schizophrenia were kept in hospitals although they were careful from then on to exhibit no behavior that was unusual (Rosenhan, 1973). The process of diagnosis was seen to cloud understanding rather than enhance it. Furthermore, recent criticism has suggested that there are biases in the minds of diagnosticians that make for inaccurate diagnoses of lower class and minority clients, and even white females. Psychiatric and psychological diagnosis is usually done in a face-to-face interview situation often supplemented by the use of personality tests. These tests vary in their format ranging from some that can be given in group formats to others that must be given in an individual situation. There is considerable literature on intellectual assessment of blacks as we have seen in Chapter 3. In general there is much less written about the assessment of personality functioning and of psychopathology in blacks and other minorities. This is partly because the clinical interpretation of some of the most widely used of these tests such as the Rorschach Test (see note 7) and the Thematic Apperception Test (telling stories to a series of pictures) is based on rather complex theories of personality. The validity of these procedures has not been easy to pin down by the usual methods of quantification for the general population or for minorities. On the other hand more has been written about the potential for racial bias in the widely used MMPI, but it would take us too far afield to deal with that or other issues of personality testing with minorities here (see Gynther & Green, 1980; Powell & Johnson, 1976; Pritchard & Rosenblatt, 1980a; Pritchard & Rosenblatt, 1980b; Smith et al., 1978).

It is true that diagnostic categories are best seen as ideal types that are rarely seen in pure and unmixed form. From this perspective they should be seen as ways of developing hypotheses about a person's behavior for further more specific investigation. It is also true that categorizing behavior has been used to put people into conceptual "pigeon holes" without due regard for their individual uniqueness, but I would argue that this is mostly a function of the way diagnostic activity is all too often carried out rather than a cogent criticism of the need for some kind of diagnosing activity Schectman, 1977).

Actually, diagnosis represents a way of conceptualizing events, that is, putting an order or frame on them. In Western society at least, some kinds of behaviors tend to occur more frequently together—for example, emotional lability and an impulsive orientation to the world—than they do with other behaviors, e.g., emotional lability and a meticulous concern for facts and details. This tends to justify groupings of some sort. Such clusterings are broadly useful in that they might give a therapist a sense of whether under pressure a person might tend to do something ill-advised or on the other hand whether (s)he might tend to be overly hesitant and indecisive. To a relatively young field of knowledge, such as abnormal psychology, events—"reality"—present themselves much as they do to the newborn, as a "blooming, buzzing confusion." It is inevitable that people must organize the data presented to them in some way or another in order to proceed. The activity of diagnosis is a particular case of what everyone has to do within a cultural context to come to know the world—we have to conceptualize it, in the humanistic sense. This does not mean as a field that we should rest too comfortably on any set of categories at which we have arrived. I am not suggesting that current diagnostic systems are satisfactory. There is much room for improvement in the way we carry on the activity of trying to understand the behavior of troubled individuals in general. Also, in the process of seeing a client, we should not be locked into the initial understanding (conceptualization) that we have of a particular person as we seek to help him or her. A diagnostic category, as the state of understanding of a given phenomenon, should be seen as a relatively temporary crystallization, a way station, to be abandoned as we develop better ones, in the *process* of coming to understand behavior. This means mental health professionals, trying to diagnose persons from other quite different backgrounds from their own, need to know as much as they can about the culture of the client and how that may affect the way that person might express him- or herself in interview or on tests. Phillips has suggested a diagnostic scheme that tries to take into account an individual's social competence as well as his or her dysfunction (1968). This would be consistent with the theme I am advocating in this book, although his theoretical perspective is different. (See also Sugarman's [1978] advocacy of diagnosis from a humanistic and humanitarian perspective.)

7. The Rorschach is the personality test that requests the subject's associations to a set of inkblots. Personality features are evaluated not only on the basis of what a person sees in the blots but also how (s)he expresses what is seen in the blots. "Thought disorder" is felt to be a hallmark of schizophrenic thinking marked by unconventional, unrealistic, illogical ways of thinking about events and stimuli. It can usually be indetified rather readily on psychological tests such as the WAIS and Rorschach (Johnston & Holzman, 1979; Weiner, 1966). Consider, for example, a subject who on the WAIS defines the word *winter* as "the ice house of the North wind," and does so without a "tongue-in-cheek" attitude or without the explicit intent to be metaphorical. If such kinds of productions amassed on this and other tests—psychologists usually do not draw such conclusions from a single response—we would have pretty good evidence for thinking disorder.

8. Block (1981) argues in her recent discussion of cross-cultural counseling that, while similar psychological principles apply to blacks as to whites, Afro-American clients tend because of their group history to accentuate different behavioral dimensions and may well respond differently to diagnostic and treatment situations. For example, she notes the reported tendency for blacks to be diagnosed paranoid schizophrenic more than whites. This may reflect the wariness and reluctance that black clients feel about disclosing themselves in cross-racial situations. Such guardedness, although characteristic of persons experiencing forms of paranoid psychosis, may often reflect the kind of vigilance and self-containment that blacks have had to develop as a means of survival historically (Grier & Cobbs, 1968). Failure on the part of the clinician to understand this may contribute to inaccurate conclusions about the presented behavior.

Raskin et al. (1975), while finding that black and white inpatients were quite similar in depressive symptomatology, also found in their sample that blacks tended to be diagnosed more as schizophrenic and whites as depressed. They suggest, as did Brody et al. (1967), that this may be because many blacks do not arrive at psychiatric facilities unless their behavior has dangerous or strikingly bizarre features. This partly reflects the feeling in black communities that you really have to be "crazy" before you go to a "shrink" or a mental hospital. This does not mean that one should not use the interview and test procedures to try and learn more about the black client's world. It means one must understand the cultural context in which the client's responses emerge.

9. In recent years a considerable literature has developed on disorders in sense of self and "narcissism" which for some theorists include the problems called "borderline" conditions (e.g., Chessick, 1977; Kernberg, 1975; Kohut & Wolf, 1978; Perry & Klerman, 1978). The term "narcissism" has been used not only to characterize features of individual personality functioning but also as a description of important aspects of American society (Lasch, 1978). Obviously we are not able to discuss these issues in depth from a clinical or sociological perspective. We have noted at various points in this book that attention to the quality of one's self-contributions to behavior, one's choices, is a necessary and desirable attitude in life. Blatt (1980) suggests the term "egocentrism" for normal self-oriented concerns and goals. Drawing on the thinking of Piaget he notes that egocentrism itself shows developmental stages over the life span. Blatt restricts use of the term "narcissism" to clinical phenomena. As such it refers to a defensive retreat from mature interpersonal relationships as a way of protecting a vulnerable and frail sense of self. (Grier & Cobbs [1968]), from a traditional psychodynamic perspective, discuss damaged "feminine narcissism" in the black woman as an effect of racism.) Although most blacks are not clinically disturbed I would suggest that such clinical language is useful in discussing some of the negative (often unconscious) pressures that the racial situation imposes on blacks, or other minorities and the poor. No person is perfectly adjusted, and understanding more about the nature of the impacts on our lives can help us deal with the tensions we experience.

10. There are specific features of a person's behavior that as a cluster would merit a diagnosis of "narcissistic personality disorder." Some of these center around such tendencies as preoccupations

with a sense of self-importance; fantasies of unlimited power, success, or ideal love; interpersonal relationships marked by exploitativeness, lack of empathy, or sense of entitlement (A.P.A., 1980). Even when such focal symptoms are not prominent, the buffeting by racism increases the risk of defensive retreats taken in order to shield the self. Thus, problems in sense of self can also manifest in low self-esteem and chronic though not incapacitating depressive feelings. A person may have a disturbance in the sense of identity not just in the area of sexuality but as well in an inability to settle on a sense of personal direction. Difficulties in sustaining gratifying, intimate interpersonal relationships may stem partly from a sense of secret shame over the person's feeling of unworthiness or from a fear that one's insignificance as a self makes one vulnerable to control by others (a feeling that might well fit the experience of the minority poor). Such symptoms per se are certainly not unique to blacks and they may well not be experienced by the black client as being related to racial experiences. Further, severe psychological symptoms of *any* kind for anyone are often accompanied by an underlying sense of inadequacy. I am suggesting, however, that weakened defensive functioning as is present in emotional disorder may also expose other psychological difficulties that may have come as a result of racism. I am not suggesting here either that all black clients manifest similar disorders or that they have developed similar personality responses to racism and other aspects of living. What I am suggesting is something that bears on psychotherapy with blacks. As we shall see, in order for therapy to work, a client must be willing to disclose intimate and painful aspects of themselves. The special reluctance that a black client may feel to do this with even a black therapist may come partly from the need (s)he has to defend the self against the hurts continually directed at him or her by the social scene.

11. The term "depression" is actually used in several ways. In common parlance it refers to the emotion of sadness that is common to us all. To be able to experience sadness after certain kinds of events is a sign that one's reactions are healthy. However, when the depressive response becomes unusually prolonged or intense, or seems to emerge without an external provocation, we begin to speak of clinical depression. Such a symptom syndrome includes not only low self-esteem and deflated mood, sometimes accompanied by irrational guilt feelings, but in the more severe forms may include striking changes in eating habits, marked loss of interest in the environment, sleep disturbances, and suicidal ideation. Clinical depression can be the primary disorder in its own right or depressive symptoms can occur secondarily to other emotional disorders such as schizophrenia or lesser problems such as the anxiety and personality disorders. Frank's concept of demoralization clearly implies that a feeling of dysphoria accompanies the sense of inability to cope effectively.

12. Clinical depressive reactions can range from the relatively mild in which an individual is able to carry on his or her activities, though with something of an emotional albatross around his/her neck, to the severe reactions and syndromes just mentioned in which an individual is not able to function effectively and may even be psychotic. As pervasive a phenomenon as depression is among mental disorders, it has not been easy to classify. It used to be the fashion in diagnosing clinical depression to differentiate between "reactive" and "endogenous" depressions (Becker, 1977). Reactive depressions were seen to be more amenable to therapeutic intervenion. Depressions of neurotic severity were labeled reactive although transient psychotic reactions were also recognized. Most writers have been willing to see the reactive depressions as attributable to psychological conflct. The more severe syndromes that people show, however, sometimes seem to occur without reference to identifiable precipitating events. These were called the endogenous depressions, the implication being that these disorders spring from some aspects of the individual's physiological functioning that has gone askew (Akiskal & McKinney, 1975).

When psychological writers talk about the "cultural depression" presumably found among Afro-Americans, they are not talking primarily about the endogenous disorders, but rather the chronic mood responses that are reactive to the external crises of social oppression imposed on them. The Crain and Weisman data may well have referred to such relatively mild, though chronic, reactions. When blacks do become clinically depressed there is some evidence of different qualitative features in the clinical picture between blacks and whites. In one study there were differences on the dimension of hostility with black men and women rating themselves higher than whites (Raskin et al., 1975). Specifically, blacks rated themselves higher on items tapping "negativism" (e.g., "When someone is bossy, I do the opposite of what he asks"; "Unless someone asks me in a nice way, I won't do what they want") and on items tapping "internalization." Internalization in this case refers to turning one's anger inward against oneself. Such a mechanism has the defensive purpose of preventing anger from escaping that would subject one to retaliatory punishment by a more powerful protagonist. (An example of an internalizing item would be "When I am mad or angry, I usually get a headache.") Black men reported themselves more ready to strike back verbally or physically when provoked. These tendencies to be more inhibiting (internalizing) or externalizing of hostility than whites are quite consistent with the conclusions drawn by Crain and Weisman (1972) that racism has forced a different handling of aggression among Afro-Americans.

Although the amount of severe clinical depression does not necessarily show racial differences, there is evidence that suicide, the lethal extreme of depressive mood, has increased in the past decade and a half among inner-city black youth. Hendin (1969) tends to locate susceptibility for suicide in the "matriarchal" black family. However, Seiden (1970) and Breed (1970) emphasize the blocking of opportunities for individual autonomy by the racist society rather than in the black family alone. Of course even using a system-blame approach, individual dynamics play a necessary part in the particular response to the depressing external circumstances.

Seiden suggests further that especially in recent years what looked like assaultive and potentially homicidal acts by young blacks may in some instances have stemmed from suicidal impulses. He cites the example of one young black man who started a commotion, seemingly with little cause, in a bar frequented by armed, off-duty policemen. He was shot to death as he pointed his loaded weapon at one of the officers. It is plausible to think that this man provoked his shooting. Seiden speculated that perhaps some "young black revolutionaries are at least partially motivated by a wish to be martyred, to be ceremoniously executed, to be destroyed in violent confrontation in which they may momentarily respect themselves and from which they will gain posthumous status [1970, p. 28]." Such feelings presumably came from the intense sense of being confronted by hopeless odds in the society. Rather than passively submit, "better to go down in an explosion of masculine rage . . . and physical power [p. 26]." Again, although individual personality factors would contribute to choosing such an alternative, Seiden's primary emphasis is on the highly stressful load placed by American social structure on black youth, especially those of lower and working-class status.

13. The notion of self-hatred among minority group members has been a popular topic (Sarnoff, 1951; Poussaint, 1972). Bailey has suggested that what she has called Ethnic Self-Hatred is an observable component of the complex of symptoms in black psychotic patients (1976). (Many of these persons were probably schizophrenic.) She devised a scale to rate the degree of ethnic self-hatred behavior displayed on a psychiatric ward and she developed a scale for assessing ethnic self-hatred attitudes. She found that the patients evidenced significantly more ethnically self-rejecting attitudes than did a control group of nonpsychotic ward personnel. Further, those patients that showed more generally psychopathological ward behavior also scored higher on her measure of ethnic self-hatred behavior. She took her results as evidence that self-hatred plays "an important and central role in the emotional disturbance of black psychotics [1976, p. 1424-B]." Bailey seems to come very close to saying that ethnic self-hatred, fostered by a dehumanizing society, is a specific cause of psychotic behavior. While such social forces make a contribution, it seems safer to say that some black persons with disturbed personalities and weakened defenses give more open expression to extreme feelings of what we might call "adaptive inferiority (Pugh, 1972)" with regard to racial self-concept. It is often the case that psychotic persons express in bold relief the experiences that others keep out of awareness or resolve effectively in their daily living. Put in terms that we used in Chapter 2, it is likely that these persons were unable to separate an extremely disturbed notion of racial self-concept from personal self-concept, as relatively normal Afro-Americans have been able to do.

14. In this regard Warheit and his colleagues (1975) found that while most of the racial difference in the mental health scales they administered disappeared when social class was controlled, on one

scale, differences remained. These items tapped the degree to which people were bothered by phobias. Blacks, particularly black women, scored higher than whites. A phobia is an intense and irrational fear of a situation, an object, or act and falls into the class of a neurotic level of disturbance. A phobia is irrational in that the thing feared actually represents only a small danger. Almost anything can become a phobic object or situation for an individual—fear of closed in places, fear of crowds, and fear of flying are familiar examples. An analysis of the items used on this scale suggested that the greater presence of phobias among blacks reflected something about the everyday realities to which they are exposed, especially in inner-city communities, in terms of bodily injury and threat from strangers. Warheit and his colleagues acknowledge that factors specific to blacks' particular social situation may not account for all the difference between groups but it is an important issue to take into account. The greater incidence of phobias in Warheit's sample (made up of blacks from the southeastern part of the United States, incidentally) is in line with Halpern's observation about the prevalence of emotional reactivity in the symptom picture of the black persons with whom she worked.

15. Many black Americans take pride in what appears to be a greater expressiveness with regard to their feelings as compared to some Euro-American groups. Some blacks feel this stems from the African cultural heritage. Rychlak emphasizes in his discussion of RV (reinforcement value) preferences that the affective assessment capacity is not a learned style, that is, a product of sociocultural "input." All groups bring affective assessment potential to life at birth. How it is expressed later is a function of learning and circumstance but the capacity is not. The implication of black/white RV differences as personality characteristics might be that a philosophical heritage that emphasized oneness with nature as in many African cultures (see Chapter 1, note 1) may have supported a more direct response to the world along affective assessment lines than those whose world view makes a sharp distinction between human beings and their rational mind on the one hand and the rest of nature on the other. It may be that people of African heritage have maintained as important the capacity to respond to the world with affective assessments than have people from other cultural groups.

16. Among the differences in approach to psychotherapy the ones that concern us most here are those between psychodynamic and behavior therapy approaches to emotional disorder. A major distinction is that psychodynamic approaches depict much of behavior as stemming from unconscious motives and forces. (The terms psychodynamic and psychoanalytic are somewhat interchangeable. I prefer the term "psychodynamic" here because the term "psychoanalytic" is often associated primarily with Freudian theoretical notions—appropriately so since the many variants in modern psychoanalytic approaches issue from Freud's work. I want to be more inclusive of other related approaches than the term psychoanalytic might appear to be.) In this view, emotional disorder stems from unconsciously motivated distortions of reality (Silverman, 1974). Psychopathology, then, can only be fully remediated when such distortions are recognized and changed. Such distortions presumably have developed as a way of reducing intolerable anxiety. The fact that distortion has occurred and still operates unconsciously to color the present situation is what makes them so powerful and so hard to change. From the humanistic perspective we might describe a distortion as a conceptualization, a structuring of reality in a way that keeps a particular sense of self intact and free from anxiety but that nevertheless in this case doesn't really square with socially constructed reality. So, without realizing it, a man responds to his wife's (in reality) reasonable demands as if they were those of his domineering mother, at least as he remembers her. The therapeutic interventions in psychodynamic psychotherapy are aimed at helping the client become as clear as he can on what the unconscious conceptualizations may be (e.g., wife = mother) that have been governing his actions and he is then in a better position to strive to put other conceptualizations into effect in behavior. It is in this sense that Edelson says, "Psychotherapy is a process that increases the capacity of its participants . . . to attain voluntarily a state of becoming more fully awake [1971, p. 117]." This is akin to the notion of what the family can contribute to the child's self-development in making it more aware (see Chap. 2, pp. 40–42).

Behavior therapies assume that an individual's current maladaptive behavior was learned as a way of reducing the anxiety aroused by a particular trauma or because the consequences in the environment produced by a particular behavior are rewarding. This is why the behavior persists, i.e., becomes a habit. No assumption is made that there are a set of unconscious conceptualizations held by the person that sustain the behavior. The therapeutic interventions in the behaviorist tradition are aimed at getting people to unlearn maladaptive habits by, for example, helping them to associate low anxiety (relaxed states) with feared situations or to associate negative and unrewarding connotations to the old habits among a variety of techniques.

Some would argue that behavior therapy approaches are more appropriate for Afro-Americans than traditional psychodynamic approaches (Hayes, 1980; Smith et al., 1978). My perspective would be that any *theory* that leaves out the role of the conceptualizing activity of the individual is inadequate to deal with the situation of Afro-Americans—or any human beings for that matter. On the other hand, many of the techniques used by behavior therapists may well be quite useful to blacks. There are trends abroad these days to attempt to integrate behavioral and psychodynamic points of view, and Afro-Americans can certainly benefit from these developments (Silverman, 1974; Wachtel, 1977).

It is customary to see psychoanalytic, behaviorist, and humanistic points of view as all differing from one another. But the humanistic position being advanced here is close in certain ways to the psychoanalytic. The notion of a conceptualizing mind guided by conscious and unconscious intentions and using the dialectical meaning inherent in symbols for the purpose of adaptation and for defense—principles basic to psychodynamic thinking—are central to the kind of humanisitc approach being adopted here.

17. The question of what happens when psychotherapy works is still unresolved. This is a particularly thorny issue in view of the large number of differing theoretical approaches which all seem to have legitimate claim to at least some success. Chessick (1969) suggests a view that I have found persuasive and that is consistent with the ideas being developed in this book. In effect he suggests that various approaches to psychotherapy can be viewed as different internally consistent ways of conceptualizing psychological issues. A person gets "better" in therapy when (s)he learns the therapist's way of conceptualizing events and applies them to life so as to live more competently. The test here is that the client is in fact able to achieve a more effective functioning of the self and has not simply slavishly adopted the therapist's style in order to please the latter. Therefore different therapists may work well with different persons. Rychlak puts that from within the teleological perspective:

> I think we could show convincingly that it is not "the" ideology which matters but "the" affirmation of *some* meaningful premise "for the sake of which" behavior can be organized and enacted that is the real therapeutic vehicle. It does not matter whether the client affirms a Freudian, Adlerian, Jungian, Binswangerian, Rogerian, or Kellyan premise regarding life. All of these formal-cause "reasons" for how to behave can prove successful to the life adjustment of any one of us [1980, p. 10].

Some persons are not as able to make sense of one kind of conceptualization, say a Freudian one, but may be able to make sense of a Jungian one. It may also be of course that a particular therapist because of his or her personal style and/or background is able to establish a relationship where other therapists have failed and thus the client is willing to relax the "resistance" to accounting for his/her life in the new model that the therapist suggests.

This has implications also for the much-debated question regarding the contribution to psychotherapeutic progress of gaining conscious "insight" into one's difficulties. Psychodynamic therapies have tended to imply that finding "the" origin of an individual's disturbance is necessary. What is being implied here is that "gaining insight" into one's difficulties involves learning a way to put one's self activities (intentions)—some of which one becomes newly aware of in psychotherapy—into a framework that "makes sense." Therapists often recognize that a client in intensive psychotherapy may resolve a specific problem even when (s)he is not clear on a specific insight into the self regarding that problem. This may be because even when a client is not able to fully acknowledge an issue as having been continually characteristic of him- or herself—and when there is good reason to believe that it is true about him or her—just the chance to discuss and experience hitherto suppressed or repressed material related to the conflict sometimes helps the individual to put it into perspective. In other words, the individual becomes better able to master these feelings—perhaps use a more mature set of defenses to handle them.

18. Of course creating a helping relationship is not the only aspect of the therapist's activity. Strupp (1973) suggests that as a second "basic ingredient" or condition of successful psychotherapy the therapist uses a well-established relationship as a kind of influence or power base, as it were, to encourage the client to reappraise defensive behavior, develop new conceptualizations, and try out new ways of acting. In the process of doing this the therapist may use "(a) suggestion (persuasion); (b) encouragement for openness of communication, self-scrutiny, and honesty . . .; (c) 'interpretations of unconscious material,' such as self-defeating and harmful strategies in interpersonal relations, fantasies, distorted beliefs about reality, etc.; (d) setting an example of 'maturity' and providing a model . . .; (e) manipulation of rewards [p. 1]."

19. Abramowitz (1978) in response to the Jones and Seagull article takes sharp issue with the idea that "black patients receive an appreciably less than fair shake from white therapists [p. 957]." His demurral comes from clinical analogue studies and from clinical judgment studies. The former are those in which subjects are not real patients and the interview is not an actual therapy session, but rather it is an interview situation in which the participants are asked to role play a session for the purposes of the research. The clinical judgment study is one in which trained clinicians (usually) evaluate a bogus case profile on several dimensions posed by the researchers. The judges are then compared for their degree of bias, for example, in the kind of diagnosis made or their feeling about the hypothetical patient's suitability for therapy. Abramowitz concludes that such data do not support a picture of negative racial expectations on the part of white clinicians toward blacks. However, he also notes that these kinds of studies do not provide compelling data. "The protocol [to be evaluated] is predetermined, the presumably evocative stimulus person is represented only skeletally, and the rater knows that his or her reactions are being monitored and do not have interpersonal consequences [1978, p. 958]." In other words, the therapist rater can give the socially acceptable response without that necessarily reflecting what his or her behavior would actually be like in a real therapy situation. Jones and Seagull didn't say that blacks must necessarily receive bad treatment from white professionals. However, they and other writers point out the pitfalls that therapists may run into on account of being products of their culture. We shall turn presently to studies of actual therapy situations.

20. As the third of his essential conditions for therapeutic change Strupp postulates that what is called for is a client who is able to profit from this kind of help. This does not refer to those qualities that critics of psychotherapy often list about successful clients, that they are young, attractive, verbal, and only moderately disturbed. For Strupp, as suggested in his first condition, the therapy situation is one that has strong elements of a benign parent-child interaction—one in which a helpful, more knowledgeable authority attempts to guide a temporarily less expert and more dependent client. Thus, the kinds of clients who can best be helped are those who are open to letting themselves be influenced by such a figure. "Psychotherapy is potentially useful when the client has remained responsive to parental-type influences, and it is essentially futile where such receptivity has either never existed or has been severely frustrated (Strupp, 1973, p. 3)." Sense of self grows out of family situations. The discussion in Chapter 2 pointed out that there have been strong sustaining influences in the black family historically. This would certainly indicate that blacks in general have the kind of background that is compatible with this condition that Strupp poses.

21. "Authoritarianism" (Adorno, et al., 1950) refers to a much-studied constellation of traits among which are attitudes of political and social conservatism associated with ethnic prejudice. This is an attitude cluster that researchers not infrequently attempt to assess in therapy clients, the typical prediction being that more authoritarian clients would do less well in psychotherapy. However, Lerner reasoned that in addition the presence of democratic-egalitarian as opposed to authoritarian values would be a particularly relevant dimension to assess in the therapist. "In the present study, it was hypothesized that the degree of authoritarianism initially manifested by clients would have no effect on outcome but that the degree of authoritarianism manifested by therapists

would have a marked effect, with less authoritarian therapists achieving significantly better results [1972, p. 88]." She devised her own scale since the widespread familiarity among social science professionals with the "F Scale," as the authoritarianism measure is called, would have made it useless with this group. Examples of some of her items were, "If they had had a successful treatment experience, most political radicals of both the right and the left would change their views on society and its ills" and "Involvement of the poor in programs planned for their welfare is essential, but, because they are mainly oriented to immedaite gratification, it is unrealistic to give them top level decision-making powers in planning such programs because long range goals would inevitably suffer [p. 89]." Responding that one strongly agrees with such statements would presumably be toward the authoritarian side.

22. A further word about authoritarianism and "authority" is in order. Because the therapist should not be authoritarian does not mean (s)he does not possess authority. Fromm, in his book *Man for himself* (1947), makes some conceptual distinctions that I have always found useful. He distinguishes between "irrational" and "rational" authority. Irrational authority is concerned with power over others. "This power can be physical or mental. . . . Power on the one side, fear on the other, are always the buttresses on which irrational authority is built [p. 9]." Its aim is to perpetuate itself and maintain others in subordination. In the political sphere the model is dictatorship. It is based on perpetuated inequality between authority and its object.

Rational authority by contrast stems from competence. The respect accruing to such a person stems from particular skill or knowledge that the authority possesses. This person's power lasts as long as (s)he competently helps those who entrusted him or her with a particular task. The relationship between authority and object is one of equality as persons; the difference between them is with regard to expertise in a particular field. In some instances the aim of the rational authority is to balance out the differences, at least somewhat, by imparting the skills to those who do not have them. The model here is of a teacher or therapist. Indeed the therapist begins with expertise about technique and soon develops knowledge about the client that the latter keeps out of consciousness and hence does not "know." Eventually however, the client gains knowledge about the self and ideally uses the kinds of techniques the therapist has taught to continue to gain self-knowledge on his or her own. The client becomes the rational authority about him- or herself. Fromm proposes that one who holds power through irrational authority represents an authoritarian stance. One who has power on the basis of rational authority is "authoritative."

It is partly in this sense that therapy partakes of a parent-child interaction. Strupp (1973) as we have seen suggests that clients in therapy are yearning for a benign and gratifying parent-child relationship. To greatly condense one view of the therapy process, the therapist with an egalitarian attitude offers a loving yet rationally authoritative relationship that substitutes for the less rational ones the client experienced in his or her life and thereby encourages trying out new and more mature behaviors in life.

23. It is useful here to consider the work of a group who have developed a variant of psychoanalytic theory which they call "Control-Mastery" theory (Sampson, 1976). It is a view of psychotherapy that is similar to competence notions that we have been advancing in this book. These writers suggest that clients presenting themselves for psychotherapeutic help, though feeling demoralized, actually bring a set of active (unconscious) coping strivings that are blocked more or less temporarily. According to this theory, while unconscious, unrealistic conceptualizations are hinderances to an individual's adaptation to reality, the client also comes to therapy with the wish to master these maladaptive urges by gradually bringing them to consciousness where (s)he can get better control over them. A fundamental tenet of the Control-Mastery view is that "a patient's most powerful unconscious motivation is to solve his problems." In the therapy the client unconsciously attempts to use the relationship to develop ways in which to make such problems more conscious

in order to increase his mastery over them. The patient must do a great deal of work to overcome the [anxiety] he would face were he to experience a mental content he had warded off by defense. He does this work by attempting to create with the analyst a relationship that would protect him from this danger (Sampson, 1976, p. 257).

A part of the therapist's growth-inducing, egalitarian attitude in Lerner's terms might well be the belief in such a mastery motivation in even severely disturbed, lower class persons.

24.   One of the key skills to be learned for blacks in interracial situations is that of separating hostile from assertive impulses and knowing when to express one or the other of these feelings. Some people cannot be assertive *for fear of* being hostile; others seem often not to be able to be assertive *without* being hostile. As we have seen, various studies have suggested that historically blacks have been kept from expressing the rage they have experienced in productive ways. It is likely that in the Crain and Weisman (1972) typology those blacks high in Internal Control (with its emphasis on inhibiting aggression in this sample) and low in self-esteem or assertiveness (the "accepters") could have profited from some "assertiveness training." Those high in assertiveness and low in Internal Control (the "militants") perhaps needed some help in expressing themselves in ways that the Establishment could respond to usefully. One of the aims of a mode of behavior therapy called "assertiveness training" (Lanyon & Lanyon, 1978) is to teach people how to stand up for themselves and advance their legitimate interests without necessarily being hostile or destructive. It involves discussion with the counselor or therapist, "role playing" in the counseling sessions, directive encouragement from the therapist, and repeated efforts in the real life situation.

Donald Cheek argues in his book *Assertive black . . . puzzled white* (1976), which he labels "a black perspective on assertive behavior," that a different approach to assertiveness training is necessary for most blacks. He notes that as blacks have recently become more assertive in their expression of self, whites have been puzzled that blacks were impatient with the pace of change. "What do you want?" was the injured question addressed to blacks in the sixties and early seventies. Cheek's approach to assertiveness training is to help blacks learn to switch language codes and behavioral styles in shifting from a black-black to a black-white interpersonal situation. He notes that what comes through as assertive in one setting, for instance, an all-black setting, may be seen as hostile in an interracial setting by a white person.

> Because of the many pressures on a black person . . . there is difficulty in finding the assertive manner of expressing oneself that is both comfortable (not giving up one's black dignity and pride) and effective (manages to get the message across without *undue* harm). The usual black response in a state of anxiety has either been passive or aggressive—either say nothing or become loud, threatening and abusive. For whites, but particularly for blacks, assertiveness is a social skill. It can open the door for many who occasionally need or want to "play the game." This doesn't mean that they must "sell out," act white or become a "handkerchief head." It means increasing choice and options in terms of ways of communicating honest feelings. It increases the repertoire of responses and makes one less subject to exploitation [Cheek, 1976, p. 65].

His approach may have particular value for students on white campuses who come from lower- and working-class backgrounds and who are prone to "withdrawing" styles or to a sole use of "separationist" or "assimilationst" styles (Gibbs, 1974).

References

Abramowitz, S. I. Splitting data from theory on the black patient-white therapist relationship. *American Psychologist,* 1978, **33**, 957–958. (Comment)

Adorno, T. W., Frenkel-Brunswik, E., Levinson, D. J., & Sanford, R. N. *The authoritarian personality.* New York: Harper, 1950.

Akiskal, H. S., & McKinney, W. T., Jr. Overview of recent research in depression. *Archives of General Psychiatry,* 1975, **32**, 285–305.

American Psychiatric Association. *DSM-III: Diagnostic and statistical manual of mental disorders.* (3rd ed.) Washington, D.C., 1980.

Ames, R. A. Protest and irony in Negro folksong. *Science and Society,* 1950, **14**, 193–213.

Amidon, E., & Hunter, E. *Improving teaching: The analysis of classroom verbal interaction.* New York: Holt, Rinehart and Winston, 1966.

Anastasi, A. *Psychological testing.* (4th ed.) New York: Macmillan, 1976.

Arieti, S. *Interpretation of schizophrenia.* (2nd ed.) New York: Basic Books, 1974.

Arieti, S., & Bemporad, J. *Severe and mild depressions.* New York: Basic Books, 1978.

Bachman, J. G. *Youth in transition, Vol. II: The impact of family background and intelligence on tenth-grade boys.* Ann Arbor, Mich.: Institute for Social Research, University of Michigan, 1970.

Bailey, S. T. Ethnic self-hatred in black psychotics (Doctoral dissertation, City University of New York, 1976) *Dissertation Abstracts International,* 1976, **37**, 1423–1424B. (Univeristy Microfilms No. 76-21, 155)

Baldwin, J. A. Theory and research concerning the notion of black self-hatred: A review and reinterpretation. *Journal of Black Psychology,* 1979, **5**, 51–78.

Banks, W. C. White preference in blacks: A paradigm in search of a phenomenon. *Psychological Bulletin,* 1976, **83**, 1179–1186.

Banks, W. C., McQuater, G. V. , & Ross, J. A. On the importance of white preference and the comparative difference of blacks and others: Reply to Williams and Morland. *Psychological Bulletin,* 1979, **86**, 33–36.

Banks, W. M. The differential effect of race and social class in helping. *Journal of Clinical Psychology,* 1972, **28**, 90–92.

Baratz, J. C. Teaching reading in an urban Negro school system. In F. Williams (Ed.), *Language and poverty.* Chicago: Markham, 1970.

Baughman, E. E. *Black Americans: A psychological analysis.* New York: Academic Press, 1971.

Becker, J. *Affective disorders.* Morristown, N.J.: General Learning Press, 1977.

Bernstein, B. A sociolinguistic approach to socialization: With some reference to educability. In F. Williams (Ed.), *Language and poverty.* Chicago: Markham, 1970.

Bibring, E. The mechanism of depression. In W. Gaylin (Ed.), *The meaning of despair.* New York: Science House, 1968. (Originally published, 1953)

Billingsley, A. *Black families in white America.* Englewood Cliffs, N.J.: Prentice-Hall, 1968.

Billingsley, A. The struggle for mental health. In D. A. Evans & W. L. Claiborn (Eds.), *Mental health issues and the urban poor.* Elmsford, N.Y.: Pergamon Press, 1974.

Blatt, S. J. Remarks prepared for discussion of symposium on "Narcissism: A Cross-Discipline Dialogue" at the annual meeting of the American Psychological Association, September, 1980.

Blatt, S.J., Wild, C. M., & Ritzler, B. A. Disturbances of object representations in schizophrenia. In D. P. Spence (Ed.), *Psychoanalysis and contemporary science*. Vol. 4. New York: International Universities Press, 1975.

Block, C. B. Black Americans and the cross-cultural counseling and psychotherapy experience. In A. J. Marsella & P. B. Pedersen (Eds.), *Cross-cultural counseling and psychotherapy*. Elmsford, N.Y.: Pergamon Press, 1981.

Bond, J.C. *Brown is a beautiful color*. New York: Franklin Watts, Inc., 1969.

Bortner, M., & Birch, H. G. Cognitive capacity and cognitive competence. In S. Chess & A. Thomas (Eds.), *Annual review and progress in child psychiatry and child development*. New York: Brunner/Mazel, 1971.

Boykin, A.W. Experimental psychology from a black perspective: Issues and examples. In W. E. Cross, Jr. (Ed.), *The third annual conference on empirical research in black psychology*. Washington, D.C.: U.S. Department of Health, Education, and Welfare, National Institute of Education, 1977.

Boykin, A. W. Psychological/behavioral verve: Some theoretical explanations and empirical manifestations. In A. W. Boykin, A. J. Franklin & J. F. Yates (Eds.), *Research directions of black psychologists*. New York: Russell Sage Foundation, 1979.

Brand, E. S., Ruiz, R. A., & Padilla, A. Ethnic identification and preference: A review. *Psychological Bulletin,* 1974, **81**, 860–890.

Breed, W. The Negro and fatalistic suicide. *Pacific Sociological Review,* 1970, **13**, 156–162.

Brody, E. B., Derbyshire, R. L., & Schleifer, C. B. How the young adult Baltimore Negro male becomes a Maryland mental hospital statistic. In R. R. Monroe, G. D. Klee & E. B. Brody (Eds.), *Psychiatric epidemiology and mental health planning* (Psychiatric research report No. 22). Washington, D.C.: The American Psychiatric Association, 1967.

Caplan, N. The new ghetto man: A review of recent empirical studies. *Journal of Social Issues,* 1970, **26**, 59–73.

Caplan, N., & Nelson, S. D. Who's to blame? *Psychology Today,* November 1974, 99–104.

Carey, P. M. Black women—a perspective. *Tenth-Year Anniversary Commemorative Monograph Series,* Vol. 1, No. 3. New York: New York University, Institute for Afro-American Affairs, May 1979.

Carkhuff, R. R., & Pierce, R. Differential effects of therapist race and social class upon patient depth of self-exploration in the initial clinical interview. *Journal of Consulting Psychology,* 1967, **31**, 632–634.

Cazden, C. B. The neglected situation in child language research and education. In F. Williams (Ed.), *Language and poverty*. Chicago: Markham, 1970.

Cheek, D. K. *Assertive black . . . puzzled white*. San Luis Obispo, Calif. Impact, 1976.

Chein, I. *The science of behavior and the image of man*. New York: Basic Books, 1972.

Chessick, R. D. *How psychotherapy heals: The process of intensive psychotherapy*. New York: Science House, 1969.

Chessick, R. D. *Intensive-psychotherapy of the borderline patient*. New York: Aronson, 1977.

Clark, C. Black studies or the study of black people? In R. L. Jones (Ed.), *Black psychology*. New York: Harper, 1972.

Clark, K. B. *Dark ghetto*. New York: Harper, 1965.

Clark, K. B., & Clark, M. P. Racial identification and preference in Negro children. In G. E. Swanson, T. M. Newcomb & E. L. Hartley (Eds.), *Readings in social psychology*. (Rev. ed) New York: Holt, Rinehart & Winston, 1952.

Cohen, R. A. Conceptual styles, culture conflict, and nonverbal tests of intelligence. *American Anthropologist,* 1969, **71**, 828–856.

Cole, M., & Bruner, J.S. Cultural differences and inferences about psychological processes. *American Psychologist,* 1971, **26**, 867–876.

Cole, M., & Scribner, S. *Culture and thought: A psychological introduction.* New York: Wiley, 1974.

Coleman, J.S., Campbell, E. Q., Hobson, C. J., McPartland, J., Mood, A. M., Weinfeld, F. D., & York, R. L. *Equality of Educational Opportunity,* U.S. Department of Health, Education and Welfare. Washington, D.C.: U.S. Government Printing Office, 1966.

Coles, R. *Children of crisis: A study of courage and fear.* New York: Dell, 1967.

Comer, J. P. *Beyond black and white.* New York: Quadrangle, 1972.

Comer, J. P., & Poussaint, A. F. *Black child care.* New York: Simon & Schuster, 1975.

Cook-Gumperz, J. *Social control and socialization: A study of class differences in the language of maternal control.* London: Routledge, Kegan & Paul, 1973.

Cooke, B. G. Nonverbal communication among Afro-Americans: An initial classification. In R. L. Jones (Ed.), *Black psychology.* (2nd ed.) New York: Harper, 1980.

Crain, R. L., & Weisman, C. S. *Discrimination, personality, and achievement: A survey of northern blacks.* New York: Seminar Press, 1972.

Cross, W. E., Jr. Black family and black identity: A literature review. *Western Journal of Black Studies,* 1978, **2,** 111–124. (a)

Cross, W. E., Jr. The Thomas and Cross models of psychological nigrescence: A review. *Journal of Black Psychology,* 1978, **5,** 13–31. (b)

Dansby, P. G. Black pride in the seventies: Fact or fantasy? In R. L. Jones (ed.,) *Black psychology,* (2nd ed.) New York: Harper & Row, 1980.

Davis, M. I., Sharfstein, S., & Owens, M. Separate and together: All-black therapy group in the white hospital. *American Journal of Orthopsychiatry,* 1974, **44,** 19–25.

Diggs, I. DuBois and children. *Phylon,* 1976, **37,** 370–399.

DuBois, W. E. B. *The souls of black folk.* New York: Fawcett, 1961.

Edelson, M. *The idea of a mental illness.* New Haven: Yale University Press, 1971.

Edelson, M. *Language and interpretation in psychoanalysis.* New Haven: Yale University Press, 1975.

Ekstein, R., & Motto, R. L. *From learning for love to love of learning.* New York: Brunner/Mazel, 1969.

Ellison, R. *Invisible man.* New York: Signet Books, 1952.

Ellison, R. That same pain, that same pleasure: An interview. In R. Ellison, *Shadow and act.* New York: Signet Books, 1964.

Ellison, R., & McPherson, J. A. Indivisible man. *Atlantic,* December 1970, 45–60.

Epps, E. G. The impact of school desegregation on aspirations, self-concepts and other aspects of personality. *Law and Contemporary Problems,* 1975, **39,** 300–313.

Epstein, S. The self-concept revisited: Or a theory of a theory. *American Psychologist,* 1973, **28,** 404–416.

Erikson, E. H. *Childhood and society.* (2nd ed.) New York: W. W. Norton, 1963.

Evans, M. C., & Chein, I. *The Movie-Story Game: A projective test of interracial attitudes for use with Negro and white children.* Paper read at the annual meeting of the American Psychological Association, Boston, September, 1948.

Fanon, F. *Black skin, white masks.* New York: Grove Press, 1967.

Farber, S. L. *Identical twins reared apart: A reanalysis.* New York: Basic Books, 1981.

Feuerstein, R. *The dynamic assessment of retarded performers: The Learning Potential Assessment Device, theory, instruments, and techniques.* Baltimore: University Park Press, 1979.

Fish, J. E., & Larr, C. J. A decade of change in drawings by black children. *American Journal of Psychiatry,* 1972, **129,** 421–426.

Flavell, J. H. *The developmental psychology of Jean Piaget.* Princeton, N.J.: Van Nostrand, 1963.

Flynn, J. T., & Anderson, B. E. The effect of test administration procedures on achievement test performance. *Journal of Negro Education,* 1976, **45,** 37–45.

Forward, J. R., & Williams, J. R. Internal-external control and black militancy. *Journal of Social Issues,* 1970, **26,** 75–92.

Francois, T. V. The engagement of adolescent black males in psychotherapy: The relation of role induction, locus of control, and depression (Doctoral dissertation, New York University, 1977) *Dissertation Abstracts International,* 1978, **38,** 6147B–6148B. (University Microfilms No. 7808524)

Frank, J. D. *Persuasion and healing: A comparative study of psychotherapy.* (2nd ed.) Baltimore: Johns Hopkins Press, 1973.

Franklin, A. J., & Fulani, L. Cultural content of materials and ethnic group performance in categorized recall. In A. W. Boykin, A. J. Franklin & J. F. Yates (Eds.), *Research directions of black psychologists.* New York: Russell Sage Foundation, 1979.

Frazier, E. F. *Black bourgeoisie.* New York: Collier Books, 1962.

Freud, S. Mourning and melancholia. In J. Strachey (Ed.), *The standard edition of the complete psychological works of Sigmund Freud.* Vol. 14. London: Hogarth Press and the Institute of Psychanalysis, 1957. (Originally published, 1917 [1915])

Friedman, N. James Baldwin and psychotherapy. *Psychotherapy: Theory, Research and Practice,* 1966, **3,** 177–183.

Fromm, E. *Man for himself.* New York: Rinehart, 1947.

Fromm, E. *The sane society.* New York: Rinehart, 1955.

Frost, R. The road not taken. In *Complete Poems of Robert Frost.* New York: Holt, 1964.

Garcia, J. IQ: The conspiracy. *Psychology Today,* September 1972, 40-43; 92-94.

Gardner, LaM. H. The therapeutic relationship under varying conditions of race. *Psychotherapy: Theory, Research and Practice,* 1971, **8,** 78–87.

Gaylin, W. (Ed.) *The meaning of despair.* New York: Science House, 1968.

Gerstein, A. I., Brodzinsky, D. M. & Reiskind, N. Perceptual integration on the Rorschach as an indicator of cognitive capacity: A developmental study of racial differences in a clinic population. *Journal of Consulting and Clinical Psychology,* 1976, **44,** 760–765.

Gibbs, J. T. Patterns of adaptation among black students at a predominantly white university: Selected case studies. *American Journal of Orthopsychiatry,* 1974, **44,** 728–740.

Gibbs, J. T. Use of mental health services by black students at a predominantly white university: A three-year study. *American Journal of Orthopsychiatry,* 1975, **45,** 430–445.

Golden, M., Birns, B., Bridger, W., & Moss, A. Social class differentiation in cognitive development among black preschool children. *Child Development,* 1971, **42,** 37–45.

Golden, M., Bridger, W. H., & Montare, A. Social class differences in the ability of young children to use verbal information to facilitate learning. *American Journal of Orthopsychiatry,* 1974, **44,** 86–91.

Gordon, E. W., & Green, D. An affluent society's excuses for inequality: Developmental, economic and educational. *American Journal of Orthopsychiatry,* 1974, **44,** 4–18.

Gordon, V. V. *The self-concept of black Americans.* Washington, D.C.: University Press of America, 1977.

Gouldner, H. *Teachers' pets, trouble-makers, and nobodies: Black children in elementary school.* Westport, Conn.: Greenwood, 1978.

Grier, W. H., & Cobbs, P. M. *Black rage.* New York: Basic Books, 1968.

Griffith, M. S., & Jones, E. E. Race and psychotherapy: Changing perspectives. In J. H. Masserman (Ed.), *Current psychiatric therapies,* Vol. 18. New York: Grune & Stratton, 1979.

Gumperz, J. J. *The sociolinguistics of interpersonal communication.* (Working papers and prepublications, No. 33) Universita di Urbino, Italia: Centro Internazionale di Semiotica e di Linguistica, 1974.

Gumperz, J. J., & Herasimchuk, E. The conversational analysis of social meaning. In R. Shuy (Ed.), *Sociolinguistics: Current trends and prospects.* Georgetown University Monographs in Language and Linguistics. Washington, D.C.: Georgetown University Press, 1972.

Gumperz, J. J., & Hernandez-Chavez, E. Bilingualism, bidialectalism, and classroom interaction. In C. B. Cazden, V. P. John & D. Hymes (Eds.), *Functions of language in the classroom.* New York: Teachers College Press, 1972.

Gurin, P., & Epps, E. G. *Black consciousness, identity, and achievement*. New York: Wiley, 1975.

Gurin, P., Gurin, G., Lao, R. C., & Beattie, M. Internal-external control in the motivational dynamics of Negro youth. *Journal of Social Issues*, 1969, **25**, 29–53.

Gurin, P., Gurin, G., & Morrison, B. M. *Personal and ideological aspects of internal and external control*. Unpublished manuscript, University of Michigan, undated.

Guthrie, R. V. *Even the rat was white: A historical view of psychology*. New York: Harper, 1976.

Gutman, H. G. *The black family in slavery and freedom, 1750-1925*. New York: Vintage, 1976.

Gynther, M. D., & Green, S. B. Accuracy may make a difference, but does a difference make for accuracy? A response to Pritchard and Greenblatt. *Journal of Consulting and Clinical Psychology*, 1980, **48**, 268–272.

Haimo, S. F., & Holzman, P. S. Thought disorder in schizophrenics and normal controls: Social class and race differences. *Journal of Consulting and Clinical Psychology*, 1979, **47**, 963–967.

Hale, J. *Black children: Their roots, culture and learning styles*. Unpublished manuscript, 1977. (Available from the author: Dept. of Elementary and Early Childhood Education, Jackson State University, Jackson, Miss. 39209)

Haley, A. *Roots: The saga of an American family*. New York: Doubleday, 1976.

Hall, W. S., & Dore, J. *Lexical sharing in mother-child interaction*. (Tech. Rep. No. 161) Urbana: University of Illinois, Center for the Study of Reading, March 1980.

Hall, W. S., & Freedle, R. O. *Culture and language*. Washington, D.C.: Halsted, 1975.

Hall, W. S., & Guthrie, L. F. *On the dialect question and reading*. (Tech. Rep. No. 121) Urbana: University of Illinois, Center for the Study of Reading, May 1979. (a)

Hall, W. S., & Guthrie, L. F. *Cultural and situational variation in language function and use: Methods and procedures for research*. (Tech. Rep. No. 148) Urbana: University of Illinois, Center for the Study of Reading, October 1979. (b)

Hall, W. S., Reder, S., & Cole, M. Story recall in young black and white children: Effects of racial group membership, race of experimenter, and dialect. *Developmental Psychology*, 1975, **11**, 628–634.

Hall, W. S., & Tirre, W. C. *The communicative environment of young children: Social class, ethnic, and situational differences*. (Tech. Rep. No. 125) Urbana: University of Illinois, Center for the Study of Reading, May 1979.

Halpern, F. *Survival: Black/white*. Elmsford, NY: Pergamon Press, 1973.

Hanley, J. H., & Barclay, A. G. Sensitivity of the WISC and WISC-R to subject and examiner variables. *Journal of Black Psychology*, 1979, **5**, 79–84.

Harding, V. The black wedge in America: Struggle, crisis and hope, 1955-1975. *Black Scholar*, 1975, **7**(4), 28–46.

Harrell, J. P. Analyzing black coping styles: A supplemental diagnostic system. *Journal of Black Psychology*, 1979, **5**, 99–108.

Harrison, A. O. Relationship between cognitive style and selective attention in black children. In A. W. Boykin, A. J. Franklin & J. F. Yates (Eds.), *Research directions of black psychologists*. New York: Russell Sage Foundation, 1979.

Harrison-Ross, P., & Wyden, B. *The black child: A parent's guide*. New York: Peter Wyden, 1973.

Hayes, W. A. Radical black behaviorism. In R. L. Jones (Ed.), *Black psychology*. (2nd ed.) New York: Harper, 1980.

Heber, R. F. Sociocultural mental retardation—a longitudinal study. In D. Forgays (Ed.), *Primary prevention of psychopathology*, Vol. II, *Environmental influences*. Hanover, N.H.: University Press of New England, 1978.

Heber, R. F., & Garber, H. The Milwaukee Project: A study of the use of family intervention to prevent cultural-familial mental retardation. In B. Z. Friedlander, G. M. Sterritt & G. E. Kirk (Eds.), *Exceptional infant*. Vol. 3. New York: Brunner/Mazel, 1975.

Hendin, H. *Black suicide*. New York: Basic Books, 1969.

Henry, W. E., Sims, J. H., & Spray, S. L. *Public and private lives of psychotherapists*. San Francisco: Jossey-Bass, 1973.

Hill, R. B. *The strengths of black families.* New York: Emerson Hall, 1971.

Hollingshead, A. B., & Redlich, F. C. *Social class and mental illness.* New York: Wiley, 1958.

Holt, R. R., Freud's mechanistic humanistic images of man. In R. R. Holt & E. Peterfreund (Eds.), *Psychoanalysis and contemporary science.* Vol. 1. New York: Macmillan, 1972.

Hoover, M. R. Community attitudes toward Black English. *Language in Society,* 1978, **7**, 65–87.

Horowitz, M. J. (Ed.) *Hysterical personality.* New York: Aronson, 1977.

Houston, S. H. A reexamination of some assumptions about the language of the disadvantaged child. In S. Chess & A. Thomas (Eds.), *Annual progress in child psychiatry and child development.* New York: Brunner/Mazel, 1971.

Houston, S. H. Black English. *Psychology Today,* March 1973, 45–48.

Hraba, J., & Grant, G. Black is beautiful: A reexamination of racial preference and identification. *Journal of Personality and Social Psychology,* 1970, **16**, 398–402.

Hughes, L. Mother to son. In *Selected poems of Langston Hughes.* New York: Alfred A. Knopf, 1926.

Jackson, A. M. Psychotherapy: Factors associated with the race of the therapist. *Psychotherapy: Theory, Research and Practice,* 1973, **10**, 273–277.

Jackson, A. M. *Treatment issues for black patients.* Paper presented at the annual meeting of the American Psychological Association, Montreal, September, 1980.

Jackson, G. G. The emergence of a black perspective in counseling. In R. L. Jones (Ed.), *Black psychology.* (2nd ed.) New York: Harper and Row, 1980.

Jencks, C. What color is IQ: Intelligence and race. *New Republic,* September 13, 1969, 25–29.

Jensen, A. R. How much can we boost I.Q. and scholastic achievement? *Harvard Educational Review,* 1969, **39**, 1–123.

Johnston, M. H., & Holzman, P. S. *Assessing schizophrenic thinking.* San Francisco: Jossey-Bass, 1979.

Jones, A., & Seagull, A. A. Dimensions of the relationship between the black client and the white therapist: A theoretical overview. *American Psychologist,* 1977, **32**, 850–855.

Jones, E. E. Social class and psychotherapy: A critical review of research. *Psychiatry,* 1974, **37**, 307–320.

Jones, E. E. Black-white personality differences: Another look. *Journal of Personality Assessment,* 1978, **42**, 244–252. (a)

Jones, E. E. Effects of race on psychotherapy process and outcome: An exploratory investigation. *Psychotherapy: Theory, Research and Practice,* 1978, **15**, 226–236. (b)

Jones, E. E. Psychotherapy outcome as a function of client-therapist race. Manuscript submitted for publication, 1979.

Jones, J. *Prejudice and racism.* Reading, Mass.: Addison-Wesley, 1972.

Jordan, W. *White over black.* Chapel Hill: University of North Carolina Press, 1968.

Kagan, J. What is intelligence? *Social Policy,* 1973, **4**, 88–94.

Kagan, J. Cognitive development. *JSAS Catalog of Selected Documents in Psychology,* 1976, **6**, 96. (Ms. No. 1338, 36 pgs.)

Kagan, J., & Klein, R. E. Cross-cultural perspectives on early development. *American Psychologist,* 1973, **28**, 947–961.

Kamin, L. J. *The science and politics of I.Q.* Potomac, Md.: Lawrence Erlbaum, 1974.

Kardiner, A., & Ovesey, L. *The mark of oppression.* Cleveland: Meridian Books, 1962. (Original edition, New York: W. W. Norton, 1951)

Karon, B. P., & VandenBos, G. R. The consequences of psychotherapy for schizophrenic patients. *Psychotherapy: Theory, Research and Practice,* 1972, **9**, 111–119.

Karon, B. P., & VandenBos, G. R. Issues in current research on psychotherapy vs. medication in treatment of schizophrenics. *Psychotherapy: Theory, Research and Practice,* 1975, **12**, 143–148.

Katz, P. A. (Ed.) *Towards the elimination of racism.* Elmsford, N.Y.: Pergamon Press, 1976.

Katz, P. A., & Zalk, S. R. Doll preferences: An index of racial attitudes? *Journal of Educational Psychology,* 1974, **66**, 663–668.

Keen, E. *Three faces of being: Toward an existential clinical psychology.* New York: Appleton-Century-Crofts, 1970.

Kernan, C. M. Language behavior in a black urban community. *Monographs of the Language-Behavior Research Laboratory,* University of California, Berkeley, 1971 (No. 2).

Kernberg, O. *Borderline conditions and pathological narcissism.* New York: Aronson, 1975.

Kohut, H. *The restoration of the self.* New York: International Universities Press, 1977.

Kohut, H., & Wolf, E. S. The disorders of the self and their treatment: An outline. *International Journal of Psychoanalysis,* 1978, **59,** 413–425.

Korchin, S. J. *Modern clinical psychology.* New York: Basic Books, 1976.

Kovel, J. *White racism: A psychohistory.* New York: Pantheon Books, 1970.

Kramer, M., Rosen, B. M., & Willis, E. M. Definitions and distributions of mental disorders in a racist society. In C. V. Willie, B. M. Kramer & B. S. Brown (Eds.), *Racism and mental health.* Pittsburgh: University of Pittsburgh Press, 1973.

Krebs, R. L. Some effects of a white institution on black psychiatric outpatients. *American Journal of Orthopsychiatry,* 1971, **41,** 589–596.

Labov, W. *Language in the inner city: Studies in the Black English Vernacular.* Philadelphia: University of Pennsylvania Press, 1972.

Lanyon, R. I., & Lanyon, B. P. *Behavior therapy: A clinical introduction.* Reading, Mass.: Addison-Wesley, 1978.

Lasch, C. *The culture of narcissism.* New York: W. W. Norton, 1978.

Lawler, J. M. *I.Q., heritability and racism.* New York: International Publishers, 1978.

Lerner, B. *Therapy in the ghetto: Political impotence and personal disintegration.* Baltimore: Johns Hopkins University Press, 1972.

Lerner, B. Is psychotherapy relevant to the needs of the urban poor? In D. A. Evans & W. L. Claiborn (Eds.), *Mental health issues and the urban poor.* Elmsford, N.Y.: Pergamon Press, 1974.

Lesse, S. (Ed.) *Masked depression.* New York: Aronson, 1974.

Lester, J. *Look out whitey! Black power's gon' get your mama!* New York: Grove, 1968.

Lewis, D. O., Balla, D. A., & Shanok, S. S. Some evidence of race bias in the diagnosis and treatment of the juvenile offender. *American Journal of Orthopsychiatry,* 1979, **49,** 53–61.

Loehlin, J. C., Lindzey, G., & Spuhler, J. N. *Race differences in intelligence.* San Francisco: Freeman, 1975.

Mahl, G. F. Conflict and defense. In I. L. Janis (Ed.), *Personality: Dynamics, development, and assessment.* New York: Harcourt, Brace & World, 1969.

Mahler, M. S. Symbiosis and individuation: The psychological birth of the human infant. In R. S. Eissler, A. Freud, M. Kris & A. J. Solnit (Eds.), *The psychoanalytic study of the child.* Vol. 29. New Haven: Yale University Press, 1974.

Malcom X. *The autobiography of Malcolm X.* New York: Grove, 1965.

Marwit, S. J., Marwit, K. L., & Boswell, J. J. Negro children's use of nonstandard grammar. In S. Chess & A. Thomas (Eds.), *Annual progress in child psychiatry and child development.* New York: Brunner/Mazel, 1973.

Marwit, S. J., & Neumann, G. Black and white children's comprehension of standard and nonstandard English passages. *Journal of Educational Psychology,* 1974, **66,** 329–332.

Maslow, A. H. *Toward a psychology of being.* (2nd. ed.) New York: Van Nostrand Reinhold, 1968.

Matarazzo, J. D., & Weins, A. N. Black Intelligence Test of Cultural Homogeneity and Wechsler Adult Intelligence Scale scores of black and white police applicants. *Journal of Applied Psychology,* 1977, **62,** 57–63.

Mbiti, J. S. *African religions and philosphy.* New York: Anchor Books, 1970.

McAdoo, H. P. The development of self-concept and race attitudes in black children: A longitudinal study. In W. E. Cross, Jr. (Ed.), *Proceedings: The third annual conference on empirical research in black psychology.* Washington, D.C.: U.S. Department of Health, Education, & Welfare, National Institute of Education, 1977.

McClelland, D. C. Testing for competence rather than for "intelligence." *American Psychologist,* 1973, **28,** 1–14.

McDonald, M. *Not by the color of their skin.* New York: International Universities Press, 1970.

Mead, G. H. Language and the development of the self. In G. E. Swanson, T. M. Newcomb & E. L. Hartley (Eds.), *Readings in social psychology.* New York: Holt, 1952.

Menninger, K. M., Mayman, M., & Pruyser, P. *The vital balance.* New York: Viking, 1963.

Mercer, J. R. *Labeling the mentally retarded.* Berkeley: University of California Press, 1973.

Mercer, J. R. *SOMPA: System of multicultural pluralistic assessment.* (Technical Manual) New York: The Psychological Corporation, 1979.

Milliones, J. Construction of a black consciousness measure: Psychotherapeutic implications. *Psychotherapy: Theory, Research and Practice,* 1980, **17,** 175–182.

Montagu, A. (Ed.) *Race and I.Q.* New York: Oxford, 1975.

Moynihan, D. *The Negro family: The case for national action.* Washington, D.C.: U.S. Department of Labor, Office of Policy Planning and Research, 1965.

Nobles, W. W. Psychological research and the black self-concept: A critical review. *Journal of Social Issues,* 1973, **29,** 11–31.

Olim, E. G. Maternal language styles and cognitive development of children. In F. Williams (Ed.) *Language and poverty.* Chicago: Markham, 1970.

Orne, M. T. On the social psychology of the psychological experiment: With particular reference to demand characteristics and their implications. *American Psychologist,* 1962, **17,** 776–783.

Page, E. B. Miracle in Milwaukee: Raising the I.Q. In B. Z. Friedlander, G. M. Sterritt & G. E. Kirk (Eds.), *Exceptional infant,* Vol. 3. New York: Brunner/Mazel, 1975.

Parker, K. The effects of subliminal merging stimuli on the academic performance of college students (Doctoral dissertation, New York University, 1977). *Dissertation Abstracts International,* 1978, **38,** 6168B. (University Microfilms No. 7808550)

Perry, J. C., & Klerman, G. L. The borderline patient: A comparative analysis of four sets of diagnostic criteria. *Archives of General Psychiatry,* 1978, **35,** 141–150.

Pettigrew, T. F. *A Profile of the Negro American.* Princeton, N.J.: Van Nostrand, 1964.

Pettigrew, T. F. *Racially separate or together?* New York: McGraw-Hill, 1971.

Phillips, L. *Human adaptation and its failures.* New York: Academic Press, 1968.

Piestrup, A. M. Black dialect interference and accommodation of reading instruction in first grade. *Monographs of the Language-Behavior Research Laboratory,* University of California, Berkeley, 1973 (No. 4).

Pines, M. A head start in the nursery. *Psychology Today,* September 1979, 56–68.

Porter, J. D. R. *Black child, white child: The development of racial attitudes.* Cambridge: Harvard University Press, 1971.

Poussaint, A. F. *Why blacks kill blacks.* New York: Emerson Hall, 1972.

Powdermaker, H. The channeling of Negro aggression by the cultural process. *American Journal of Sociology,* 1943, **48,** 750–758.

Powell, G. J. Self-concept in white and black children. In C. V. Willie, B. M. Kramer, & B. S. Brown (Eds.), *Racism and mental health.* Pittsburgh: University of Pittsburgh Press, 1973.

Powell, L., & Johnson, E. H. The Black MMPI profile: Interpretive problems. *Journal of Negro Education,* 1976, **45,** 27–36.

Pritchard, D. A., & Rosenblatt, A. Racial bias in the MMPI: A methodological review. *Journal of Consulting and Clinical Psychology,* 1980, **48,** 263–267. (a)

Pritchard, D. A., & Rosenblatt, A. Reply to Gynther and Green. *Journal of Consulting and Clinical Psychology,* 1980, **48,** 273–274. (b)

Pugh, R. W. *Psychology and the black experience.* Monterey, Calif. Brooks/Cole, 1972.

Rainwater, L. Crucible of identity: The Negro lower-class family. In T. Parsons & K. B. Clark (Eds.), *The Negro-American.* Boston: Houghton Mifflin, 1966.

Raskin, A., Crook, T. H., & Herman, K. D. Psychiatric history and symptom differences in black and white depressed inpatients. *Journal of Consulting and Clinical Psychology,* 1975, **43,** 73–80.

Reeves, C. An exploratory study: Modification of color concepts of low income black preschool youngsters (Doctoral dissertation, Stanford University, 1976). *Dissertation Abstracts International,* 1976, **37,** 2751A–2752A. (University Microfilms No. 76–26, 064)

Rice, B. Brave new world of intelligence testing. *Psychology Today,* September 1979, 27–41.

Robins, L. N. Negro homicide victims—who will they be? *Trans-action,* June, 1968, 15–19.

Robins, L. N., Murphy, G. E., Woodruff, R. A., Jr., & King, L. J. Adult psychiatric status of black schoolboys. *Archives of General Psychiatry,* 1971, **24,** 338–345.

Rohwer, W. D., Jr. How the smart get smarter. *Quarterly Newsletter of the Laboratory of Comparative Human Cognition,* 1980, **2,** 35–39.

Rosen, H. Language and class: A critical look at the theories of Basil Bernstein. *Urban Review,* 1974, **7,** 97–114.

Rosenberg, M., & Simmons, R. G. *Black and white self-esteem: The urban school child.* Washington, D.C.: American Sociological Association, 1971.

Rosenhan, D. L. On being sane in insane places. *Science,* 1973, **179,** 250–258.

Rosenthal, R. The pygmalion effect lives. *Psychology Today,* September 1973, 56–63.

Rosenthal, R., & Jacobson, L. Self-fulfilling prophecies in the classroom: Teachers' expectations as unintended determinants of pupils' intellectual competence. In M. Deutsch, I. Katz & A. R. Jensen (Eds.), *Social class, race, and psychological development.* New York: Holt, 1968.

Rotter, J. B. Generalized expectancies for internal versus external control of reinforcement. *Psychological Monographs,* 1966, **80** (1, Whole No. 609).

Rumsey, J. M., & Rychlak, J. F. The role of affective assessment in intelligence testing. *Journal of Personality Assessment,* 1978, **42,** 421–425.

Rychlak, J. F. *Introduction to personality and psychotherapy: A theory-construction approach.* Boston: Houghton Mifflin, 1973.

Rychlak, J. F. Is a concept of "self" necessary in psychological theory, and if so why? A humanistic perspective. In A. Wandersman, P. J. Poppen & D. F. Ricks (Eds.), *Humanism and behaviorism: Dialogue and growth.* Elmsford, N.Y.: Pergamon Press, 1976.

Rychlak, J. F. *The psychology of rigorous humanism.* New York: Wiley, 1977.

Rychlak, J. F. *Discovering free will and personal responsibility.* New York: Oxford University Press, 1979.

Rychlak, J. F. *Teleology as logical phenomenology: Some therapeutic implications.* Paper presented at the annual meeting of the American Psychological Association, Montreal, September 1980.

Rychlak, J. F. *Introduction to personality and psychotherapy: A theory-construction approach.* (2nd ed.) Boston: Houghton Mifflin, 1981.

Rychlak, J. F. Logical learning theory: Propositions, corollaries, and research evidence. *Journal of Personality and Social Psychology,* in press.

Rychlak, J. F., & Barna, J. D. Causality and the proper image of man in scientific psychology. *Journal of Personality Assessment,* 1971, **34,** 403–419.

Rychlak, J. F., & Ingwell, R. H. Causal orientation and personal adjustment of hospitalized veterans. *Journal of Personality Assessment,* 1977, **41,** 299–303.

Sacks, S. R. Influence of Black is Beautiful program on black adolescents' drawings and high status job selections. Unpublished manuscript, Teachers College, Columbia University, 1972.

Sampson, H. A critique of certain traditional concepts in the psychoanalytic theory of therapy. *Bulletin of the Menninger Clinic,* 1976, **40,** 255–262.

Samuda, R. J. *Psychological testing of American minorities: Issues and consequences.* New York: Harper, 1975.

Sarason, S. B. Mental subnormality. In F. C. Redlich & D. X. Freedman, *The theory and practice of psychiatry* (Chapter 19). New York: Basic Books, 1966.

Sarnoff, I. Identification with the aggressor: Some personality correlates of anti-semitism among Jews (Doctoral dissertation, University of Michigan, 1951). *Microfilm Abstracts,* 1951, **11,** 753–754. (Publication No. 2647)

Sattler, J. Racial "experimenter effects" in experimentation, testing, interviewing, and psychotherapy. *Psychological Bulletin,* 1970, **73,** 137–160.

Scarr-Salapatek, S. Race, social class and I.Q. *Science,* 1971, **174,** 1285–1295.

Scarr, S. Genetic effects on human behavior: Recent family studies. Paper presented in Master Lecture Series on Brain and Behavior Relationships at the annual meeting of the American Psychological Association, San Francisco, September, 1977.

Scarr, S., & Weinberg, R. A. I.Q. test performance of black children adopted by white families. *American Psychologist,* 1976, **31,** 726–739.

Scarr, S., & Weinberg, R. A. The rights and responsibilities of the social scientist. *American Psychologist,* 1978, **33,** 955–957. (Comment)

Schacht, T., & Nathan, P. E. But is it good for the psychologists? Appraisal and status of DSM-III. *American Psychologist,* 1977, **32,** 1017–1025.

Schafer, R. *A new language for psychoanalysis.* New Haven: Yale University Press, 1976.

Schafer, R. Danger-situations. In P. W. Pruyser (Ed.), *Diagnosis and the difference it makes.* New York: Aronson, 1977.

Schectman, F. Provocative issues in psychiatric diagnosis: A dialogue. In P. W. Pruyser (Ed.), *Diagnosis and the difference it makes.* New York: Aronson, 1977.

Schuman, H. Racial attitude change: Are whites really more liberal? Blacks aren't impressed. *Psychology Today,* September 1974, 82–86.

Scott, J. P., & Senay, E. C. (Eds.) *Separation and depression.* Washington, D.C.: American Association for the Advancement of Science, 1973.

Scrofani, P. J., Suziedelis, A., & Shore, M. F. Conceptual ability in black and white children of different social classes: An experimental test of Jensen's hypothesis. *American Journal of Orthopsychiatry,* 1973, **43,** 541–553.

See, J. J., & Miller, K. S. Mental health. In K. S. Miller & R. M. Dreger (Eds.), *Comparative studies of blacks and whites in the United States.* New York: Seminar Press, 1973.

Seiden, R. H. We're driving young blacks to suicide. *Psychology Today,* August 1970, 24–28.

Seligman, M. E. P. *Helplessness: On depression, development, and death.* San Francisco: Freeman, 1975.

Silverman, L. H. Some psychoanalytic considerations of non-psychoanalytic therapies: On the possibility of integrating treatment approaches and related issues. *Psychotherapy, Theory and Research,* 1974, **11,** 298–305.

Silverman, L. H. Psychoanalytic theory: "The reports of my death are greatly exaggerated." *American Psychologist,* 1976, **31,** 621–637.

Silverman, L. H. The subliminal psychodynamic activation method: An overview. In J. Masling (Ed.), *Empirical studies of psychoanalytic theory.* New York: Erlbaum, in press.

Simons, H. D. Black dialect, reading interference and classroom interaction. Unpublished manuscript, University of California, Berkeley, 1976.

Smith, O. S., & Gundlach, R. H. Group therapy for blacks in a therapeutic community. *American Journal of Orthopsychiatry,* 1974, **44,** 26–36.

Smith, W. D., Burlew, A. K., Mosley, M. H., & Whitney, W. M. *Minority issues in mental health.* Reading, Mass.: Addison-Wesley, 1978.

Smitherman, G., & McGinnis, J. Black language and black liberation. In R. L. Jones (Ed.), *Black psychology.* (2nd ed.) New York: Harper, 1980.

Society for the Psychological Study of Social Issues (SPSSI). Guidelines for testing minority group children. *Journal of Social Issues,* 1964, **20,** 127–145. (Supplement)

Steele, R. E. Clinical comparison of black and white suicide attempters. *Journal of Consulting and Clinical Psychology,* 1977, **45,** 982–986.

Stewart, W. A., Toward a history of American Negro dialect. In F. Williams (Ed.), *Language and Poverty.* Chicago: Markham, 1970.

Strupp, H. H. On the basic ingredients of psychotherapy. *Journal of Consulting and Clinical Psychology,* 1973, **41,** 1–8.

Sue, S., McKinney, H., Allen, D., & Hall, J. Delivery of community mental health services to black and white clients. *Journal of Consulting and Clinical Psychology,* 1974, **42,** 794-801.

Sue, S. Community mental health services to minority groups: Some optimism, some pessimism. *American Psychologist,* 1977, **32,** 616-624.

Sugarman, A. Is psychodiagnostic assessment humanistic? *Journal of Personality Assessment,* 1978, **42,** 11-21.

Sullivan, H. S. Peculiarity of thought in schizophrenia. In H. S. Sullivan, *Schizophrenia as a human process.* New York: Norton, 1962. (Originally published, 1925-26)

Szasz, T. S. *The myth of mental illness: Foundations of a theory of personal conduct.* New York: Hoeber-Harper, 1961.

Szasz, T. S. *The myth of psychotherapy: Mental healing as religion, rhetoric, and repression.* Garden City, N.Y.: Anchor Press/Doubleday, 1979. (Originally published, 1978)

Taylor, O. Black language and what to do about it: Some black community perspectives. In R. L. Williams (Ed.), *Ebonics: The true language of black folks.* St. Louis, Mo.: Institute of Black Studies, 1975.

Taylor, R. L. Psychosocial development among black children and youth: A reexamination. *American Journal of Orthopsychiatry,* 1976, **46,** 4-19.

Temoshok, L., & Attkisson, C. C. Epidemiology of hysterical phenomena: Evidence for a psychosocial theory. In M. J. Horowitz (Ed.), *Hysterical personality.* New York: Aronson, 1977.

Terrell, F., Taylor, J., & Terrell, S. L. Effects of type of social reinforcement on the intelligence test performance of lower-class black children. *Journal of Consulting and Clinical Psychology,* 1978, **46,** 1538-1539.

Thomas, A., Hertzig, M. E., Dryman, D., & Fernandez, P. Examiner effect in IQ testing of Puerto-Rican working-class children. *American Journal of Orthopsychiatry,* 1971, **41,** 809-821.

Thomas, A., & Sillen, S. *Racism and psychiatry.* New York: Brunner/Mazel, 1972.

Thomas, C. W. Different strokes for different folks: Jo Ann E. Gardner (women's lib) and Charles W. Thomas (black psychology) in a conversation with T. George Harris. *Psychology Today,* September 1970, 49-53; 78-80.

Thomas, C. W., & Thomas, S. W. Something borrowed, something black. In C. W. Thomas (Ed.), *Boys no more.* Beverly Hills, Calif.: Glencoe, 1971.

Tomes, H. The impact of cultural influences on psychotherapy. In J. L. Claghorn (Ed.), *Successful psychotherapy.* New York: Brunner/Mazel, 1976.

Tonks, C. M., Paykel, E. S., & Klerman, G. L. Clinical depression among Negroes. *American Journal of Psychiatry,* 1970, **127,** 329-335.

Trudgill, P. *Sociolinguistics: An Introduction.* Harmondsworth, England: Penguin Books, 1974.

Tuckett, R. B. *The effects of subliminal merging stimuli on the academic performance of emotionally handicapped students.* Unpublished doctoral dissertation, New York University, 1980.

Tuma, A. H., & May, P.R.A. Psychotherapy, drugs and therapist experience in the treatment of schizophrenia: A critique of the Michigan State Project. *Psychotherapy: Theory, Research and Practice,* 1975, **12,** 138-142.

Vosk, J. S. Study of Negro children with learning difficulties at the outset of their careers. *American Journal of Orthopsychiatry,* 1966, **36,** 32-40.

Wachtel, P. L. *Psychoanalysis and behavior therapy: Toward an integration.* New York: Basic Books, 1977.

Waite, R. The Negro patient and clinical theory. *Journal of Clinical and Consulting Psychology,* 1968, **32,** 427-433.

Ward, M. C. *Them children: A study in language learning.* New York: Holt, Rinehart, & Winston, 1971.

Ward, S. H., & Braun, J. Self-esteem and racial preference in black children. *American Journal of Orthopsychiatry,* 1972, **42,** 644-647.

Warheit, G. J., Holzer, C. E., III, & Schwab, J.J. An analysis of social class and racial differences in depressive symptomatology: A community study. *Journal of Health and Social Behavior,* 1973, **14**, 291-299.

Warheit, G., Holzer, C. E., III, & Arey, S.A. Race and mental illness: An epidemiological update. *Journal of Health and Social Behavior,* 1975, **16**, 243-256.

Watson, P. I.Q.: The racial gap. *Psychology Today,* September 1972, 48-50; 97-99.

Weiner, I. B. *Psychodiagnosis in schizophrenia.* New York: Wiley, 1966.

Weiss, B. L., & Kupfer, D. J. The black patient and research in a community mental health center: Where have all the patients gone? *American Journal of Psychiatry,* 1974, **131**, 415-418.

White, K. P. Toward a definition of the black self-concept: An analysis of meaning ascriptions (Doctoral dissertation, New York University, 1977). *Dissertation Abstracts International,* 1978, **38**, 7249A. (University Microfilms No. 7808572)

White, R. W. Motivation reconsidered: The concept of competence. *Psychological Review,* 1959, **66**, 297-333.

White, R. W. Ego and reality in psychoanalytic theory. *Psychological Issues,* 1963, (**3**, Serial No. 11).

White. R. W., & Watt, N.F. *The abnormal personality.* (5th ed.) New York: Wiley, 1981.

Williams, F. Language, attitude, and social change. In F. Williams (Ed.), *Language and poverty.* Chicago: Markham, 1970.

Williams, J. E., & Morland, J. K. *Race, color, and the young child.* Chapel Hill: University of North Carolina Press, 1976.

Williams, J. E., & Morland, J. K. Comment on Bank's "White preference in blacks: A paradigm in search of a phenomenon." *Psychological Bulletin,* 1979, **86**, 28-32.

Williams, R. L. Developing cultural specific assessment devices: An empirical rationale. In R. L. Williams (Ed.), *Ebonics: The true language of black folks.* St. Louis, Mo.: Institute of Black Studies, 1975.

Williamson, J. V. A look at Black English. In R. L. Williams (Ed.), *Ebonics: The true language of black folks.* St. Louis, Mo.: Institute of Black Studies, 1975.

Willie, C. V., Kramer, B.M., & Brown, B.S. (Eds.), *Racism and mental health.* Pittsburgh: University of Pittsburgh Press, 1973.

Wilson, L., & Rogers, R. W. The fire this time: Effects of race of target, insult, and potential retaliation on black aggression. *Journal of Personality and Social Psychology,* 1975, **32**, 857-864.

Winslow, C. N., & Brainerd, J. E. A comparison of the reactions of whites and Negroes to frustration as measured by the Rosenzweig Picture-Frustration Test. *American Psychologist,* 1950, **5**, 297.

Wright, R. Black English. *Language in Society,* 1975, **4**, 185-198.

Wylie, R. *The self-concept: A review of methodological considerations and measuring instruments.* (Rev. ed.) Lincoln: University of Nebraska Press, 1974.

Yando, R., Seitz, V., & Zigler, E. *Intellectual and personality characteristics of children: Social-class and ethnic-group differences.* Hillsdale, N.J.: Lawrence Erlbaum, 1979.

Zigler, E. Familial mental retardation: A continuing dilemma. In S. Chess & A. Thomas (Eds.), *Annual progress in child psychiatry and child development.* New York: Brunner/Mazel, 1968.

Zigler, E. F. Project Head Start: Success or failure? In S. Chess & A. Thomas (Eds.), *Annual progress in child psychiatry and child development.* New York: Brunner/Mazel, 1974.

Zigler, E., Abelson, W. D., & Seitz, V. Motivational factors in the performance of economically disadvantaged children on the Peabody Picture Vocabulary Test. In S. Chess & A. Thomas (Eds.), *Annual progress in child psychiatry and child development.* New York: Brunner/Mazel, 1974.

Zigler, E. & Butterfield, E.C. Motivational aspects of changes in I.Q. test performance of culturally deprived nursery school children. *Child Development,* 1968, **39**, 1-14.

Zigler, E., & Tricket, P. K. IQ, social competence, and evaluation of early childhood intervention programs. *American Psychologist,* 1978, **33**, 789-798.

AUTHOR INDEX

SUBJECT INDEX

About the Author

Adelbert H. Jenkins (Ph.D., University of Michigan) is Associate Professor of Psychology in the Faculty of Arts and Science at New York University. His primary interests are in such areas as the training of clinical psychologists, the conceptual and theoretical underpinnings of clinical psychology, and the delivery of mental health services to minority communities. A founding member and past Chair of the New York Chapter of the Association of Black Psychologists, he received its "Psychologist of the Year" Award in 1976. A Fellow of the Society for Personality Assessment, he has served as member and Chair of the Committee on Accreditation and the Board for Convention Affairs of the American Psychological Association. For three years he was Co-Director of the clinical psychology internship at Bellevue Psychiatric Hospital. Other activities have included private practice and work as a training and human relations consultant with the Veterans Administration, mental hospitals, and school systems.

Pergamon General Psychology Series

Editors: Arnold P. Goldstein, Syracuse University
Leonard Krasner, SUNY, Stony Brook